ZEN BUDDHISM AND ENVIRONMENTAL ETHICS

Zen Buddhism and Environmental Ethics explores the implications of Zen Buddhist teachings and practices for our moral relations with the natural world. At once an accessible introduction to Zen and an important contribution to the debate concerning the environmental implications of the tradition, this book will appeal both to readers unfamiliar with East Asian thought and to those well versed in the field.

In elucidating the philosophical implications of Zen, the author draws upon both Eastern and Western philosophy, situating the Zen understanding of nature within the Buddhist tradition, as well as relating it to the ideas of key Western philosophers such as Aristotle, Kant and Heidegger. These philosophical reflections on Zen are used to shed light on some prominent debates in contemporary environmental ethics concerning such issues as the intrinsic value of nature.

D1611523

Ashgate World Philosophies Series

The Ashgate World Philosophies Series responds to the remarkable growth of interest among English-language readers in recent years in philosophical traditions outside those of 'the West'. The traditions of Indian, Chinese, and Japanese thought, as well as those of the Islamic world, Latin America, Africa, Aboriginal Australian, Pacific and American Indian peoples, are all attracting lively attention from professional philosophers and students alike, and this new Ashgate series provides introductions to these traditions as well as in-depth research into central issues and themes within those traditions. The series is particularly designed for readers whose interests are not adequately addressed by general surveys of 'World Philosophy', and it includes accessible, yet research-led, texts for wider readership and upper-level student use, as well as research monographs. The series embraces a wide variety of titles ranging from introductions on particular world philosophies and informed surveys of the philosophical contributions of geographical regions, to in-depth discussion of a theme, topic, problem or movement and critical appraisals of individual thinkers or schools of thinkers.

Series Editors:
Professor David E. Cooper, University of Durham, UK
Professor Robert C. Solomon, University of Texas, Austin, USA
Professor Kathleen M. Higgins, University of Texas, Austin, USA
Associate Professor Purushottama Bilimoria, Deakin University, Australia

Other titles in this series:
Buddhism, Knowledge and Liberation
David Burton

Comparative Approaches to Chinese Philosophy
Edited by Bo Mou

An Introduction to Madhva Vedanta
Deepak Sarma

Mencius, Hume and the Foundations of Ethics
Xiusheng Liu

Personal Identity and Buddhist Philosophy
Mark Siderits

Zen Buddhism and Environmental Ethics

SIMON P. JAMES
University of Durham, UK

ASHGATE

Published by
Ashgate Publishing Limited
Wey Court East
Union Road
Farnham
Surrey GU9 7PT
England

Ashgate Publishing Company
Suite 420
101 Cherry Street
Burlington, VT 05401-4405
USA

Ashgate website: http://www.ashgate.com

Reprinted 2010

British Library Cataloguing in Publication Data
James, Simon P.
  Zen Buddhism and environmental ethics. – (Ashgate world
philosophies series)
  1. Buddhist ethics 2. Environmental ethics 3. Zen Buddhism –
Essence, genius, nature
  I. Title
  294.3'420427

Library of Congress Cataloging-in-Publication Data
James, Simon P.
  Zen Buddhism and environmental ethics / Simon P. James.
      p. cm. – (Ashgate world philosophies series)
  Includes bibliographical references and index.
  ISBN 0-7546-1367-4 (hd. : alk. paper) – ISBN 0-7546-1368-2 (pbk. : alk. paper)
      1. Zen Buddhism–Doctrines. 2. Environmental ethics. 3. Human ecology–
Religious aspects–Zen Buddhism. I. Title. II. Series.

BQ9268.3.J36 2003
294.3'5691–dc22
                                                                    2003063022

ISBN 13: 978-0-7546-1368-8 (pbk)

Mixed Sources
Product group from well-managed
forests and other controlled sources
www.fsc.org Cert no. SGS-COC-2482
© 1996 Forest Stewardship Council

Printed and bound by TJI Digital, Padstow, Cornwall

Contents

Acknowledgements

In writing this book, I have benefited from the help of many people. I would especially like to thank the following: David E. Cooper, for his guidance and support; Michael McGhee, for his perceptive and helpful comments, and for allowing me to publish parts of my article 'Zen Buddhism and the Intrinsic Value of Nature' (*Contemporary Buddhism* 4, no. 2, 2003) in Chapter 4; my students, for reminding me why it is we study these things; Sarah Lloyd and Sarah Charters at Ashgate, for their sound and prompt advice; Bruce Morito, for permission to publish sections of my article 'Heidegger, the body and environmental virtue' (*The Trumpeter* 18, no.1, 2002) in Chapter Five; Reverend Shōhaku Okumura for giving a beautiful talk at Bloomington, Indiana, and so unwittingly inspiring my interest in Zen; Dave Morgan of the Durham ITS Service for helping me out with the Romanized Sanskrit fonts; Michel Mohr, for his thoughts on the non-existence of 'Zen thought'. Last, but not least, I would like to thank my family, and especially my mother, to whom I dedicate this book.

Linguistic Conventions

Sanskrit has been used throughout, rather than Pali, so the goal of Buddhist practice has, for example, been given as *Nirvāṇa*, rather than *Nibbāna*, and the founder of Buddhism is referred to as Siddhartha Gautama rather than Siddhattha Gotama. I have rendered words denoting Chinese people or phenomena in (Romanized) Chinese (according to the Wade-Giles system) and words denoting Japanese people or phenomena in (Romanized) Japanese. So, for instance, the sixth Patriarch of Ch'an is given as 'Hui-neng', not 'Eno'.

For the sake of simplicity, I have referred to figures by their most familiar names. So Ma-tsu is simply Ma-tsu, not Ma-tsu Tao-I, Dōgen is simply Dōgen, not Dōgen Kigen. Moreover, I have generally chosen to omit honorific titles such as *rōshi* or *zenji*.

Introduction

This book is about the implications of Zen Buddhist teachings and practices for our moral relationship with nature. But more generally, it is a book about philosophy, and since it is a book about philosophy, I feel I ought to begin by saying something about the philosophical study of Zen.[1]

It is difficult – and in a certain sense, impossible – to say what Zen is, but most writers on the subject are agreed that it is not a philosophy, for a philosophy is a rational inquiry into the nature of things and Zen, whatever it is, is certainly not that. For writers such as D. T. Suzuki, the (alleged) irrationality of Zen represents a (thoroughly 'Eastern') virtue. For many clearheaded Western thinkers, it is a (thoroughly 'Eastern') vice. But in neither case is Zen thought to have much in common with the philosophical inquiries that have preoccupied Western thinkers for millennia. To be sure, Zen Buddhists might sometimes address similar questions – concerning the nature of the self, for instance, or time, or the existence of objects – but they do not try to answer these questions by formulating rational arguments, nor do they express their insights systematically in the form of philosophical treatises. They sit in meditation, contemplate seemingly nonsensical riddles, and indulge in other non-philosophical activities, all with the aim of achieving a direct insight into the mysteries of the universe.

This is a crude conception of Zen. For one thing, it overlooks figures like the thirteenth-century Zen master, Dōgen, who is widely regarded as having been a profound philosopher as well as a spiritual adept. Nonetheless, despite its shortcomings, this conception of Zen does contain some truth. In an important sense, Zen is anti-philosophical. Philosophical understanding is not necessary in order to practise Zen; in fact, philosophical reflections can sometimes obstruct one's practice – for example, if one's attempts to meditate are hindered by philosophical speculations on what exactly one is supposed to realize through meditation. Hence, I feel the need to begin this book by defending my explicitly philosophical approach to Zen.

So what do I think a philosophical inquiry into Zen can achieve? In short, I believe it may be of benefit to people who doubt the intellectual credibility of the tradition, and who may reject the idea of practising Zen as a result. These may be sceptics who dismiss Zen as mystical nonsense, and who believe that its speculations on the nature of things would not be able to withstand any very

---

[1] To refer to the tradition, I use the nouns 'Zen' and 'Zen Buddhism' interchangeably. To refer to a practitioner of Zen, I use the term 'Zen Buddhist', instead of the rather ugly 'Zennist'.

probing intellectual analysis. Or they may be people who, though intrigued by Zen, have been dogged by worries that the thoughts expressed in the tradition cannot be justified philosophically. In response to both these views, I hope to show in this book that Zen is philosophically robust.

To do this, my main strategy will be to look to the various philosophical traditions on which Zen is based and whose ideas are implicit in its practice: Taoism, for example, or Confucianism, or (in Japan) Shintō. For the most part, I will look to the philosophy of Buddhism.

But there is a danger here. It is possible that this demand for philosophical justification could lead one to identify Zen with a set of philosophical propositions. One might be led to think that Zen holds certain theses about how the world is, that 'all things are one', for instance, or that the self does not exist. The danger here is that one would then rest satisfied with a philosophical picture of Zen rather than Zen itself, that one would mistake the moon for the finger that points to it, to adapt a traditional saying.

My aim in this book will, therefore, not be to congeal the Zen tradition into a set of philosophical theses, but to, so to speak, clear a space for the practice of Zen, to do just enough conceptual work to show that Zen is not so vulnerable to philosophical criticism as it is often presumed to be. If I can convince cynics of that, then hopefully they will be more ready to turn to the practice of Zen; and it is in practice that the 'real' Zen may be found.

I will try to clear a space for the practice of Zen by clearing away some misconceptions about what Zen is. And since this is not a general philosophical investigation of Zen but, specifically, a book about environmental ethics, the misconceptions I will be tackling are all related to our moral relations with the natural world. Thus, Chapters Two through Five can be thought of as responses to particular criticisms of the idea of a Zen Buddhist environmental ethic. In responding to these criticisms, I hope to develop a philosophical account of our moral relations with the natural world. So if the negative aim of this book is to refute some objections to the idea that Zen Buddhism might have anything to offer environmental ethics, the positive aim is to develop an environmental ethic inspired by Zen.

More precisely, Chapters Two through Five address the following issues. Chapter Two addresses the charge that Zen is inimical to the whole business of morality, and so cannot yield an ethic of any sort. Chapter Three responds to the accusation that Zen is anthropocentric, that is, perniciously concerned with the well-being of humans, and so cannot yield an environmental ethic. Chapter Four addresses the charge that, by virtue of its commitment to the teaching of emptiness, Zen is unable to account for the value natural beings have 'in themselves', rather than as resources for our use. Chapter Five responds to the charge that Zen is irredeemably escapist and quietist, and so cannot motivate action in support of environmental objectives.

First, however, it is necessary to explain what Zen is. This is what I set out to do in Chapter One.

Chapter One

A Short History of Zen

The main purpose of this chapter is to explain what Zen is by looking at its historical development.[1] Another aim is to introduce the concepts, individuals and historical episodes I will be referring to in subsequent chapters, so that when I refer later in the book to the 'emptiness teaching' or to 'Dōgen Zenji', for example, readers will know to what or to whom I am referring.

The Buddha

If, as is conventionally held, Bodhidharma is the father of the tradition, then Zen was born in what is now modern day China around the turn of the sixth century CE. We will consider Bodhidharma presently. For the moment, it can be noted that even if this birth certificate is accurate, it is far from illuminating. Zen did not coalesce out of thin air, springing fully-fledged from the furrowed brow of Bodhidharma. To determine the nature of the tradition one must look back to times that even by the sixth century were considered ancient history, and one must look further afield than China. Most obviously, Zen is a form of Buddhism,[2] and to understand its nature one must look to the ancient Indian traditions of Buddhism from which it evolved.

Buddhism can of course be traced back to the Buddha himself, and so a good place to start in our history of Zen is with an account of the Buddha's life. (Or rather, an account of how his life has been traditionally understood. I leave the task of sifting the factual elements of it from the legend to historians.) The first thing to note here is that the word 'Buddha' means 'Awakened One', one who has, as it were, awoken from his spiritual slumber to perceive things as they really are. The title 'Buddha' can, moreover, be applied to any beings that have thus awoken, so

---

[1] For a more detailed history see Heinrich Dumoulin's two-volume *Zen Buddhism: A History* (New York: Macmillan, 1988, 1990).

[2] I am aware that this claim has been disputed in recent years by Noriaki Hakamaya and other exponents of the school of Critical Buddhism. For reasons that I will not canvass here, I do not believe their claims are well founded. For discussion of this issue see Jamie Hubbard and Paul L. Swanson (eds), *Pruning the Bodhi Tree: The Storm over Critical Buddhism* (Honolulu: University of Hawai'i Press, 1997).

that one can speak, as many Buddhists do, of a plurality of Buddhas, scattered throughout time and space. However, when people refer to *the* Buddha, they mean one Buddha in particular, Siddhartha Gautama, the historical figure credited with founding the Buddhist religion.

Gautama was born around 480 BCE in present-day Nepal, the son of a ruler of the Śākya people (hence his occasional title, Śākya-muni, the Sage of the Śākyas). As a prince, he grew to manhood surrounded by the luxuries of royal life: fine clothes, fragranced air, beautiful women, evenings spent strolling in the royal gardens. His was a life of ease and pleasure. But it was also a closeted life, one thoroughly insulated from the suffering of the world. His father, keen to persuade his son of the value of courtly life and to thereby secure a successor, ensured that it was kept that way.

Such an artificial existence could not, however, be sustained, and at the age of twenty-nine Gautama was suddenly brought face to face with the brutal facts of life.[3] On three consecutive excursions beyond the confines of the palace he came across, in turn, an old man, a sick man and a corpse, and so was exposed for the first time to the universal truths of aging, sickness and death. Life, he realized, was shot through with impermanence and suffering.

This realization was said to have hit home like a poisoned arrow, and now the prince found that he could find no contentment in his royal life and no solace in sensual pleasure. In the hope of finding some peace, he rode out, once again, from the palace. On this journey, Gautama is said to have encountered another startling and life-changing sight – a holy man, his head shaved and his face serene. This, he realized, was someone who had devoted himself entirely to overcoming suffering. That night, inspired by the holy man's commitment, the troubled prince stole out from the palace and took to the road, his aim to become a wandering ascetic himself and thereby to solve the problem of suffering. Eager for spiritual guidance, he turned first to the practice of yogic meditation. Yet he felt that even the rarefied modes of consciousness he managed to attain through these techniques fell short of his goal. So leaving his gurus, Gautama sought out another path, that of self-mortification. Now he subjected himself to the most terrible hardships, eating only a few drops of bean soup a day, exposing himself to withering heat and freezing cold, sleeping on thorns – all in an effort to break his attachment to sensual pleasures. But after several years of such austerities, Gautama was still not satisfied. Although he had excelled as an ascetic, his physical health was ruined and his mind was still in turmoil. He had not solved the problem of suffering.

Thus it was that having abandoned both his early life of sensual pleasure and the path of self-mortification, Gautama sat himself one evening under the famous *Bodhi*-tree at what is now Bodh-Gayā in northern India, and entered a state of deep meditation. At dawn, he had a great insight into the nature of the world, known as awakening or enlightenment. The problem of suffering, he realized, had now been solved. Gautama had now earned the title of Buddha.

---

[3] At least this is the story given in later *Sūtras*. See Peter Harvey, *An Introduction to Buddhism: teachings, history and practices* (Cambridge: Cambridge University Press, 1998), pp.17-18.

The religion, Buddhism, stems ultimately from Gautama's insight. Its core teachings are expressed as four 'Noble Truths':

> Suffering is inherent in life.
> Suffering is caused by craving.
> Craving and hence suffering can be destroyed.
> The Holy Eightfold Path is the course leading to this.[4]

These four statements can be explained according to an analogy drawn from medicine, in which the Buddha is portrayed as a kind of spiritual doctor. First, the Buddha diagnoses a disease: life is suffering (*duḥkha*). By this he means, not that life is an unremittingly painful journey – although in his time, as now, for many people it was – but that even those moments when life seems to be going well are marked by a sense of dissatisfaction. This could be the realization that even the best of times cannot last, or it could be a vague feeling that there is something lacking in life, that what is really important is being overlooked in one's day to day existence. In either case, claims the Buddha, life, even the life of a mollycoddled prince or a nectar-sipping god, is marked by dis-ease, *duḥkha*.

It is important to realize that the Buddha is not referring to a single life here. He is not claiming that one is born, suffers and then dies, and that death brings an end to suffering. On the contrary, to suffer is to be reborn time and time again, and so to suffer again and again in a cycle of rebirths known as *saṃsāra*. To be sure, some rebirths bring more suffering than others. According to the law of *karma*, if one's actions in one's past life were wholesome, one will enjoy a relatively happy rebirth, such as that of a fortunate human or a god. If, on the other hand, one's past actions were largely unwholesome, one will be reborn into a less auspicious station in the cosmic order – that of an animal, perhaps, or a ghost. But even in a divine existence, one's life will still be marked by a certain amount of *duḥkha*.

While the first Truth diagnoses the disease, the second identifies its cause: craving, or literally 'thirst' (*tṛṣṇa*). Included here are a host of strong and often seemingly uncontrollable desires: craving for things one wants, such as the sensual pleasures of sex, food and drink; craving to be rid of things one does not want; and craving directed towards oneself – selfish craving, the desire to enhance one's ego, for instance. It is craving that causes us to suffer in each of our lives, and it is, moreover, a craving for existence that ensures that we are reborn time and again in the cycle of *saṃsāra*.

After identifying the cause of the disease, the Buddha proceeds to determine whether it can be cured. Direct experience tells him that it can: the Buddha's enlightenment is said to have been an experience of *Nirvāṇa*, literally a 'quenching' of the 'fires' of craving, and hence the cessation of suffering.

Finally, like any doctor, the Buddha prescribes a course of treatment. To extinguish the fires of craving, he advises, one must develop the virtues set out in the Holy Eightfold Path: 1) right understanding, 2) right thought, 3) right speech, 4) right action, 5) right livelihood, 6) right effort, 7) right mindfulness, and 8) right

---

[4] From Harvey, *An Introduction to Buddhism*, p.23.

concentration. The Path lays out what it means to live a good life, that is, a life conducive to the extinction of craving and the cessation of suffering. One who lives such a life understands the true nature of the world; he thinks before he speaks and tells the truth; he abstains from harming living beings and from stealing; he makes an honest living; he keeps his mind alert through the mindfulness and concentration developed through meditation.

It would be wrong to think of the Eightfold Path as a set of instructions for how to escape reality and attain a state of blissful tranquillization. For Buddhism, craving is inseparable from ignorance, and to free oneself from craving one must develop one's understanding of the world. That is why right understanding is accorded the first and most important place on the Eightfold Path. Far from representing a flight from reality, Buddhism advocates a greater understanding of the world. Rather than transcending the world, one who is enlightened sees the true nature of things, the reality that but for the constant distractions of *saṃsāra* would have been evident all along.

For Buddhism, to understand the world correctly is to see that there is no such thing as an abiding self. First and foremost, this is a statement on personal identity: prefiguring David Hume, the Buddha contended that there is no essential 'you' that persists, unchanged, throughout 'your' life. Instead, there is only a collection of constantly changing elements (*skandhas*). On this point, the Buddha argued that the dominant religion of his day, Brahmanism, had got it wrong: the goal of life was not to realize one's true self (*ātman*), for there is no good reason and no compelling evidence to suggest that such an entity exists. There is no essence, no inner nature, no soul that makes someone who they are. Moreover, the mistake of thinking that an abiding self exists is not the sole province of Brahmins. Our everyday 'samsaric' existence is said to be predicated on the idea of such a self. This does not mean that ordinary folk subscribe to the philosophical proposition that such an entity exists. It means that our everyday actions, shot through, as they are, with self-centred craving, presuppose the existence of such a fictitious entity. When I crave a beer, I crave it for my*self*. Startled by the vehicle in the wing mirror, I fear for my*self*. Uneasy in front of the audience, I wonder how they are seeing *me*. And so on. Moreover, this truth of 'not-self' (*anātman*) is taken to apply to all beings, not just to humans. The Buddha maintained that nothing has a self-like essence which determines that it is one thing rather than another. All things are said to be empty (*śūnya*) of such a self.

This does not mean that no things exist. But it does mean that no things enjoy the kind of independent existence they would have if they were imbued with a soul or self. For Buddhism, the world is said to be marked by 'conditioned arising' (*pratīya-samutpāda*), which is to say that things are what they are, not because of some self-like essence inhering in them, but because of the presence of various conditions seemingly outside themselves. They arise when these conditions cohere, they persist as long as they obtain, and they disappear when the conditions disappear. And so as well as being empty of an abiding self, all things (bar *Nirvāṇa*) are said to be impermanent (*anitya*). Once this fact is thoroughly digested, it is said that one will stop craving objects but will instead view them with equanimity as mere shadows on the water.

This is a very rough sketch of the basic tenets of 'the *Dharma*', the Buddhist teachings. Readers who have found it all rather too much to take in would be well advised to consult a standard introduction to the religion before continuing with this book. Yet even on the basis of this sketch it is clear that the aim of Buddhism was from the beginning decidedly practical: the religion provides a set of practical guidelines for leading a life free from suffering, a happier, more fulfilling life. In a truly pragmatic spirit, the Buddha eschewed speculations that had no bearing on the problem of *duḥkha*, and he famously refused to indulge in metaphysical speculations for their own sake. To convey this point he used a memorable simile of a man struck by a poisoned arrow. Such a man would be foolish if he refused to be treated until he knew everything about his situation. He would be dead before he had learnt who shot the arrow and what the arrow was made of and all the details of its construction.[5] As we shall see, this fiercely pragmatic stance was to receive a special emphasis in Zen.

In line with this pragmatism, the ultimate aim of Buddhism is not (or not only) to arrive at an intellectual understanding of the core doctrines, but to realize them, to actually experience the conditioned arising of things, the truth of not-self, and so on. Enlightenment is said to be something that has to be experienced directly. It is the world as seen after awaking from a dream. That is why one who awakes is called a Buddha, an Awakened One.

The Mahāyāna

These early teachings are accepted, for the most part, by all Buddhist traditions; they constitute what one might call orthodox Buddhism. Some schools tried to preserve the core of this message in a pristine form, encouraging new interpretations of the old doctrines but resisting attempts to add new teachings. Theravāda Buddhism, which nowadays flourishes in Sri Lanka, Myanmar and Thailand, is the only surviving example of a school of this sort (in fact, 'Theravāda' is a Pali word meaning 'Ancient teaching'). Other Buddhist traditions were, however, less conservative.

The most influential of these more liberal schools were accounted to be part of the Mahāyāna tradition of Buddhism, which began to take shape from around 150 BCE. This movement was centred on the '*Bodhisattva* Path' of practice leading to Buddhahood. In early Buddhism, full Buddhahood was considered a lofty goal, one that could be attained only by following a long path of practice spanning innumerable rebirths. This was the path walked by *Bodhisattvas* ('beings-for-enlightenment'), spiritual virtuosos who aimed at the liberation of countless beings.[6] The great majority of practitioners, however, were advised to follow the path leading to the goal of *Arhat*-ship – roughly, sainthood – which nonetheless

---

[5] From the 'Minor Discourse with Māluṅkyāputta', discourse no.63 in the *Majjhima Nikāya; Middle Length Sayings*, translated by I. B. Horner, *Middle Length Sayings*, Vol.1. (London: PTS, 1954-9), 1.426-32.
[6] See Harvey, *An Introduction to Buddhism*, p.93.

involved the not insignificant rewards of release from the cycle of rebirth and entry into *Nirvāṇa*. By contrast, the Mahāyāna set up Buddhahood as a spiritual goal to which all beings ought to aspire. Moreover, if all beings should aspire to such a lofty goal, Mahāyāna texts such as the *Lotus Sūtra* maintained not only that Buddhahood was a goal that all beings could attain, but that, given enough rebirths, it was one that all beings *would* eventually reach.

A Buddha was seen as being more compassionate than an *Arhat*, and the way of the *Bodhisattva* was conceived as being a more altruistic path than that set out in the early teachings. Since it aimed at the salvation of countless beings, the Mahāyāna distinguished itself as the 'Great Vehicle', the vehicle 'capable of ferrying all sentient beings to the other shore of Buddhahood'.[7] The Śrāvakayāna or vehicle of the 'hearers', those who were held to have actually heard the Buddha, was disparaged as 'Hīnayāna', the 'Inferior Vehicle', and those who sought *Arhat*-ship were thought not only to have sold themselves short in striving for a lesser spiritual goal, but as being infected with a subtle form of selfishness. This was an unfair charge and I shall avoid the pejorative label 'Hīnayāna' in this book. Nevertheless, whatever the justification of its caricatures of other schools, the Mahāyāna certainly accorded altruistic action a central role on the spiritual path, and indeed made compassion a pre-eminent virtue (of which more presently).

The Mahāyāna was also marked by developments in other areas of Buddhist philosophy, notably in the teaching of emptiness (*śūnyatā*). References to emptiness were present in the Buddha's teachings from the beginning: it was because things were empty (*śūnya*) of self-existence that they were said to depend for their existence on conditions seemingly outside themselves. In some Buddhist schools – the Vaibhāṣika Abhidharma school, for instance – this general commitment to the emptiness of things was taken to mean that the objects that populate our everyday world exist, not 'in themselves', but as combinations of basic elements called *dharmas*.[8] It was in this sense that things were said to be empty of self-existence. By contrast, *dharmas*, being the fundamental elements of reality, *were* held to be self-existent.

This understanding of emptiness was not accepted by all Buddhist schools, however, and it was not accepted by the schools of the Mahāyāna.[9] A more radical interpretation of the teaching of *śūnyatā* is evident in the collection of Mahāyāna *Sūtras* known as the Perfection of Wisdom literature. It is also evident in the work of the second century CE Indian philosopher-monk, Nāgārjuna, and in the school of Mahāyāna based on his teachings, the Madhyamaka or 'middle way' school. According to this more radical understanding, *all* things are held to be empty of self-existence, where for our purposes we can take this set to include anything you care to name: selves, sentient beings, language, thoughts, emotions, and so on. On this understanding, then, and against Vaibhāṣika Abhidharma, even *dharmas* are

---

[7] Takeuchi Yoshinori (ed.), *Buddhist Spirituality: Indian, Southeast Asian, Tibetan, Early Chinese* (London: SCM Press, 1994), p.xxi.

[8] To be distinguished from *Dharma*, the Buddhist teachings.

[9] Which is not to say that all the schools that rejected the self-existence of *dharmas* were originally classified as Mahāyāna. See Paul Williams, *Mahāyāna Buddhism: the doctrinal foundations* (London: Routledge, 1996), pp.16, 43, 46-7.

considered to be empty. Indeed, from the standpoint of Madhyamaka, even so lofty an 'object' as *Nirvāṇa* is thought to depend for its existence upon *saṃsāra*. (It is the *Bodhisattva's* realization of this that enables him to walk a 'middle way' between the two realms, immersing himself in the manifold sufferings of *saṃsāra*, but without being stained by craving and without being caused to suffer. In this way he is said to be able to work most effectively to alleviate the suffering of his fellow beings.) Moreover, if *Nirvāṇa* should not be thought of as self-existent then neither should *śūnyatā*. For according to Madhyamaka, emptiness is not a noun denoting an entity, but an adjectival quality of things, and as such depends upon the existence of various things which can be said to be empty of self-existence.[10] For this reason, *śūnyatā* should not be thought of as some sort of metaphysical absolute, along the lines of the Christian creator-God, say, or Vedānta's *Brahman*.

The final truth expounded in the Perfection of Wisdom literature and by Nāgārjuna is therefore emptiness, the teaching that all things – emptiness included – are conditioned. For Nāgārjuna, this is the real meaning of the teaching of conditioned arising: that all things arise and persist in dependence upon other things.[11] It is, moreover, important to note that this conditioning is not merely causal; for Nāgārjuna the dependence between things referred to is conceptual or logical, so that it does not make sense even to *imagine* an abstract whole, for instance, existing independently of its parts, or an abstract 'now' existing apart from a past and a future.

It would, however, be misleading to suppose that Nāgārjuna claimed this as a *thesis* about the world or that the school deriving from his teachings, the Madhyamaka, subscribes to the philosophical *proposition* that all things are empty of self-existence. On the contrary, Nāgārjuna's aim was not to congeal his account of emptiness into a theory but to put it to *work*. In his *Mūlamadhyamakakārikā* (*Fundamentals of the Middle Way*) he did this by turning his attention to the positions espoused by the philosophers of his day. Too often, it seemed, scholars had tried to capture the true nature of things in a set of philosophical propositions. And too often these propositions had stopped being illuminating (i.e., conducive to one's spiritual practice) but had instead become objects of attachment, groups of scholars defending their respective positions like bands of soldiers huddled round standards raised in the midst of battle. In opposition to these tendencies to theorization, the *Mūlamadhyamakakārikā* consists of a series of attacks on philosophical views, Nāgārjuna showing, in each case, how any standpoint that might be taken on a particular philosophical question is untenable. For instance, in one chapter he shows how no view that can be proffered regarding the identity of cause and effect can be upheld in the light of analysis. There are only four possible views on the matter, and none of them, he holds, are tenable: either (1) cause and effect are completely identical, or (2) not identical in any way, or (3) both identical and not identical, or (4) neither identical nor not identical.[12]

---

[10] Harvey, *An Introduction to Buddhism*, p.99.
[11] Inada, Kenneth K. *Nāgārjuna: A Translation of his Mūlamadhyamakakārikā with an Introductory Essay* (Tokyo: The Hokuseido Press, 1970), Chapter 24, Verse 18 (p.148).
[12] Ibid. Chapter 1.

Explaining Nāgārjuna's argument for this conclusion would take us to too far off track.[13] For present purposes, it will suffice to note that his aim in the *Mūlamadhyamakakārikā*, and elsewhere, was not to propound a philosophical thesis of his own regarding emptiness but to show emptiness in action, as it were, in the dissolution of philosophical problems. Madhyamaka philosophy is therefore therapeutic, as, on one interpretation, is the later work of Wittgenstein. Recognizing the pathology of philosophical thought, it aspires to be a universal solvent for all philosophical views, rather than a view itself. Its aim is to inspire the reader to break free of all attachments to particular theses, and to thus experience the true nature of things firsthand.

Aside from the Madhyamaka, the other major Indian school of the Mahāyāna was the Yogācāra or Cittamātra school, founded by Asanga (fourth or fifth century) and developed by his half-brother Vasubandhu.

Like all schools of Buddhism, Yogācāra maintains that the world does not exist in the way we ordinarily perceive it to exist. The apparently hard-edged, self-existent things that surround us are said to be the projections of our unenlightened 'samsaric' consciousness, and in this respect like illusions. Yogācāra provides a theory of mind to account for how this mental construction occurs and to explain its relation to enlightenment.

From the standpoint of Yogācāra, portraying things as illusory encourages practitioners to withdraw themselves from the 'samsaric' world. Seeing things as mental constructions, as 'mind-only' or 'thought-only' (*citta-mātra*), one becomes less attached to them, less bound to them. Moreover, as this view is internalized through meditation, one becomes aware that just as there are no independently existing 'external' objects, so there is no 'inner' subject that apprehends them (for in the absence of an object, how could a subject exist?). With this realization, it is said that the active functions of one's mind, which normally project the everyday world, abruptly cease, and one becomes directly, intuitively aware of their source, a profound level of mind known as the 'storehouse consciousness' (*ālaya-vijñāna*). The *ālaya* is said to be a non-dual and ineffable source of the world, a universal reality lying 'within' all beings.[14]

Another tradition of the Mahāyāna that held that the ultimate nature of things is, so to speak, 'within' us was the Tathāgata-garbha tradition. The Mahāyāna teaching, expounded in texts such as the *Lotus Sūtra*, recall, was that all beings are potential Buddhas, indeed that all beings are destined to become Buddhas. The Tathāgata-garbha tradition went further in claiming that all beings are imbued with an intrinsically pure 'Buddha-nature', which meant that all beings are not potential Buddhas, but actual Buddhas who are but unaware of their enlightenment. Enlightenment is accordingly not a matter of becoming something that one is not, but of realizing one's inherently enlightened nature. We shall see below that this idea was to have an important influence on Zen.

---

[13] For a digestible account of Nāgārjuna's reasoning here see Thomas P. Kasulis, *Zen Action, Zen Person* (Honolulu: University of Hawaii Press, 1985), pp.20-1.

[14] Harvey, *An Introduction to Buddhism*, p.108.

Although, in Yogācāra, the *ālaya* was thought to be empty of the subject-object duality, *pace* the Madhyamaka, it was not considered to be empty of self-existence. Similarly, for the Tathāgata-garbha tradition, the Buddha-nature was said to be empty of 'defilements' such as greed, hatred and delusion, but not empty of the good qualities one would associate with Buddhahood. On the contrary, it was described in positive terms as being brightly shining and pure. Enlightenment was said to involve removing the defilements that normally encrust one's true nature to allow this inherent purity to shine forth.

China

Buddhism initially spread from India to China in the first centuries of the Common Era, transmitted along the trade routes running north through Kashmir, Pakistan and Afghanistan, before turning east to join the Silk Route, linking the great Chinese capital of Ch'ang-an with the Mediterranean. Its establishment in China must, however, be to a large extent credited to the pilgrims, translators and missionaries who brought Buddhists texts to China, Indians like Kumārajīva (344-413) and Chinese like Hsüan-tsang (596-664).

These men delivered the scriptures to a land whose culture was dominated by two philosophies, Confucianism and Taoism. Confucianism, for its part, was (and is) a comprehensive body of thought, at once a socio-political ideology and a rich philosophy, incorporating speculations on topics ranging from metaphysics to ethics to epistemology. In attempting to summarize it, I will concentrate on the thought of its founder, Confucius (Ch. K'ung Fu-tzu; b.551 BCE). One of Confucius's primary concerns was to provide an account of the ideal life, the life of the *chun tzu* or 'superior person'. Such a life was said to be marked by the cultivation of *jen*, a quality conventionally translated as 'benevolence', but which seems also to connote a sort of moral *gravitas* that enables the *chun tzu* to live his life with assurance, immune from the anxieties that cause lesser men to veer off course.[15] As well as being, in this latter respect, 'at one' with himself, the *chun tzu* was said to be in harmony both with the workings of 'heaven' (*t'ien*) and with his essential nature, a nature which Mencius (Ch. Meng-tzu; *c.*372-289 BCE) was later to argue was intrinsically good. For our purposes, it is important to note that the *chun tzu* was said to express his moral excellence by adhering to *li*, the catalogue of duties and responsibilities that attend one's station in life. These are social responsibilities, both to society as a whole and to one's family. Indeed, special importance is attached to the latter, qualities such as filial piety, the virtue expressed in honouring one's parents and, by extension, one's ancestors, being deemed especially praiseworthy. By adhering to *li* in this way, a man was said to fulfil his proper role in the strict hierarchy that constitutes the universe.

---

[15] See David E. Cooper, *World Philosophies: an historical introduction, 2nd edition* (Oxford: Blackwell, 2003), pp.68-9.

Taoism[16] is chiefly associated with two texts: the *Tao te Ching* or *Lao Tzu*, which was traditionally held to have been composed by Lao-tzu in the sixth century BCE, but which modern scholars now believe to be a compilation of older teachings assembled in the fourth century BCE; and the *Book of Chuang Tzu*, whose titular author lived in the third or fourth century BCE. Like Confucianism, Taoism is centrally concerned with providing an account of the ideal life, but its conception of what that life must involve is diametrically opposed to the Confucian account of the *chun tzu*. Put simply, for Taoists the ideal life is a life lived in accordance with the way of things, the *Tao*, where the *Tao* is portrayed as a mysterious, creative force which both flows through and gives rise to all things. However, any attempt to determine more precisely the nature of this enigmatic 'force', and thus what it might mean to live in harmony with it, immediately encounters the problem that the *Tao* is held to be ineffable (as the *Tao Te Ching* famously states: 'The way that can be spoken of/Is not the constant way').[17] But although it is said that the *Tao* cannot be determinately captured in words, its nature is conveyed in Taoist texts by the use of several metaphors. We learn that the *Tao* is yielding and pliant, like water flowing around obstacles. To live in accord with the *Tao* is, moreover, to become soft and pliant like the *Tao* itself, to become 'submissive', 'weak', 'feminine', 'yielding', and so on. To act in harmony with the *Tao* is not to force matters but to 'go with the flow'. This manner of acting is exemplified by the man who, to adopt Martin Heidegger's apt phrase, 'lets things be'. It is the seamless harmony with things exemplified by the deft strokes of the skilled woodcarver working with the grain of the wood, or by the green-fingered gardener sensitively responding to the turning of the seasons. It even characterizes the more cerebral life of the sage who through contemplation has brought himself into accord with the true nature of things.

But it would not seem to be the sort of action encouraged by Confucianism. Chuang-tzu especially derided the Confucian adherence to customs and responsibilities, claiming that the man whose life is dominated by social conventions, etiquette and all the other trappings of civilized life had settled for a lesser life. Traditionally, Taoism has therefore been associated with the ideal of a simple, solitary existence, lived in some natural setting far removed from the trappings of civilized culture. As we shall see, some Zen Buddhists came to advocate a similar ideal.

Buddhism did not readily take root on Chinese soil, the foreign religion being – or rather being perceived to be – too otherworldly to appeal to the Chinese, who were generally more down to earth (and inveterately suspicious of all things foreign to boot). Buddhist aims at escaping the everyday, familiar world of *samsāra* jarred with the thisworldly spirit of Chinese thought, wherein the main goals of life – longevity, for instance – were to be found in the world rather than 'beyond' it. The otherworldly nature of the foreign religion was thought to be exemplified in the social structure of monasticism. Since the *Vinaya* rules for

---

[16] I am here concerned with 'philosophical' Taoism as opposed to the 'popular' Taoism associated with divination, alchemy and a number of other occult practices.

[17] *Tao Te Ching*, translated by D. C. Lau (Middlesex: Penguin, 1982), p.57.

monastic life explicitly prohibited productive labour, sceptical commentators noted that the Buddhist monastic community or *Saṃgha* (usually rendered in the Pali as *Saṅgha*) would always be economically parasitic on society, monks having to rely on the seemingly ignoble practice of almsgiving. Moreover, their celibacy was seen as harming the ancestral line, and their relinquishment of family ties was seen as unfilial. More generally, it was charged that Buddhists saw themselves as apart from, and often above, the concerns of society, demonstrating a disregard for the social hierarchies so important for Confucians. At first, they even refused to bow to the emperor – a shocking display of disrespect in the eyes of the Chinese.

Buddhism, then, might initially be thought to have fallen on stony ground in China; yet history shows that it did nonetheless take root in the land. Indeed, in later centuries the foreign religion was thoroughly absorbed by the Chinese: by the T'ang dynasty (618-907) Mahāyāna Buddhism was the dominant religion in the country. A key event in the rise of Chinese Buddhism was the disintegration of the Confucian-dominated Han dynasty in the early years of the third century CE. In the ensuing Period of Disunity, which lasted from 221 to 589, many thinkers disillusioned with the social philosophy of Confucianism turned for solace to Taoism. In its lack of interest in socio-political matters and its emphasis on a simple, selfless life lived at one with nature, Taoism had much in common with Buddhism, and the foreign religion accordingly took root in an intellectual climate dominated by Taoist thought. Or, more precisely, the intellectual scene at the time was dominated by Neo-Taoism, a rather more scholastic, philosophically inclined form of the religion which explored metaphysical and ontological questions in terms of the broad categories of understanding set out in the work of Lao-tzu and other old masters. Buddhist teachings therefore came to be translated by and interpreted using a broad set of metaphysical and ontological categories derived from Taoism. For instance, the idea of emptiness (*śūnyatā*; Ch. *k'ung*) was interpreted – rightly or wrongly, as the case may be – in terms of the Neo-Taoist conception of *wu* or non-being, a term often used to denote the nature of the *Tao*.

These Neo-Taoist interpretations of emptiness were arguably at odds with Madhyamaka since they tended to conceive *śūnyatā* in ontological terms as an ineffable source of the world rather than as an adjectival quality of things (according to which references to emptiness always denote the absence of some specific property). They seemed to have more in common with the more positive accounts of emptiness articulated in the Yogācāra and Tathāgata-garbha traditions, according to which *śūnyatā* was taken to represent an ultimate reality (the *ālaya*, the Buddha-nature) which could be discovered through introspection. Accordingly, in two of the most influential texts in Chinese Buddhism, the *Laṅkāvatāra Sūtra* and the Chinese-composed *Treatise on the Awakening of Faith in the Mahāyāna*, one finds the Yogācāra and Tathāgata-garbha traditions combined; indeed, the *Laṅkā* identifies the Buddha-nature with both the *tathāgata-garbha* (the 'embryonic Buddha') and the *ālaya*.[18]

---

[18] D. T. Suzuki (trans), *The Laṅkāvatāra Sūtra* (London, Routledge & Kegan Paul, 1973), Chapter 6, Section 82.

The idea of the Buddha-nature proved especially popular amongst Chinese thinkers. For Confucians, it chimed with the idea of the innate goodness of man. For Taoists, its status as a mysterious, ineffable reality recalled accounts of the *Tao*.[19] Furthermore, both the *Laṅkā* and *Awakening* stressed that, in keeping with the ineffability of the Buddha-nature, enlightenment must consist in ceasing the discursive activity of the mind and thus returning it to a state of quiescent stillness in which the pure radiance of the Buddha-nature could shine forth.[20] For if our natures are already pure, why, it was asked, do we need to think our way out of our delusions? This stance struck a chord with the Taoist idea that the true nature of things cannot be captured in language and that the *Tao* is attained, not through discursive thought, but through acting spontaneously in accord with our essential nature.

For Tao-sheng (*c*.360-434), this kind of realization could only come all at once, for it made no sense to suppose that insight into the indivisible Buddha-nature could come piecemeal. His conception of 'sudden enlightenment' met with much opposition, no less a man than Seng-chao (384-414), one of the greatest figures in early Chinese Buddhism, being called upon to defend the 'gradualist' alternative.[21] As we shall see, the idea of sudden enlightenment would win more favour in later years, when it would come to be associated with the school of Ch'an (Zen) Buddhism.[22]

Another characteristically Chinese Buddhist concept that was to have an important influence on the development of Zen was the idea that the whole of reality is contained in each and every individual phenomenon. This view was associated with two Buddhist schools in particular: the syncretic T'ien-t'ai (Jp. Tendai) School and the Hua-yen (Jp. Kegon) school, both of which flourished in the T'ang dynasty (618-907). In the main text of the latter school, the enormous *Avataṃsaka Sūtra* (*Flower Ornament Sūtra*), the idea is famously expressed by the metaphor of the 'Jewel Net of Indra'. The *Sūtra* describes a net extending infinitely in all directions, a single sparkling jewel set into each of its infinite 'eyes'. The net and the jewels have been arranged in such a way that each jewel reflects every other jewel (and its reflection in the other jewels), and so on to infinity. In this manner, the entire net finds itself reflected in each and every particular jewel. This is a grandiose image, and the metaphysics behind it is abstruse; however, the conception of a universe in which individual phenomena are each invested with a supreme significance served as an affirmation of the phenomenal world which resonated with the Taoist idea that one could realize one's unity with the *Tao* through everyday, practical actions. In an idea that was to achieve its consummation in Zen, enlightenment was not a remote goal, but a reality evident

[19] John P. Keenan, 'Yogācāra in China' in Yoshinori (ed.), *Buddhist Spirituality: Indian, Southeast Asian, Tibetan, Early Chinese*, p.366.
[20] See Williams, *Mahāyāna Buddhism*, p.111.
[21] Whalen Lai, 'The Three Jewels in China' in Yoshinori (ed.), *Buddhist Spirituality: Indian, Southeast Asian, Tibetan, Early Chinese*, p.308.
[22] Though perhaps not because of the influence of the Tao-sheng himself. See Dumoulin, *Zen Buddhism, Vol.1*, p.77.

here and now in one's dealings with ordinary things. In this way, *Nirvāṇa* was said to be present in the midst of one's everyday 'samsaric' life.

Ch'an

So far we have been considering the salient features of the intellectual landscape which gave birth to Zen. Now it is time to turn to the history of Zen itself. The first thing to note is that 'Zen' is a Japanese word; for the Chinese stage of its evolution, Zen ought more properly to be referred to as 'Ch'an'. (In this chapter I will honour this distinction, but in later chapters I will ignore it for the sake of convenience.)

According to tradition, the school of Ch'an can be traced to Bodhidharma, an Indian monk who arrived in China sometime around the late fifth century CE. Legends portray him as an eccentric figure, iconoclastic, unperturbed by authority and, moreover, fiercely dedicated to the practice of a remarkably austere form of sitting meditation. One of the most famous stories about him tells of his meeting with Emperor Wu of Liang (502-550 CE). Wu was a very pious ruler, who during his reign had been an enthusiastic patron of Buddhism – on several occasions, he even pledged himself as a serf to a temple so that the royal court had to ransom him back.[23] Face to face with the strange Indian, the Emperor asked how much merit he had accrued from his patronage of Buddhism. 'No merit,' replied Bodhidharma. Somewhat taken aback, the Emperor tried another question: 'What is the highest meaning of the holy truths?' 'Vast emptiness, no holiness,' came the reply. 'Who are you to say this?' the Emperor demanded. 'I do not know,' answered Bodhidharma, and left.

The word 'Ch'an' is a transliteration of the Sanskrit *dhyāna*, a term meaning meditation, and as one would therefore expect, the Ch'an school was marked from its very beginning by a special emphasis on the practice of meditation. Indeed, if Bodhidharma's eccentricities and disrespect of authority remind one of the stories of Taoist sages, accounts of his commitment to meditation recall the feats of Indian yogis. He is, for instance, said to have spent nine years meditating before a wall in a monastery – so long that according to one legend his legs fell off.

The following succinct description of Ch'an is attributed to Bodhidharma:

> A special transmission outside the scriptures;
> Without depending on words and letters;
> Pointing directly to the human mind;
> Seeing the innate nature, one becomes a Buddha.[24]

The deprecation of scriptural knowledge in this account is one of the most distinctive features of Ch'an. It provides the basis for the later stories of Zen

---

[23] Whalen Lai, 'The Three Jewels in China', p.309. Bodhidharma's encounter with the Emperor is the first incident recorded in the *Hekiganroku*, a Sung dynasty compilation. I have followed the translation provided in Tenshin Fletcher and David Scott, *Way of Zen* (Barcelona: Vega, 2001), p.58.

[24] I use the version quoted in Harvey, *An Introduction to Buddhism*, p.154.

masters burning the Buddhist scriptures – the rationale for such a stance being, presumably, that attachment, even to so lofty an object as a Mahāyāna *Sūtra*, is nonetheless an attachment and hence an obstacle on the spiritual path. That said, it would perhaps be naïve to take these stories of *Sūtra*-burning monks at face value, it being likely that they functioned solely as rhetorical devices, rather than accounts of actual incidents.[25] In fact, notwithstanding his insistence that Ch'an did not depend on words and letters, Bodhidharma himself was said to have been a champion of the *Laṅkāvatāra Sūtra*, and the conception of enlightenment expressed in the short description above is entirely in accord with the teachings of that *Sūtra*.[26] On that conception, enlightenment consists in realizing the innate purity of one's mind, where this is achieved without the intermediary of language, indeed by cutting off discursive thought. For this reason it is said that, when interrogated about the nature of insight, a genuinely enlightened man or woman might respond with silence – as the lay-*Bodhisattva* Vimalakīrti does when questioned about such matters in the Mahāyāna *Sūtra* bearing his name.

Yet this account of enlightenment would seem to create problems for a religious tradition. If awakening really is such an esoteric affair, consisting solely in one's personal acquaintance with one's essential nature, then how could the authentic understanding be preserved in a tradition? After all, there could be no possibility of crystallizing the Ch'an insights into a text which could then be held up as embodying the essence of the tradition. In the face of these problems, Ch'an was said to rely on an intimate teaching relationship, a 'special transmission', as Bodhidharma puts it, from master to pupil. The blueprint for such a transmission was taken to be the Buddha's communication of the *Dharma* to his disciple Mahākāśyapa. The story of that event tells how the Buddha, facing an audience eager for profundity and teaching, responded by quietly and simply holding out a flower. Surveying the sea of perplexed faces before him, he saw that only Mahākāśyapa was smiling. This monk, the Buddha recognized, was his *Dharma* heir, and he proclaimed to his baffled audience that he was entrusting the teaching to him. This incident is considered so important in Zen that Mahākāśyapa is traditionally considered the first Indian Patriarch of Ch'an. Bodhidharma is traditionally considered the first Chinese Patriarch of Ch'an, or the twenty-eighth since the Buddha.

Bodhidharma transmitted his teaching to Hui-k'o (the second Patriarch), who transmitted it to Seng-ts'an. Tao-hsin (580-651), the fourth Patriarch, did much to adapt Ch'an to its Chinese setting, tempering its individualistic, anti-societal tenor, and making it more amenable to the communitarian Chinese. Relaxing the prohibition on productive labour, he made the Ch'an monasteries more self-sufficient and less dependent on alms. Though all the Ch'an chronicles agree that Hung-jen (601-674) was the fifth Patriarch, the subsequent line of transmission became the subject of dispute. Nowadays, all Zen schools recognize Hui-neng (638-713) as the sixth Patriarch; however, the actual lineage is open to question.

---

[25] See Dale S. Wright, *Philosophical Meditations on Zen Buddhism* (Cambridge: Cambridge University Press, 1998), pp.127-8, 140.

[26] See David J. Kalupahana, *A History of Buddhist Philosophy: continuities and discontinuities* (Delhi: Motilal Banarsidass, 1994), p.230.

According to tradition, Hung-jen, eager to secure a *Dharma* heir, had announced that if candidates composed verses demonstrating their levels of insight (a common method for assessing understanding in Ch'an), he would choose his heir based on the quality of the verses composed. Two verses were written on the monastery wall. The first had been composed by Shen-hsiu (600-706), the head monk:

> The body is the Bodhi [enlightenment] tree,
> The mind is like a clear mirror.
> At all times we must strive to polish it,
> And must not let the dust collect.

Next to it was the following response:

> Bodhi originally has no tree,
> The mirror also has no stand.
> Buddha-nature is always clear and pure;
> Where is there room for dust?[27]

Hung-jen saw that the greater insight was expressed in the second verse, and that the title of *Dharma* heir must rightfully belong to its author. It transpired, however, that the second verse had been composed by Hui-neng, an uneducated kitchen helper at the monastery, who, being illiterate, had dictated it to a friend. Concerned lest the other monks be angry at being bested by a mere servant, Hung-jen called Hui-neng to his room in secret. There he taught him the *Diamond Sūtra*, and Hui-neng, suddenly enlightened, was made the sixth Patriarch.

This, then, is the traditional story of how Hui-neng became the sixth Patriarch. Its lesson is clear: Shen-hsiu was the representative of an outdated conception of enlightenment, the idea that awakening is achieved through a gradual purification of the mind. This was superseded by Hui-neng's new conception of practice, centred on the idea of a sudden insight into the emptiness of all things.

Yet the story is largely that, an invention. The traditional account of Hung-jen's transmission was invented by a monk called Shen-hui (668-760) to legitimate the lineage of the particular school of Ch'an he represented. That school was the so-called 'Sudden' or Southern school, which claimed the *Diamond Sūtra* rather than the *Laṅkā* as its guiding text, and which held that enlightenment took the form of an instantaneous insight into emptiness. It pitched itself in opposition to the school Shen-hui dubbed the 'Gradual' or Northern school of Ch'an, which recognized Shen-hsiu, not Hui-neng, as the sixth Patriarch, and which was associated with the idea that enlightenment is achieved through a gradual purification of the mind. The opposition between the 'sudden' and 'gradual' approaches was, however, to a great extent constructed: by the time of Shen-hui the Northern school admitted the importance of sudden insights in practice, while Southern Ch'an, for its part, did not dismiss the importance of gradual development in practice. (In fact, schools such as the Niu-t'ou (Oxhead) school

[27] Both verses are from *The Platform Sutra of the Sixth Patriarch*, translated by Philip B. Yampolsky (New York: Columbia University Press, 1967), p.130. My annotation.

saw their teachings as consistent with both traditions.)[28] Nevertheless, Shen-hui did not believe that Shen-hsiu should be considered the sixth Patriarch; that title, he proclaimed, belonged to his teacher, Hui-neng. Hence the legend.[29]

Shen-hui's story clearly did little to enhance the reputation of the Northern School; however, the main reason for the demise of that school in the eighth century was political. Notwithstanding his rather demeaning caricature in the *Platform Sūtra* of Hui-neng, Shen-hsiu did much to promote Buddhism at the court of Empress Wu (625-705 CE), and his teaching became closely associated with the T'ang rule. But the benefits of these royal associations proved in the end to be double-edged. When the T'ang court began to lose ground in the mid-eighth century, the Northern school began to decline as well.

The decline of the Northern Ch'an of the cities coincided with the rise of other schools in the rural areas of the south. The influence of Shen-hui can be seen in the fact that they all traced their lineage to Hui-neng.[30] One master of this period was Shih-t'ou (700-790). His school emphasized the value of a solitary life, lived out on the open road or in secluded mountain retreats. Communion with nature was highly valued, and Shih-t'ou himself composed several poems conveying his sympathy with the natural world and its connection with practice.

The most famous school of this period was, however, the school of Hung-chou Ch'an, which derived from the teachings of Ma-tsu (*c.*709-788). This was a school of rustic Ch'an. For Ma-tsu and his followers, practice was not a matter of retiring to some cloistered existence to spend one's days in meditation, but of living in the midst of the world close to ordinary people, and teaching in the colloquial language to which they could relate. In line with this new conception of practice, Hung-chou Ch'an embodied a new conception of meditation. The early schools of Ch'an had followed Bodhidharma in setting meditation at the centre of their practice. Ma-tsu, however, had been convinced by his teacher, Nan-yüeh (677-744), that trying to attain Buddhahood solely through the practice of meditation was like trying to make a mirror by rubbing a tile.[31] For Hung-chou Ch'an, our Buddha-nature is already pure, it does not need to be purified, it needs only to be realized. And it can be realized in any activity, be it chopping wood, carrying water or washing dishes. Moreover, beings lost in the dream of *saṃsāra* are best shaken awake, shocked into suddenly realizing their inherently pure Buddha-nature. To this purpose, the Hung-chou masters employed a variety of shock tactics as 'skilful means' for jolting their pupils to realization: sudden shouts, irrational retorts, even physical beatings. Attention was now shifted onto the way a master taught, not just what he taught, and records of the master's words and actions were collected together to

---

[28] Thomas P. Kasulis, 'Ch'an Spirituality' in Takeuchi Yoshinori (ed.), *Buddhist Spirituality: Later China, Korea, Japan, and the Modern World* (London: SCM Press, 1999), p.28.

[29] See Philip Yampolsky, 'Ch'an: a historical sketch' in Yoshinori (ed.), *Buddhist Spirituality: Later China, Korea, Japan, and the Modern World*, pp.6-10.

[30] Ibid. p.11.

[31] Dale Wright, 'Four Ch'an Masters' in Yoshinori (ed.), *Buddhist Spirituality: Later China, Korea, Japan, and the Modern World*, p.35. But compare Philip Kapleau, *The Three Pillars of Zen* (London: Rider and Company, 1985), pp.23-5.

form a new breed of literature, the *yu-lu* (J. *go roku*) or 'Discourse Record' texts. These records have a very Chinese flavour: the illogical and often amusing stories of eccentric masters recalling the tales of the laughing, carefree Taoist sages of old.

Meanwhile, far from the rural haunts of Shih-t'ou and Ma-tsu, the T'ang government, weakened by a draining civil war, was in economic crisis. To replenish its coffers it turned its greedy eye towards the powerful and influential Buddhist establishment. Thus began the great persecution of Buddhism of 845-6. Monks and nuns were forced to disrobe, temples were looted and their land was confiscated. Although establishment Buddhism was decimated in these years, the rural schools were, again, little affected. Five schools of Ch'an survived, of which two were particularly important for the subsequent development of the tradition, the schools of Lin-chi and of Ts'ao-tung.

In his early years as a teacher, Lin-chi (J. Rinzai; d.866) continued the aggressive, hands-on Hung-chou style of instruction he had learnt from his teacher, Huang-po (d.850?), and he became known for his use of the shout and the stick as means of prompting his students to realization. The Lin-chi school came to emphasize the use of the famous Ch'an *kung-ans* (J. *kōans*), short stories or questions that could be used both to inspire students to realize their true natures and to test their degree of insight. *Kung-ans* are often baffling; consider the following one from Chao-chao (J. Jōshū; 778-897):

> A monk asked Chao-chao: 'Has a dog the Buddha-nature?'
> The Master replied: '*Wu*!' (No!)

This famous *kung-an* has been the object of countless studies. It is said that penetration into its meaning can only come about as a result of awakening. Although the Chinese word *wu* (usually rendered in Japanese as *mu*) is a negation, Chao-chao is not simply denying that the dog has the Buddha-nature: such a response would, for one thing, contradict the Mahāyānist *Mahāparinirvāṇa Sūtra*'s teaching that all sentient beings have the Buddha-nature. Or rather, he is not rejecting the idea that *the dog* has some property Buddha-nature; he is rejecting the idea that the dog has some *property* Buddha-nature, as if the dog and the non-dual Buddha-nature were separate beings. So the *kung-an* ought not to be considered a denial of the doctrine of universal Buddhahood. But how, then, should it be understood? The answer is that it ought not to be understood at all – and certainly not in this detached, intellectual way. A *kung-an* is not a riddle. It is rather an object of meditation, the purpose of which is to occasion an existential crisis, a 'Great Doubt', in the mind of the meditator, in which discursive thought ceases, and from which awakening can spontaneously arise. So in the form of *kung-an* meditation known as *hua-t'ou*, for example, the meditator does not ponder the 'meaning' of the *kung-an*, but focuses instead only on its 'critical phrase'. In the example above, he concentrates only on Chao-chao's single word: *wu*. When this word comes to fill his mind entirely, discursive thought ceases and the mind is said to be primed to awaken.

In the Sung dynasty (960-1279), the Lin-chi school flourished, and the *kung-ans* which it used were collected into anthologies like the 12th century *Pi-yen lu* (*Blue Cliff Records*) and the 13th century *Wu-men kuan* (*The Gateless Gate*). The schools of T'ang dynasty Ch'an, and in particular, the Hung-chou school, were now looked back to as epitomizing a 'golden age' of Ch'an, and much of the literature on these schools was composed during this period. Another important body of literature composed in the Sung were the various lineages legitimizing Ch'an as a school of Buddhism and portraying the Ch'an masters as the rightful heirs of the historical Buddha. Tao-yüan's *Ch'ing-te ch-uan-teng lu* (*The Transmission of the Lamp*) was an example of one such work.

The Ts'ao-tung (J. Sōtō) school was founded by Tung-shan (807-869) in the ninth century. It continued the less confrontational lineage of Ch'an deriving from Shih-t'ou, and accorded a central role to sitting meditation (*tso-ch'an*; J. *zazen*) and the realization of the natural radiance of the enlightened mind. Just as there had been a certain amount of conflict between the Northern and Southern schools, so there was some tension between this school's promotion of meditation and the Lin-chi school's emphasis on sudden enlightenment attained through *kung-an* study. The differences were not so great as they are often made out to be, however. Although Ta-hui (1089-1163), the 'second Lin-chi' and a great promoter of *kung-an* practice, attacked the Ts'ao-tung emphasis on 'silent illumination' (*mo-chao*; J. *mokushō*), he was good friends with Hung-chih of the Ts'ao-tung lineage (1091-1157). The latter, for his part, advocated the use of *kung-ans* and even compiled a *kung-an* collection of his own (the *Ts'ung-jung-lu* or *Book of Serenity*).[32]

After the intellectualism and scholasticism of the T'ang, practice-orientated and anti-intellectual schools flourished in the Sung. Pure Land schools, which emphasized chanting and faith in the saving power of the Buddha Amitābha (J. Amida), became very popular. Ch'an also remained an important school, but in time its practices and those of the Pure Land schools became amalgamated, so that by the fourteenth century it had ceased to exist as a distinct school altogether.[33] Moreover, Confucianism was revived, and Ch'an was increasingly attacked by Neo-Confucian scholars who, though borrowing extensively from Ch'an practice, railed against what they saw as its nihilism and moral degeneracy.

Yet while Ch'an was waning in Sung China, it was waxing in other lands. In north Vietnam, it was flourishing in the monasteries. In the tenth century, under state patronage, Thien (Ch'an) monks had become established amongst the intellectual elite.[34]

In the ninth century Ch'an took root in Korea, and became a major force in a land already dominated by Buddhism. The history of Son (Ch'an) is marked by efforts to reconcile the textual study advocated by the doctrinal (Kyo) schools – in particular, the Hwaom (Hua-yen) schools – with the Son rejection of scriptural study in favour of meditation. The most influential figure in the history of Son, Chinul (1158-1210), made great efforts, in his early writings at least, to reconcile these two approaches, producing what is essentially a synthesis of Son and Hwaom.[35] Another live debate at the time was (once again) that between the

---

[32] Fletcher and Scott, *Way of Zen*, p.70.
[33] See Julia Ching, 'The Encounter of Ch'an with Confucianism' in Yoshinori (ed.), *Buddhist Spirituality: Later China, Korea, Japan, and the Modern World*, p.45.
[34] Harvey, *An Introduction to Buddhism*, p.159.
[35] Ibid. p.160.

respective advocates of the sudden and gradual conceptions of enlightenment. Drawing upon Hwaom philosophy, Chinul proposed that the two teachings were not at odds, arguing that sudden insights must often be matured through a process of gradual cultivation of wholesome states. Chinul's later writings show a special concern with Lin-chi methods, and indeed Son was to become dominated by the Lin-chi *kung-an* method in the fourteenth century.[36] One particularly influential method in Korea was the aforementioned investigation of the 'critical phrase' (*hwadu*, Ch. *hua-t'ou*).

Japan

Son has a rich heritage in Korea, and even today it remains the dominant school of Korean Buddhism. Yet it was in Japan that Ch'an was to evolve into the set of traditions we nowadays refer to as Zen.

By the time Ch'an arrived on its shores in the early years of the Kamakura period (1185-1333), Japan, like Korea, had been Buddhist for centuries. The dominant schools of Japanese Buddhism at the time were the Tendai (Ch. T'ien-t'ai) and Shingon (Tantric) schools. Though both were Mahāyāna schools, the Mahāyāna virtues of restraint and non-violence were less than evident in the practices of many of their followers. By the mid-twelfth century, relations between the various factions of the increasingly decadent Tendai establishment had degenerated to the point of open conflict.[37] 'Warrior-monks' now took up arms to settle matters, and pessimistic onlookers diagnosed that they had entered the 'period of the latter-day *Dharma*' (*mappō*), the 'Last Days' of Buddhism.

It would, of course, be a mistake to suppose that all Tendai monks were so neglectful of the Mahāyāna ideal. Some more pious priests saw the decadence of the Buddhist establishment as a call to reform their own practice. Two such men, Myōan Yosai, usually known as Eisai (1141-1215) and Dōgen (1200-1253) were responsible for the introduction of Ch'an to Japan. There are several similarities between the lives of the two men and their approaches to Buddhism. As well as beginning their monastic careers as Tendai priests, both travelled to China and brought back separate lines of Ch'an: Eisai introduced Rinzai (Ch. Lin-chi) to Japan in 1191; Dōgen introduced Sōtō (Ch. Ts'ao-tung) in 1227. Both were, moreover, keen to lay a firm foundation for Zen practice and so emphasized the ethical guidelines embodied in the precepts and monastic rules (Dōgen even looked to 'Hīnayāna' texts for inspiration). Both were therefore opposed to the teachings of contemporaries such as Dainichi Nōnin (d. *c*.1196), a self-proclaimed master, who deemed practice unnecessary. Finally, in opposition to the traditional Zen insistence on 'No dependence on words and letters' both men criticized neglect of the *Sūtras*.

One might imagine that Eisai, as the founder of Rinzai, would have promoted the use of *kōans* (Ch. *kung-ans*) above all other practices, while Dōgen, as the

---

[36] Ibid.
[37] Fletcher and Scott, *Way of Zen*, p.74.

founder of Sōtō, would have promoted the practice of sitting meditation or *zazen*. Matters were not, however, quite so simple. During the Kamakura period, the respective methods of Rinzai and Sōtō were not sharply distinguished: Eisai did not teach pure Rinzai, but rather an eclectic mix of Ch'an, Tendai and Shingon teachings, while Dōgen, for his part, had trained in both Rinzai and Sōtō traditions, and probably used *kōan* practice with some of his students. Nevertheless, Dōgen is famous for his advocacy of sitting meditation or *zazen*, and in his later years he promoted this practice above all others.

Zazen is quite easy to describe but significantly more difficult to practise.[38] Maintaining the correct bodily posture is very important: one should sit upright, ideally in the lotus position, chin drawn slightly in, eyes half-closed and slightly lowered, mouth shut with the tongue resting lightly on the back of one's incisors; one's dominant hand should rest gently on the other, the tips of the thumbs gently touching. The breath should not be forced. In all, one should be in a stable, relaxed position. Thoughts should neither be suppressed nor dwelt upon; instead they should be allowed to naturally arise and disappear. For Dōgen, meditating in this way was not a means to achieve enlightenment. It was rather an entirely natural way of manifesting or 'authenticating' our inherently enlightened natures. To sit in *zazen* is to realize the way of the Buddhas.

Dōgen is also famous for his conception of Buddha-nature. The Mahāyānist *Mahāparinirvāṇa Sūtra* had asserted that 'All sentient beings without exception have the Buddha-nature'. Dōgen translated the line as 'All is sentient being, all beings are (all being is) the Buddha-nature'.[39] In translating the line in this way he meant to reject the notion that beings *possess* Buddha-nature as, say, a seed destined to ripen into Buddhahood (cf. our discussion of Jōshū's *Mu* above). On the contrary, for Dōgen they *are* Buddha-nature. Moreover, by referring to 'all beings', he dismissed the idea that Buddha-nature may be restricted to the set of sentient beings. For Dōgen, *all* beings are Buddha-nature. Dōgen also rejected the idea, expressed, for instance, in the Tathāgata-garbha tradition, that Buddha-nature is permanent, proclaiming, on the contrary, that 'the very impermanency of grass and tree, thicket and forest, is the Buddha-nature'.[40] This extension of Buddha-nature to the natural world resonated with indigenous Shintō beliefs in the ubiquity of natural spirits, while his emphasis on impermanence chimed with the Japanese love of change and the ephemeral nature of things.[41] For Dōgen, the cherry blossom is Buddha-nature.

In 1244 Dōgen founded a new training centre called Eihei-ji, dedicated to austere and strict practice, and in his later years he increasingly cloistered himself there. After his death, his successors – Keizan (1268-1325), in particular – worked tirelessly to promote Sōtō, and the school became more and more influential, partly

---

[38] For a good guide to practising *zazen*, see Kapleau, *The Three Pillars of Zen*, pp.327ff.
[39] Williams, *Mahāyāna Buddhism*, p.114.
[40] Quoted in Dumoulin, *Zen Buddhism: A History. Vol.2*, p.85.
[41] Williams, *Mahāyāna Buddhism*, p.115.

by engaging with the people through public works and services.[42] Thus Sōtō became known as a 'farmers' Zen', a Zen for the people.

Rinzai, by contrast, grew to prominence under the protective wing of the samurai, a partnership which had been forged by Eisai himself, who had secured the protection of the Shōgun at the capital, Kamakura.[43] That the military supported a branch of Mahāyāna Buddhism, ostensibly committed to the ideals of compassion and non-violence, may seem surprising. But Zen appealed to the military rulers for several reasons. The rigorous training in Zen fostered virtues that were clearly of value in military life – mindfulness, for instance, and equanimity in the face of death. Moreover, the direct, pragmatic teaching methods employed by Zen masters seemed to be well suited to the training of military men. A dose of good old Hung-chou style Zen, it seemed, was just the thing to knock soldiers into shape.

Supported by the military establishment, the Rinzai schools flourished. In the Ashikaga period (1333-1573), the most prominent temples of the school were organized in a complicated hierarchical system, the Gozan or 'five mountain' classification scheme. These temples became closely associated with the ruling Ashikaga shoguns, and as the latter grew in power and influence, so too did they. The flipside of this was that as the power of the Ashikaga Shogunate declined in the late fifteenth and early sixteenth centuries, so too did the power of the Gozan temples.

While the power of the Gozan temples diminished, the power of others grew. Pre-eminent among these were two non-Gozan Rinzai temples, Daitoku-ji and Myōshin-ji. Both these temples adhered to the Ōtōkan school of Zen, which taught strict *kōan* practice, unmixed with other elements.[44] This school came to dominate Rinzai from the seventeenth century on.

Nowadays, the best known Zen master from this period is probably Ikkyū (1394-1481), a highly gifted religious man, and a master of the 'art of tea', calligraphy and painting. Continuing a venerable Zen tradition, he was famously eccentric and iconoclastic, and for most of his life he rejected the monastic establishment, which he saw as corrupt, for a life lived close to the people. In his later years, no doubt somewhat mellowed, he was appointed abbot of Daitoku-ji. Myōshin-ji, for its part, became very powerful in the years following the Ōnin War (1467-1477), and eventually took over even the Gozan monasteries. Over time, however, the traditional elements of Zen practice were neglected, and the temple became increasingly decadent.

The arts flourished during the Ashikaga period, and it was during this period that Zen came to have a great influence on Japanese literature, gardening, painting, calligraphy, theatre and architecture. This was the period in which the Zen priest Sen no Rikyū (1521-1591) brought the art of tea to its consummate expression in a simple ceremony that embodied the four principles of harmony (*wa*), reverence

---

[42] Philip Yampolsky, 'Zen: a historical sketch' in Yoshinori (ed.), *Buddhist Spirituality: Later China, Korea, Japan, and the Modern World*, pp.263-4.

[43] Christopher Ives, *Zen Awakening and Society* (Honolulu: University of Hawaii Press, 1992), p.57.

[44] Yampolsky, 'Zen: a historical sketch', p.269.

(*kei*), purity (*sei*) and tranquillity (*jaku*).[45] The Ashikaga period also saw great advances in painting. The *sumi-e* style of ink painting, which like so many arts had been imported from Sung China, flourished under the patronage of the Shogunate. As so often in the art of this period, it bears the indelible stamp of Zen. The ideal in many *sumi-e* paintings was to bring out the life of things in only a few spare traces of ink: three or four deft brush strokes coalescing into the distinct form of a withered tree against the blank background of the parchment, for instance; the emptiness of the parchment accentuated by the lonely presence of the tree. The action of painting was itself thought of as a spiritual practice, the painter composing himself, brush laden with *sumi* ink, waiting for it to suddenly, spontaneously, descend to the paper and make its mark. The influence of Zen is not hard to discern.

Zen also had a great influence on the art of gardening. The garden at Ryoan-ji in Kyoto was completed in 1513, an outstanding example of the *kare-sansui* or 'dry landscape' style: fifteen natural stones, arranged in five groups and set in a rectangular sea of white sand enclosed by a low wall. Just as the master of *sumi-e* achieves much with only a few brush strokes, so here a vision of profound stillness and serenity is conveyed with the barest of means. Not all Japanese gardens are so austere, however. Another major style of garden, the *tsukiyama* or landscape garden, typically comprises a richer set of features combined to produce a natural effect: a stream, perhaps, crossed by stepping stones, running into a small lake flanked by white sand; a moss-covered path winding its way through a shady grove, dappled by sunlight filtering through the canopy. In contriving to produce a natural effect by apparently unnatural means, Zen gardens illustrate a conception of nature which, if not distinctively Zen Buddhist, is entirely in keeping with the spirit of the religion. To aim at a natural effect through art is to deny the bifurcation, so prominent in the West, of wilderness and artifice. In the context of a Zen garden, and indeed in Zen art generally, the natural is not considered a realm opposed to the human, and art is not conceived as artificial. On the contrary, just as the gardener aims at achieving a natural effect, so his gardening is thought of as an entirely natural, even a consummately natural, activity.

The Tokugawa or Edo era (1603-1867) began with the battle of Sekigahara in 1600, which ended two centuries of civil war and brought Japan under the sway of a single military dictatorship. The islands closed their doors to the world. Buddhism, for its part, was brought under strict state control, and in 1614 it was established as the state (that is, compulsory) religion. Stifled by strict government control from the Shogunate, Buddhism stagnated, and Zen had less influence on Japanese culture than it had had in the Ashikaga period. Yet some aspects of Zen practice underwent something of a revival, recovering some of the authenticity that had been lost in the sixteenth century.

One figure who kept far from the reach of the establishment was the layman Bashō (1644-94). He is especially important for our purposes because of the deep appreciation of nature evident in his writings; his importance for the history of Zen generally is that it was through his exemplary efforts that the seventeen-syllable

---

[45] See Dumoulin, *Zen Buddhism: A History. Vol.2*, pp.237ff.

haiku verse was turned into a religious art form. Bashō lived a life on the road close to nature, recalling the ideals exemplified by Shih-t'ou and the Taoist masters. 'Follow nature and return to nature!' he advised.[46] But his was not a passionate love of the natural world, of the sort one finds in the ecstatic verse of Romantics such as Wordsworth. It is quiet, serene, and shot through with the poignancy borne of an acute sense of impermanence (*aware*), of the sun setting on all things, and with the feeling Japanese refer to as *sabi*, a sense of natural solitude and restfulness. For Bashō, as for Dōgen, the Buddha-nature was evident in even the most fragile and ephemeral phenomena; indeed, perhaps it was especially evident in these things. Only a few lines of verse were needed to capture it:

> White shines the stone
> Of the mountain rock; whiter yet
> The autumnal wind.[47]

The key figure in Tokugawan Zen is Hakuin (1686-1769). Hakuin came from the Myōshin-ji line of the Ōtōkan tradition of Rinzai, and he revived the strict emphasis on *kōan* practice that that tradition had been formerly known for. Inspired by the examples set by Ta-hui and other Lin-chi masters, he warned against attempts to understand *kōan* intellectually. Such superficial practice, he inveighed, could not result in true awakening. If, however, *kōan* practice was authentic it would lead to a 'Great Doubt', an existential crisis that would prepare the ground for an experience of awakening (*kenshō* or *satori*). (We will consider some of Hakuin's detailed accounts of this experience in the next chapter.) To achieve this aim, Hakuin promoted the study of Jōshū's *mu*, in particular, and the famous 'Sound of the Single Hand' (popularly, 'One Hand Clapping'), a *kōan* he himself devised.

Hakuin was, by all accounts, a popular and compassionate teacher, travelling extensively, and often working for the poor. In the history of Zen, he is chiefly known for his reorganization of *kōan* practice. Details of Hakuin's precise contribution in this area are, however, rather unclear: it is not clear that the five successive types of *kōan* conventionally attributed to him were in fact his invention.[48] Nevertheless, regardless of the specific details of his contribution in this area, Hakuin is rightly known as the father of modern Rinzai, and his reformulation of Rinzai practice is said to have laid the foundations for what would in later years become a sharp division between the strict *kōan* study of Rinzai and the *zazen* of Sōtō.

---

[46] Quoted in Ibid. p.351.
[47] Quoted in Ibid. p.352.
[48] See Michel Mohr, 'Hakuin' in Yoshinori (ed.), *Buddhist Spirituality: Later China, Korea, Japan, and the Modern World*, pp.316ff.

The West

In 1853, Commodore Matthew Perry of the US Navy dropped anchor off the coast of Japan, and with the persuasive muscle lent by two fully armed steamships, negotiated a treaty that effectively opened up Japan to trade. The islands had been largely isolated from the international community for almost 400 years. Anger at the foreign incursion led to a *coup d'etat* which, in turn, resulted in the resignation of the Tokugawa Shōgun in 1867 and the restoration of imperial rule under Emperor Meiji. During the ensuing Meiji period (1867-1912) Zen was at first persecuted, both because in contrast to the state-sanctioned Shintō it was considered a foreign religion, and because it was seen as an embarrassing reminder of Japan's feudal past. But the religion recovered, and, no doubt sensitive to the charge of being foreign, emphasized its connection with the Japanese people. Indeed, as the nation militarized, the Zen establishment actively supported the government.[49]

With the opening up of Japan to trade, Zen now had the opportunity to step onto the international stage, a chance it duly seized. A key event in provoking Western interest in Zen was the Rinzai abbot Shaku Sōen's (1856-1919) talk presented to the World Parliament of Religions in 1893. But it was his lay student Daisetz Teitaro Suzuki (1870-1966) who was largely responsible for the transmission of Zen to the West. The conception of Zen Suzuki transmitted was partisan in at least two respects. On the one hand, he promoted a strongly nationalistic conception of Zen in tune with the nationalistic sentiments of the time in his home country. For him, Zen expressed a characteristic Japanese ability to experience the true nature of things directly, and so was a quintessentially Japanese phenomenon – though, of course, one from which the West could learn. On the other hand, the Zen discussed in Suzuki's books was predominately Rinzai; Sōtō and the practice of *zazen* hardly get a mention.

For our purposes, it is important to note that Suzuki emphasized the connection between Zen Buddhism (and hence the Japanese people) and the natural world. For him, 'Zen helped a great deal to deepen the aesthetic sensibility of the Japanese mind and finally to root it in the religious intuitions that rise from a mystic understanding of Nature'.[50] It was through Zen that the Japanese people learnt 'how to be in touch with the life running through all objects'.[51] To appreciate this 'life', he maintained, was to bear witness to a beautiful vision of things as groundless manifestations of emptiness; a vision that would naturally foster an attitude of respect, even love, for the natural world. As well as being quintessentially Japanese, in Suzuki's eyes Zen was also inherently 'eco-friendly'.

Suzuki's books were followed by other accounts of Zen, notably from Christmas Humphreys (1901-83) and Alan Watts (1915-73), and the enigmatic Eastern religion soon attracted a following in the West. One prominent group of thinkers who were particularly impressed were the Beat Generation, and through

---

[49] Ives, *Zen Awakening and Society*, p.67.

[50] D. T. Suzuki, *Zen and Japanese Culture* (Princeton, NJ: Princeton University Press, 1973), p.386.

[51] Ibid. p.381.

the work of 'beat' writers and poets like Allen Ginsberg, Jack Kerouac and Gary Snyder a distinctive conception of 'Beat Zen' gradually filtered into popular consciousness. Zen now became associated with a freewheeling enthusiasm for life, shot through with a sense of the mystical and expressed in spontaneous art – in many respects, a Taoism for the twentieth century. With the onset of the sixties and the era of Flower Power, this interpretation of Zen only became more appealing. Interest in all things Eastern burgeoned, and Zen soon found itself caught up in a maelstrom of counter-cultural ideas, from Aldous Huxley's 'Perennial Philosophy' to Timothy Leary's cult of LSD. There can be no denying that the perception of Zen as some sort of tie-dyed, Californian fashion has persisted, and it is no doubt because of such associations that some people continue to doubt the intellectual credibility of the tradition.

But it would be a mistake to suppose that Western interest in Zen has been merely superficial. Since the early years of the twentieth century many Zen teachers from a variety of lineages have come to the West to teach. Japanese teachers have had the greatest influence, in particular those teachers such as Nyogen Senzaki, Sokei-An, Shunryu Suzuki and Taizan Maezumi who travelled to the United States and remained to teach. Over time, Western students who had studied under these or other Japanese masters received transmission and began to teach in their own right – men such as Bernie Glassman, John Daido Loori, Robert Aitken and Philip Kapleau and women like Jiyu Kennett. Many centres for the study of Zen have also been founded in Western countries: in the States, the San Francisco Zen Center, the Zen Center of Los Angeles, the Rochester Zen Center and the Koko-An Zendo in Hawaii, for instance; in France, Thich Nhat Hanh's *Thien* community; in England, Throssel Hole Priory in Northumberland.

Zen and environmental concerns

This breakneck tour through the history of Zen has, I hope, provided some small insight into the nature of the tradition. It is now time to consider the historical connections between Zen and modern environmental concerns.

Let us return in our history to the 1960s. *Silent Spring*, Rachel Carson's seminal study of the effects of DDT, had been published in 1962. The book had heralded in a growing awareness of the harmful effects of human actions upon the natural environment, and indeed in some quarters a growing sense that our relations with nature had deteriorated to such an extent that we were now entering a period of environmental crisis, if, that is, we were not embroiled in it already. One writer who was convinced that such a crisis was already upon us was the historian Lynn White, and in 1967 he published his views in an essay entitled 'The historical roots of our ecologic crisis'. The main point of this essay was to lay the blame for the environmental crisis at the feet of traditional Judaeo-Christian attitudes towards our relations with the natural world, according to which, White argued, humans are conceived as being superior to nature and hence justified in putting it to whatever use they want. But in the following famous and influential passage White also had something to say about the question of Zen Buddhism and environmental concern:

> More science and more technology are not going to get us out of the present ecologic crisis until we find a new religion, or rethink our old one. The beatniks, who are the basic revolutionaries of our time, show a sound instinct in their affinity for Zen Buddhism, which conceives of the man-nature relationship as very nearly the mirror image of the Christian view. Zen, however, is as deeply conditioned by Asian history as Christianity is by the experience of the West, and I am dubious of its viability among us.[52]

White presents the reader with a dilemma: either we abandon our traditional ways of conceiving our relations with the natural world and turn to an entirely new way of understanding these matters (such as that embodied in Zen), or we reject such attempts to flee our heritage and instead devote our attention to the possibility of reforming our traditional Western understanding from the inside, as it were. This dilemma has been reflected in subsequent debates concerning the implications of Zen for environmental ethics.[53] On the one hand, are arrayed those who maintain that we ought to turn our attention to the East; on the other, those who argue that we ought to keep our attention focused on the West, and who accordingly deride attempts to draw upon Zen Buddhist ideas.

Throughout the short history of environmental ethics, the first position has been chiefly associated with thinkers towards the more radical pole of the environmental spectrum.[54] The most prominent of these thinkers rally under the banner of 'deep ecology', and it is on this group that I would like to focus for the moment.

'Deep ecology' was originally conceived as an 'umbrella term', intended to incorporate a variety of positions sharing certain broad views on the resolution of what is perceived to be our environmental crisis. Deep ecologists are united in holding that the environmental crisis is not a technical problem that can be 'fixed' by the application of appropriate technology. Nor do they believe its ultimate solution is to be found in political or economic reforms. What they believe is called for is a change in consciousness, a new way of seeing the natural world and our relation to it. This is not (or not only) a call for us to revise our intellectual understanding of what the world is; it is a call for us to change the way we actually experience the world.

In articulating what sort of experience is required, deep ecologists turn to a variety of sources: philosophers like Baruch Spinoza and Martin Heidegger; the

---

[52] 'The historical roots of our ecologic crisis' reprinted in Louis P. Pojman, *Environmental Ethics: readings in theory and application* (Belmont, CA: Wadsworth, 2001), p.18.

[53] As suggested by Eugene C. Hargrove in his foreword to Callicott and Ames, *Nature in Asian Traditions of Thought* (Albany: State University of New York Press, 2001), p.xiv ff.

[54] Which is not to say that there have not been thinkers from other quarters who have recommended that environmental thinkers turn to Buddhism – some scholars of Buddhism have, for instance, advocated this. See, for example, the essays collected in Mary Evelyn Tucker and Duncan Ryūken Williams (eds), *Buddhism and Ecology: the interconnection of dharma and deeds* (Cambridge, Massachusetts: Harvard University Press, 1997).

worldviews of indigenous peoples such as the Native Americans; writers and poets such as Henry Thoreau and Robinson Jeffers; and reflective environmentalists such as the American forester Aldo Leopold. Many have turned to Buddhism and some have turned specifically to Zen. Zen has proven attractive to deep ecologists because it is focused on a particular mode of experiencing the world, one that apparently leads people to behave in 'eco-friendly' ways. If Suzuki, for instance, is right then the Zen Buddhist, seeing the sapling as the Buddha-nature will treat it with respect, and not view it as nothing more than a resource to be used for her benefit. Having thoroughly digested the teaching of *anātman*, she will feel less need to greedily secure resources for her own use. And so on. Deep ecologists also feel an affinity with Zen's reluctance to produce sets of rules prescribing how one ought and ought not to behave: for Zen, as for deep ecology, it would seem, on the face of it at least, that acting appropriately is not a matter of obeying certain rules – ethical rules, for instance – but of seeing the world in a certain way and coming naturally to behave in ways appropriate to that vision.

So nowadays references to Zen in the environmental literature usually occur in the writings of radical environmental thinkers such as deep ecologists. Unfortunately, many – but not all – of these works present a rather uncritical portrait of Zen, set out in overly pious and saccharin language. As a result, many of the books treating the topic of Zen and environmental ethics are to be found in the 'Mind, Body, Spirit' section of the local bookstore, in the shady company of treatments of New Age thought, numerology, astrology, and the like.

Let us turn now to the second stance on Zen and environmental ethics, the position adopted by those sceptical of the value of turning to Zen for inspiration. For a good example of this view one can do no better than John Passmore's *Man's Responsibility for Nature* (1974). Like White, Passmore rejects the idea that environmental thinkers ought to turn to a 'new religion' in order to deal with the environmental crisis. But whereas White seems to think that a widespread turn to Eastern religions such as Zen would be a good thing if only it were feasible, Passmore holds that there is considerable danger in looking to the East.[55] The danger here, he claims, is that Eastern religions such as Zen are essentially mystical and hence opposed to our tradition of rational criticism and science. While traditions like Zen seek to mystify nature, to imbue it with a '"mysterious life" which it is improper, sacrilegious, to try to understand or control', science seeks to dispel mystery, to understand the world.[56] And it is science, not mysticism, that will provide the solutions to the environmental problems the world faces. Indeed, Passmore suggests that sanctifying nature could militate against attempts to preserve it. For if nature is sacred, then who are we to interfere with it? He maintains that this view is supported by the observation that nations like the Japanese, which have been hailed for their love of nature by Suzuki and others, have appalling environmental records. In Passmore's view, we already have the tools to tackle the environmental crisis with: independent rational thought and

---

[55] See John Passmore, *Man's Responsibility for Nature: Ecological Problems and Western Traditions*, 2nd ed. (London: Duckworth, 1980), pp.173-6.
[56] Ibid. p.175.

science. There is no need and considerable peril in turning to Eastern religions such as Zen.

I have sketched two responses to the proposition that Zen might have something to offer environmental ethics: wholesale, but often uncritical, acceptance, and complete dismissal. I do not mean to suggest that these two categories are exhaustive: as we shall see, some writers have proposed more balanced views on the topic. Nonetheless, I do believe that the field can be roughly divided in this way.

The reader will have to make up his or her mind as to where they stand on the matter of Zen Buddhism and the environment. Hopefully, this book will enable them to do so. But it is now high time we got started with the philosophical investigation of Zen. We will begin by examining the role of ethics in the tradition.

Chapter Two

Zen Ethics?

The charge of amorality

Before turning to the matter of environmental ethics, it is necessary to determine what Zen Buddhism has to say about ethics in general. And this would seem a particularly important issue to address, for there are reasons for thinking that Zen is singularly hostile to the whole business of morality.[1] I will call the general charge that Zen rejects morality the charge of amorality.[2] This chapter is my response to it.

The charge of amorality can take a variety of forms. In its most extreme form, it holds that, for Zen, the desire to do right or be good in fact constitutes an *obstacle* to awakening. Consider, for example, Mumon's (Jp.; Ch. Wu-men, 1183-1260) claim that 'Thinking good and evil is attachment to heaven and hell'.[3] The rationale here is presumably that the distinction between good and evil is the result of a dualistic and hence unawakened consciousness, and that awakening, by contrast, involves the cessation of discriminative thought (as per the Tathāgata-garbha tradition).[4] To agonize about right and wrong or good versus evil is to fall short of the non-dual consciousness realized in awakening.

In a slightly milder form, the charge of amorality holds that although morality does not actually constitute an obstacle to awakening, it is nevertheless irrelevant to one's spiritual practice. There are at least two claims that could be being made here. On the one hand, the claim could be that Zen practice is ontological rather than ethical in orientation since its sole aim is the development of a special kind of insight into reality (*prajñā*) – seeing things as they really are, as it is sometimes put. And although compassionate behaviour might naturally result from such insight, one could argue that attaining that insight is a matter of developing one's

---

[1] I use the terms 'ethics' and 'morality' interchangeably.

[2] As we shall see, I am using the term 'amoral' in a loose sense to encompass the accusation that Zen is in fact *im*moral. Historically, the charge that Zen is amoral or even immoral and anyway too little concerned with society has been often raised by Confucian and Neo-Confucian critics. On this, see James Whitehill, 'Is There a Zen Ethic?' *The Eastern Buddhist* 20, (Spring 1987), pp.11-13.

[3] Katsuki Sekida (translator) and A. V. Grimstone (ed.), *Two Zen Classics: Mumonkan and Hekiganroku* (Tokyo: Weatherhill, 1977), p.138.

[4] Cf. Paul Williams' discussion of the views of the Ch'an monk, Mahāyāna. *Mahāyāna Buddhism: the doctrinal foundations* (London: Routledge 1989), pp.193-7.

understanding of the nature of things rather than behaving ethically. On the other hand, the claim could be that since we are already imbued with an intrinsically pure Buddha-nature there can be no point in striving to attain it; hence any sort of practice is unnecessary. A laissez-faire approach to practice perhaps inspired by this thought has occasionally been associated with Zen. Thomas Cleary notes that attitudes of this sort were rife during the Sung dynasty, and quotes one Sung master's complaints of a 'false teaching... according to which discipline, meditation, and knowledge are unnecessary; and it is unnecessary to cultivate virtue or get rid of craving.'[5] Indeed, even as great a figure as Dōgen is said to have been troubled, in his early years at least, by the apparent paradox involved in striving to attain the Buddha-nature that we are said to already have.

In an even less extreme – but still, I think, potentially damaging – form, the charge of amorality can concede (but admittedly does not need to concede) that morality is a component of the path to liberation, but holds that moral concerns are ultimately transcended in awakening. James Whitehill writes that for one who has fallen into this 'transcendence trap' the ideal moral life is thought to consist of 'a non-rational expressiveness, something natural, spontaneous, non-linguistic, and uncalculating', which leads to an 'ontological dismissal of morality and ethics'.[6] He argues that D. T. Suzuki's overemphasis on 'the "awakening" dimensions of Buddhist soteriology, to the detriment of the moral, "virtuous" dimensions'[7] encourages this notion, a claim that would seem to be supported by the following quotation from Suzuki himself:

> Morality is always conscious of itself; it speaks of decisions and individual responsibilities... Morality can never be innocent, spontaneous, self-forgetful and divinely or devilishly above all worldly concerns. The saintly man is, therefore, to be distinguished from the moral man.[8]

On this reading, then, the Zen master has transcended morality; one might say that he is in this respect beyond good and evil.

The idea that the awakened individual is in some sense 'above' conventional moral norms raises the worrying possibility that awakening need not express itself in spontaneously good actions, but could manifest itself in evil actions, the master being beyond good and evil in this more troubling sense. Certainly, some accomplished Zen Buddhists are reported to have behaved in ways that would by the lights of common sense morality seem at the very least morally questionable. The Hung-chou masters are particularly susceptible to this charge (as were the samurai, who admired them, and whose behaviour was sometimes far from saintly). In one oft-cited story, Nan-ch'uan (J. Nansen, 748-834) holds up a cat and

[5] Thomas Cleary (translator), *Rational Zen: the Mind of Dōgen Zenji* (Boston: Shambhala, 1992), p.14.
[6] James Whitehill, 'Buddhism and the Virtues' in Damien Keown (ed.) *Contemporary Buddhist Ethics* (Richmond: Curzon, 2000), p.21.
[7] Ibid.
[8] Quoted in A. D. Brear 'The nature and status of moral behavior in Zen Buddhist tradition', *Philosophy East and West* 24(4) (1974), p.429.

challenges his students to tell him what it is he is holding. If they cannot do this, the master announces, he will cut the animal in two. When his students fumble and stutter, unsure how to reply, Nan-ch'uan keeps to his word and cuts the poor creature in half. Are we really to believe that such actions only seem to be evil from our unawakened perspective, but that they are in reality rendered acceptable by virtue of their being performed by a Zen master?

In *Zen Awakening and Society*, Christopher Ives would seem to be subscribing to a version of the charge of amorality when he claims that for the tradition

> the pivotal question is that of what one should *be*, not what one should *do*. Zen goes a step beyond ethics in the ordinary sense in that it calls into question the moral agent rather than simply dwelling on a critique of the agent's actions.[9]

The implication is that ethics 'in the ordinary sense' is concerned – solely concerned, presumably – with what one should do rather than with what one should be. But is this correct? In order to answer this question, we will have to pause to consider some general features of modern ethics.

The possibility of a Buddhist virtue ethic

Ives is correct in thinking that ethics is usually concerned with formulating rules by which the actions of agents may be judged to be right or wrong. Modern ethics has been dominated by theories purporting to provide rules setting out how we ought or ought not to act. (Indeed, nowadays the view prevails that this is simply what ethics means.) Thus, as their name suggests, consequentialist theories hold that actions may be judged right or wrong according to their consequences, an action being deemed right if it produces a good outcome and wrong if it produces a bad outcome. For the most prominent tradition of consequentialism, utilitarianism, actions are held to be right if they produce the greatest good for the greatest number, where this good is usually defined as happiness or the absence of suffering. By contrast, deontological thinkers maintain that some actions are inherently right or wrong, irrespective of their consequences.[10] Thus a deontologist such as Kant could argue that lying or, more plausibly, torturing, is always wrong, even if it happened to result in a good outcome. A case can be made for saying that modern ethics has largely consisted of the debate between consequentialists and deontologists over what makes some actions right and other actions wrong.

The defining question in modern ethics has therefore been 'What is the right thing to do?' But ethics is not a distinctively modern phenomenon, and this is not the only question with which ethicists through the ages have been concerned. One type of ethic – one primarily associated with *pre*-modern thinkers – begins with a

---

[9] Christopher Ives, *Zen Awakening and Society* (Honolulu: University of Hawaii Press, 1992), p.109. Emphasis in original.

[10] Or more precisely, regardless of their connection to the good. As we shall see presently, for a virtue ethicist such as Aristotle virtuous actions are good 'in themselves' because they are constitutive of the human good.

quite different question. A *virtue ethic* begins with reflection on the question of what sort of person one wants to be.

Imagine you were able to survey the whole of your life. What sort of life would you hope to have led? What sort of life would have been best? A virtue ethic argues that there is a general answer to this question, one that holds for all. It holds, in other words, that there is such a thing as *the* best sort of life. Moreover, it provides a reasoned account of what sort of life that would be. It argues that such a life would exemplify certain character traits (virtues), and that other, opposing traits (vices) could not be part of such a life. So a virtue ethic could argue, for instance, that a monastic life is, for various reasons, the best sort of life to live, and it could then flesh this claim out by arguing that a monastic life would exemplify virtues such as humility, patience and piety (and would, of course, be free of the corresponding vices of pride, impatience and impiety). Another virtue ethic could argue that the best sort of life is the life of a man of action, exemplifying courage, impulsiveness and pride.

This, then, is a rough – *very* rough – sketch of how I will be understanding virtue ethics in this chapter. It is not, I think, a very controversial account; the text-book list of virtue ethicists – Plato, Aristotle, Epicurus, the Stoics – all come out as virtue ethicists according to it. However, the question of how a virtue ethics might be defined as such has been hotly debated of late, and a number of different definitions have been proposed.[11] My account would not be accepted by all writers on the subject (perhaps it would not be accepted by writers such as Michael Slote who reject the idea that an account of the virtues must be allied to some substantive conception of human well-being).[12] Nevertheless, when I refer to virtue ethics, I will be referring to an account of ethics that fits the very general outline presented above.

I will have more to say about what virtue ethics is presently. For the moment, let us return to Ives' claim. Ives is, I think, correct in saying that Zen is centrally concerned with the question of what sort of person one ought to be. Although, as we shall see later, Zen embodies ethical rules in the shape of the precepts, its primary focus is on self-development. Thus, for Dōgen the point of *zazen* is 'to become a certain man';[13] for Yamada Kōun Roshi, 'The purpose of Zen practice is the perfection of character'.[14] But, far from lying outside the domain of ethics altogether, these concerns can, I suggest, be helpfully framed in terms of virtue ethics. I will devote the rest of this chapter to trying to demonstrate this, and in doing so I hope to present a rejoinder to the charge of amorality. But, first, let us turn to some recent studies in Buddhist virtue ethics.

---

[11] For an introduction to this debate see the essays collected in Daniel Statman (ed.), *Virtue Ethics: A Critical Reader* (Edinburgh: Edinburgh University Press, 1997).

[12] See his discussion of agent-based virtue ethics in Marcia W. Baron, Philip Petit and Michael Slote, *Three Methods in Ethics: A Debate* (Oxford: Blackwell, 1997), pp.206ff.

[13] Damien Keown, quoting Robert Gimello, *The Nature of Buddhist Ethics* (Basingstoke: Palgrave, 2001), p.81.

[14] Quoted in Robert Aitken, *The Mind of Clover: Essays in Zen Buddhist Ethics* (San Francisco: North Point Press, 1984), p.155.

Virtue ethics has undergone something of a revival in philosophical circles in recent years, as has the study of Buddhist ethics amongst scholars of Buddhism. It should therefore come as no surprise that the possibility of framing Buddhist teachings and practices in terms of virtue ethics has recently received a fair amount of attention. Writers such as Alan Sponberg and James Whitehill have argued that virtue ethics captures the point of Buddhist practice in a way in which other ethical traditions do not.[15] The most thorough study so far produced of Buddhism and virtue ethics is Damien Keown's *The Nature of Buddhist Ethics*, and it is on this book that I would like to focus for the moment.

Keown compares the Buddhist teachings with the ethical theory developed in the fourth century BCE by the most influential of virtue ethicists, Aristotle. He argues that Aristotle and Buddhism are alike in thinking that, over and above the many competing ends that we try to achieve in our lives (money, pleasure, fame, contentment, etc.) there is a final end which is desired for its own sake and for the sake of which all other ends are desired.[16] Aristotle names this overarching good *eudaimonia*. This is not some desirable mental state – as the conventional translation of *eudaimonia* as 'happiness' misleadingly suggests – but a 'good life', a life which one could look back on with pride on one's deathbed. For Aristotle, such an exemplary life would be one that itself exemplified various 'excellences' or virtues: a *eudaimōn* life would be one that exemplified courage, magnanimity, justice, and so on. The virtues are therefore integral to *eudaimonia*: as Keown puts it, they 'are not simply instrumental means to an end [*eudaimonia*] which transcends them... they participate in and *constitute* the end'.[17] So Aristotle does not consider courage or justice virtues because they allow one to achieve *eudaimonia* in the way that a bus ticket allows one to ride on a bus, or a glass or two of wine enables one to get a good night's rest. Living well, in the sense of living a *eudaimōn* life, consists in acting courageously, justly, and so on, so that one cannot define what *eudaimonia* is without referring to these virtuous ways of acting.

For Buddhism, *Nirvāṇa* provides a final end. Just as for Aristotle the virtues are integral to *eudaimonia*, so Keown makes a convincing case that the components of the Buddhist path (the factors of the Eightfold Path, for instance) are not merely means to *Nirvāṇa* that can be dispensed with once one achieves enlightenment; instead they are constitutive of enlightenment, in the sense that an enlightened life consists in acting wisely, compassionately, truthfully, and so on.

In these very general respects, then, there are some formal similarities between Aristotle's virtue ethics and the Buddhist teachings. But there are also some illuminating differences between the two. These differences can be brought out through a discussion of the role of the 'practical' and 'theoretical' modes of wisdom in Aristotle.

---

[15] See Alan Sponberg, 'Green Buddhism and the Hierarchy of Compassion' in Mary Evelyn Tucker and Duncan Ryūken Williams, (eds), *Buddhism and Ecology: the interconnection of dharma and deeds* (Cambridge, Massachusetts: Harvard University Press, 1997), pp.351-76; Whitehill 'Buddhism and the Virtues'.

[16] Damien Keown, *The Nature of Buddhist Ethics* (Basingstoke: Palgrave, 2001), pp.196-9.

[17] Ibid. p.194. Keown's emphasis, my annotation.

The virtue of practical wisdom (*phronēsis*) plays a key role for Aristotle in picking out the virtuous course of action in any given situation. The *phronimos* or practically wise man (for Aristotle, it is always a man) knows when courage slides into bravado or when caution becomes cowardice. More precisely, in any situation, practical wisdom enables him to steer a rational course between two classes of inappropriate actions; as Aristotle puts it, practical wisdom determines virtue as a 'mean' between two kinds of vice. Thus, with regard to fear, the *phromimos* sees that the virtue of courage lies on a mean between the vices of recklessness and cowardice; with regard to giving and taking money, he sees that the virtue of generosity lies on a mean between the vices of extravagance and stinginess; with regard to amusing one's fellows, he sees that wittiness lies between buffoonery and boorishness. In general, the *phronimos* perceives the right, i.e., virtuous, thing to do in any particular situation.[18]

Keown makes some interesting comparisons between *phronēsis*, and the other components of Aristotelian psychology, and Buddhist concepts such as choice (*cetanā*). I do not intend to recapitulate his conclusions here. What I would like to note is that Keown focuses on Aristotle's account of 'moral' virtue, that is, virtue guided by practical wisdom, rather than his account of the 'intellectual' virtue of theoretical wisdom (*sophia*). Yet Aristotle treats both forms of reason in his *Ethics*, and even implies that of the two theoretical wisdom is the more illustrious. For while practical wisdom determines how best to act in worldly situations, theoretical wisdom is said to concern loftier things – the abstract truths of mathematics, say, or of metaphysics. Aristotle contends that it is possible to be theoretically wise without being practically wise, and he cites as evidence cases of young people who have extraordinary insight into mathematics or metaphysics but have acquired little practical wisdom.[19] For Aristotle, one can have these kinds of insight into reality without the practical wisdom necessary to know how to behave appropriately.

Insight

Let us extend Keown's analysis by comparing Aristotle's account of theoretical wisdom with the Mahāyāna philosophy on which Zen is based. Where Aristotle speaks of theoretical wisdom, the Mahāyāna speaks of *prajñā*, the insight into the nature of things achieved by someone who has fully understood the teaching of emptiness (*śūnyatā*). Keown maintains that 'There is a close similarity between *sophia* and [*prajñā*]',[20] and he would seem to be right. Both are insights into the nature of reality, even if Aristotle sees *sophia* as insight into the immutable truths of metaphysics or mathematics, while *prajñā* is the realization of the impermanence and emptiness of all phenomena. But whereas Aristotle admits the possibility of having *sophia* without *phronēsis*, for the Mahāyāna *prajñā* and

---

[18] See *Nicomachean Ethics*, translated by David Ross, revised by J. L. Ackrill and J. O. Urmson (Oxford: Oxford University Press, 1998), 1143a, b (pp.152-3).

[19] Ibid. 1142a (p.31).

[20] *The Nature of Buddhist Ethics*, p.205. My annotation.

practical wisdom are inseparable. For Mahāyāna traditions such as Zen, *prajñā* would seem to involve practical wisdom.

Let me explain. For the Mahāyāna, and indeed for Buddhism generally, *prajñā* is not propositional knowledge; it is not simply a matter of assenting to certain statements about how the world is. Instead, it must be internalized, taken to heart. The Zen literature abounds with condemnations of merely theoretical or propositional knowledge of the *Dharma*. The deficient understanding of the student who seems to have only an intellectual understanding of Buddhist philosophy – who affirms that all things are empty, and so on, but whose actions show that these insights have not been deeply cultivated – is invariably exposed by a sudden strike or an unexpected cry of *Katsu!* from the master.[21] Huang-po is railing against a merely intellectual understanding of the *Dharma* in the following passage:

> In these days people only seek to stuff themselves with knowledge and deductions, seeking everywhere for book-knowledge and calling this 'Dharma-practice.' They do not know that so much knowledge and deduction have just the contrary effect of piling up obstacles. Merely acquiring a lot of knowledge makes you like a child who gives himself indigestion by gobbling too much curds... When so-called knowledge and deductions are not digested, they become poisons, for they belong only to the plane of *saṃsāra*.[22]

For Zen, as for other forms of Buddhism, *prajñā* must be internalized so that it ceases to be a matter of mere intellection but rather spills out into one's practical being, informing the way one sees the world and the way one acts in it. So Zen refuses to allow the kind of 'gap' between insight into the nature of things and comportment in life that Aristotle allows. Insight into emptiness does not constitute a merely intellectual understanding of the world; it is a form of practical wisdom which expresses itself in the way one sees the world and acts in it.

Let us consider in more detail how *prajñā* affects the way one sees the world. It is a general thesis of Buddhism that our ordinary perception of the world is distorted by attachments. In the rush and bustle of *saṃsāra* we are portrayed as being thrown helplessly this way and that, pulled towards the things we crave and repulsed by the things we seek to avoid. From the Buddhist standpoint, we are in this sense slaves to (our cravings for) things; in normal life we are, as Philip Kapleau puts it, 'acted upon' by our cravings, 'driven' by them.[23] We are led through the world by desirable things (sexual images, fashionable products, the promise of fame or fortune), which dangle before our noses like carrots on sticks. Or we try to avoid things we fear, even when, like aging and death, we know them

---

[21] See, for instance, Nyogen Senzaki and Paul Reps (translators), *Zen Flesh, Zen Bones* (Middlesex: Penguin, 1957), p.75.

[22] *The Zen Teaching of Huang Po on the Transmission of Mind*, translated by John Blofeld (London: The Buddhist Society, 1968), p.56. See Dale S. Wright's discussion of this passage in *Philosophical Meditations on Zen Buddhism* (Cambridge: Cambridge University Press, 1998), p.31.

[23] Philip Kapleau, 'Responsibility and Social Action' in Stephanie Kaza and Kenneth Kraft, *Dharma Rain: Sources of Buddhist Environmentalism* (Boston: Shambhala, 2000), p.242.

to be inevitable, because we are ultimately attached to the idea of an abiding self that we seek to protect from harm.

When it is internalized, the emptiness teaching can change all this. For, once it has been thoroughly digested in the form of *prajñā*, the destructive light of *śūnyatā* can be turned on any particular object of attachment. Thus the student whose obsession with a new woman at the Zen Centre is disturbing his practice is asked to contemplate the fact that even the object of his lust is empty of self-existence. He reflects that the entity we conventionally designate as 'her' is nothing but a bag of bones and flesh, to paraphrase one Zen story. Or the teacher recommends that the student whose practice is disturbed by a fear of failure contemplate *what* exactly she is concerned to protect. 'What is this self you want to keep safe from humiliation? Show me!' The substantial self the student seeks to protect, it turns out, cannot be thus grasped; indeed, it does not exist at all. Of course a teacher will not always be around to identify these attachments and administer remedies. But as the student develops his understanding he will become better able to identify his own attachments, those moments when he feels the pull of clinging, and he will also learn to apply the emptiness teaching in such a way that it dissolves the objects of his attachment.

An analogy can be made with Aristotle's ethics here. We saw that for Aristotle learning ethics consists of learning how to discern virtue as a mean between two vicious (vice-ous) extremes, learning what it is to be courageous rather than reckless or cowardly, for instance. Similarly, for the Mahāyāna progressing on the spiritual path is to a large extent a matter of learning to recognize harmful attachments, which one could think of as vicious desires (i.e., cravings), pulling and pushing one from the middle way. As one internalizes the emptiness teaching and becomes more proficient at recognizing attachments, one's perception of the world will become increasingly less distorted. One will begin to see the new woman at the Centre in a new light. One will come to see one's own failure as the insignificant event it is in the great scheme of things. In general, one will develop a clearer, more realistic way of seeing the world. Contrary to popular opinion, then, Zen is not a form of mysticism. In a sense, it is we unenlightened beings who are the mystics. For we are the ones who find ourselves faced by a world projected by our cravings and spiritual ignorance. It is we who see the world as if in a dream.[24]

The development of insight therefore has implications for how one sees the world: to see things through the eye of *prajñā* is to see the world free from distorting attachments. But it also has consequences for how one acts. For just as Aristotle's *phronēsis* does not consist solely of an intuitive appreciation of situations but also results in appropriate action (hence it is *practical* wisdom), so for the Mahāyāna the *Bodhisattva's* undistorted perception expresses itself in distinctive ways of acting. When one's perception of the world has been cleansed by the emptiness teaching, one does not just see a different world, one acts differently too. Hence *prajñā* involves a kind of practical wisdom. Someone who

---

[24] In case 40 of the *Hekiganroku* Nan-ch'uan points to a flower and remarks that 'People of these days see this flower as though they were in a dream'. See Sekida and Grimstone, *Two Zen Classics*, p.255.

has thoroughly digested the emptiness teaching and who has consequently become sensitive to her attachments will be less likely to be buffeted in her life by desires and aversions. She will be calmer, surer, more level-headed, less prone to distraction, and, as we shall see presently, more sensitive to the feelings of others.

In the Mahāyāna, the practical function of *prajñā* can be thought of in terms of the conception of skilful means (*upāya kausālya*). This idea originally referred to the Buddha's ability to gauge his teachings to different audiences, to preach to laypeople in lay terms, to Brahmin in terms of Brahmanism, and so on. (This, at any rate, is one meaning of the phrase – we will encounter another meaning later.) A commitment to skilful means is implicit in Zen. Consider the following quotation from Ives:

> The ability to discern another person's state of mind and to respond to it on the spot is often attributed to Zen teachers... [Lin-chi] says to his disciples, 'Whoever comes to me, I do not fail the person: I know exactly where the person comes from'.[25]

Lin-chi does not fail whoever comes before him because he has developed the intuitive ability to perceive the right thing to do in any particular situation, the ability Aristotle articulates in terms of the concept of *phronēsis*, and which the Mahāyāna refers to (in certain contexts) as *upāya*. One of the reasons he has this ability is because he has thoroughly internalized the emptiness teaching and has therefore achieved a truer vision of the world, one undistorted by harmful attachments. In a similar vein, T. P. Kasulis describes how a Zen master might skilfully respond to a student's question:

> the master replies to the *student*'s question rather than the student's *question*. If a student reveals a nihilistic attitude, the master might say there is an essence to the person. If the student is bound to categories, the master might say there is no essence to the person.[26]

So for Zen, as for the Mahāyāna generally, *prajñā* would seem to involve, not just an insight into the true nature of things, akin in some very general respects to Aristotle's *sophia*, but also a practical wisdom which manifests itself in one's practical being in the world – notably in one's ability to perceive situations clearly and to act appropriately.

Compassion

So far, we have been considering Zen as a form of Mahāyāna Buddhism, explaining the words and actions of Zen Buddhists in terms of Mahāyāna conceptions of *prajñā*. However, Mahāyāna Buddhism is distinguished from other

---

[25] Ives, *Zen Awakening*, p.28. My annotation.
[26] Thomas P. Kasulis, *Zen Action, Zen Person* (Honolulu: University of Hawaii Press, 1985), p.127. Kasulis's emphasis.

traditions of Buddhism, not by its emphasis on *prajñā* per se, but by the central role it accords the virtue of compassion (*karuṇā*). As we saw in Chapter One, the Mahāyāna is centred on the *Bodhisattva* Path, where one is motivated to embark upon this path by the compassionate wish to lead all beings to Buddhahood. Indeed, the Dalai Lama has said, from the standpoint of Madhyamaka, that although there are no absolutes in Mahāyāna thought, if there were one it would be compassion.[27]

Is compassion a virtue in Zen? Before answering this, let us consider the general question of how one determines which character traits may be considered virtues. In order to ascertain whether a particular trait is a virtue one could try to imagine whether it would be possible for someone of an exemplary character to lack it. So Aristotle would (presumably) maintain that one could not imagine a 'good life' that did not exemplify courage (and truthfulness and justice, and so on). Conversely, he would maintain that one could imagine a good life that did not exemplify humility, say. Therefore, by Aristotle's lights, courage, truthfulness and justice are virtues, while humility is not (in fact, for Aristotle, it would seem to count as a 'vice of deficiency' relative to magnanimity).[28]

Let us apply this test to the character trait of compassion in Zen. Does the Zen tradition allow the possibility that one could be compassionate but not awakened? In trying to answer this question we encounter a problem. In his lectures on ethics, Aristotle would have been able to appeal to the intuitions of his audience. He would have been able to ask questions like 'Can we imagine a *eudaimōn* life – the life of Pericles, for instance – lacking courage?' And because his audience were all young Athenian aristocrats, he could have expected a fairly uniform reply. But in trying to determine whether an enlightened life could lack compassion I encounter a problem of authority. For who am I to judge which character traits are or are not integral to enlightenment? For this reason, I defer to the Zen tradition.

But in turning to the tradition we encounter another problem: the 'Zen tradition' is a many-headed beast and it does provide a univocal answer to the question of whether an enlightened life must exemplify compassion. I must admit that I have not conducted an empirical inquiry into the thoughts of Zen Buddhists on this matter, but I do not think it too controversial to say that most Zen traditions answer this question in the affirmative: a life that did not exemplify compassion would not be an enlightened life. Even when Zen masters are described as beating their students with fists or sticks, it is generally recognized that these are acts of 'grandmotherly kindness' aimed at provoking the students to realize their true natures and thus free themselves from suffering. It would seem, then, that for Zen compassion is a virtue constitutive of enlightenment just as it is for other Mahāyāna traditions. To be sure, Zen traditions do seem to present some counterexamples here – the apparently enlightened Nan-ch'uan killing the cat, for instance, or the samurai adapting the emptiness teaching to the needs of warfare – and we will consider these cases presently. Moreover, I think it has to be admitted that Zen thinkers tend to place less emphasis on *karuṇā* than *prajñā*. As Masao

---

[27] Williams, *Mahāyāna Buddhism*, p.198.

[28] See *Nicomachean Ethics*, 1125a (pp.94-5).

Abe notes of the views of D. T. Suzuki: 'In the view of Suzuki, a Zen person is apt
to make too much of *prajñā*, the great wisdom, rather neglecting *karuṇā*, the great
compassion'.[29] But, all things considered, I think that compassion is a virtue in Zen
as it is in other Mahāyāna traditions.

What is the connection between compassion and *prajñā*? Consider the
following argument. The emptiness teaching, when internalized in the form of
prajñā, undermines a student's sense of self. A student who has thoroughly
digested the emptiness teaching will be selfless (that is, not selfish, non-attached to
her self, rather than excessively self-abnegating). And because she is selfless she
will naturally act in a compassionate and altruistic way. So, *prajñā* entails
selflessness, and selflessness entails compassion.

This line of reasoning is often repeated in the literature on Zen, and where it is
not explicit it is often implicit. It is not wrong in maintaining that an enlightened
master must be selfless. But it is, I think, wrong in assuming that selflessness must
entail compassion.

No convoluted arguments are needed to refute the idea that selflessness entails
compassion; it will suffice to conceive of someone who is selfless but not
compassionate. If such a figure is conceivable, then selflessness might be
necessary for compassion but it cannot be sufficient. I would like to suggest that an
example of just such a figure could be the samurai, emboldened by his study of
Zen, selflessly hacking his way through the battlefield (or, more likely, through
some assembly of unfortunate medieval peasants). The following instructions
given to a samurai by the Zen master Takuan (1573-1645) imply that such a figure
could be both selfless and callous:

> Do not get your mind stopped with the sword you raise; forget about what you are
> doing, and strike the enemy. Do not keep your mind on the person before you.
> They are all of emptiness, but beware of your mind being caught in emptiness.[30]

Takuan's samurai is selfless in the sense that he has 'forgotten' about what he
is doing, but he is hardly compassionate.[31] If we are to show that compassion is
constitutive of awakening, we therefore have to show that the samurai's realization
is lacking in some respect. To do this, it will be necessary to consider the
Madhyamaka teaching of emptiness in more detail.

On the face of it, the emptiness teaching would seem to be inherently
destructive ('postmodern' thinkers may prefer the term 'deconstructive'). We have
already seen how the destructive force of the teaching can be directed at objects of

[29] Masao Abe, *Zen and Western Thought* (Honolulu: University of Hawaii Press, 1989),
p.79. Note how this portrayal of Suzuki seems to conflict with the idea, mentioned earlier,
that the man thought of Zen as being in some sense amoral.
[30] Quoted in Aitken, *The Mind of Clover*, p.5.
[31] Compare Bernard Williams' reference to a 'pure and selfless malevolence... a malice
transcending even the agent's need to be around to enjoy the harm that he wills'. (Bernard
Williams, *Ethics and the Limits of Philosophy* (London: Fontana/Collins, 1985), p.13.)
Perhaps the samurai, if he is selfless, will in a sense not be 'around' to witness the harm he
causes.

attachment. But Madhyamaka texts make it clear that like all medicines the teaching of *śūnyatā* should not be taken carelessly, for it has the power to destroy not only one's sense of self (the older teaching of *anātman* did that), but any security one might find in external things.[32] To see the world in the light of *prajñā*, one might suppose, would be to see things as being insubstantial and to that degree unreal, to find oneself in a world in which nothing can be relied upon.

In order to determine what it might *feel* like to see things in this way, I would like to turn to the phenomenon Zen Buddhists refer to as the 'Great Doubt'. Here is Hakuin's description of his experience of the phenomenon:

> Night and day I did not sleep! I forgot both to eat and rest. Suddenly a great doubt manifested itself before me. It was as though I were frozen solid in the midst of an ice sheet extending tens of thousands of miles. A purity filled my breast and I could neither go forward nor retreat. To all intents and purposes I was out of my mind and the *Mu* alone remained. Although I sat in the Lecture Hall and listened to the master's lecture, it was as though I were hearing a discussion from a distance outside the hall. At times it felt as though I was floating through the air.[33]

To experience the Great Doubt is, I suggest, to be aware that whatever one can see, hear, touch, taste or smell is not real. It is to see things as illusory, as, so to speak, dissolving into the void. Hakuin describes it as being faced with 'a vast, empty abyss... with no place to set your hands and feet'.[34] In his discussion of Hakuin's awakening, Kasulis suggests that in the Great Doubt 'everything blurs into a monistic whole'.[35] He refers to it as the experience of being 'engulfed' by 'the nothingness of complete annihilation', of being frozen in a state in which one feels 'almost dead'.[36] I am clearly speculating here on a matter which has to be experienced at first hand; however, it does not seem unreasonable to suggest that someone who found himself completely engulfed by this 'nothingness' would be selfless (as Hakuin puts it 'the *Mu* alone remained'). But it would not seem that such a person could be compassionate, for compassion surely requires a certain warmth of emotion, not just the cold, uncanny *Angst* of someone absorbed in the Great Doubt.[37]

I will return to these thoughts presently. For the moment, let us consider the relation between the Great Doubt and awakening. Zen teachers such as Hakuin stress that the Great Doubt does not constitute enlightenment proper but only a

---

[32] See in this connection Peter Harvey, *An Introduction to Buddhist Ethics* (Cambridge: Cambridge University Press, 2000), p.133.

[33] *The Zen master Hakuin: Selected Writings*, translated by Philip B. Yampolsky (New York: Columbia University Press, 1971), p.118.

[34] Ibid. p.135.

[35] Kasulis, *Zen Action, Zen Person*, p.112.

[36] Ibid. p.113.

[37] I am alluding to Heidegger's *Being and Time*, in which he describes *Angst* in terms reminiscent of Hakuin's account of the Great Doubt. *Angst* is described as being an uncanny (*unheimlich*, literally, 'unhomelike') state in which everyday things lose their significance. See *Being and Time*, translated by John Macquarrie and Edward Robinson (Oxford: Blackwell, 1996), pp.231ff.

precursor to true enlightenment. For the experience of the Great Doubt would still seem to be marked by a subtle attachment: an attachment to emptiness at the expense of form. One could say that someone who had become engulfed by the Great Doubt would have become fixated with the void (their mind, as Takuan says, would have become 'caught' in emptiness). They would not have *thoroughly* digested the teaching of *śūnyatā*, but would be still harbouring a lingering attachment to emptiness. They would have failed to realize that emptiness is itself empty of self-existence and only exists relative to form. If they could only realize that then they could awaken. Kasulis also sees the Great Doubt as a delusion:

> When frozen in the Great Doubt, Hakuin heard the voice of the Zen master as if it were coming from afar. In other words, his primary experience was that of the empty stillness metaphorically expressed as the great expanse of ice... The sheet of ice was a delusion...[38]

In order to prepare the ground for awakening, the experience of the Great Doubt must be de-centred, so that emptiness becomes not, so to speak, a noun, an object of attachment, but an adjective, a description of the mind that is not fixed on any thing but is instead held open, ready to welcome whatever thing presents itself of its own accord. To advance from the Great Doubt to awakening one must resist being beguiled by emptiness but must open one's mind so that the world can, as it were, rush back in to fill the empty space of consciousness. To achieve this would be to have freed yourself of everything, to have undergone the Great Death, to have awoken. Kasulis again:

> To experience the Great Death, one must revive from the monistic nondifferentiation of the Great Doubt, that frozen state of negation Hakuin called the great expanse of ice. To die to that empty monism is to be born to presence.[39]

What 'presences' here are things. The mirror-like openness of the mind becomes suddenly filled with the raw 'thereness' of a thing – the morning star, the temple bell, the splash of a frog in a pond – and one finds oneself enlightened, to paraphrase Dōgen, by things. Moreover, in this there can be no sense of the thing as an object standing over against a spectating subject – there is only the seamless whole of the thing-presenting-itself. I will have more to say about this phenomenon in Chapter Four; for the moment, I would like to speculate on how it is connected with the virtue of compassion. In order to see this connection, consider what would happen if one's consciousness was not filled by a thing – a temple bell, or whatever – but by another *person*. In that special kind of interpersonal 'presencing' there would only be the single unbroken event of that fellow being laughing or smiling or frowning or crying – no distraction, no self-centred thoughts or feelings, no lingering fixation with the emptiness of all things – just that man, woman or child. We saw earlier that selflessness is not sufficient for compassion. Neither is

---

[38] Kasulis, *Zen Action, Zen Person*, p.115.
[39] Ibid. p.114.

empathy (no one is as sensitive to human suffering as the master torturer).[40] But in this phenomenon we find selflessness and empathy combined, and hence, it would seem, compassion.

I have argued that it is possible to have internalized *prajñā* to the extent that one is selfless, but at the same time to be lacking in compassion. My account has suggested that in some cases enlightenment can arise spontaneously out of this cold, nihilistic state, bringing compassion in tow. In suggesting this I am disagreeing with commentators like Whitehill who claim that in Zen morality must always be cultivated as a virtue in order to precipitate awakening. Whitehill et al are, I think, correct in the sense that this is generally speaking the case. However, Zen traditions are not all of a piece on this matter, and some seem to admit the possibility of someone not cultivating compassion prior to enlightenment but rather becoming spontaneously compassionate upon awakening. This is not to deny that compassion is a virtue, however, for to deny that the trait needs to be cultivated is not to reject the idea that it is nonetheless integral to enlightenment.

Returning to the example above, I would want to say of our samurai that he had a deficient understanding of *prajñā*, one that was to an extent cultivated, but not deeply enough, for it was still tainted with an attachment to emptiness. Though I would hesitate to say that he had been struck by the Great Doubt, I would want to say that his understanding of emptiness was similarly 'cold'. He realizes that all things are empty but takes this to mean that they are only illusions. 'They are all of emptiness,' he thinks. The void looms ever larger in his mind, and he becomes increasingly cold and unfeeling. In this way, the samurai falls short of true enlightenment and fails to achieve the compassion by which it is marked. In conclusion, it is interesting to note that Takuan warns the samurai not to let his mind get 'caught' in emptiness. If the samurai indeed managed to free himself of his attachment to emptiness, then my account would predict that he would become spontaneously compassionate, and would, presumably, have to give up his vocation altogether. It is comforting to imagine Takuan Zenji as employing skilful means in his teaching, knowing that if his instructions took effect they would soften the heart of his samurai pupil![41]

Practice and virtue

I have identified two virtues in Mahāyāna Buddhism, which seem also to be present in Zen: 1) *prajñā* (which involves both an insight into the nature of things, analogous to Aristotle's *sophia*, and a form of practical wisdom, analogous to Aristotle's *phronēsis*); and 2) *karuṇā*, compassion. In this section, I consider how these virtues develop in the practice of Zen.

---

[40] Williams, *Ethics and the Limits of Philosophy*, p.91.

[41] I am not offering this as a serious historical conjecture. However, it is interesting to note that the literature of Zen does contain stories of samurai who were inspired by their practice of Zen to put down their arms.

tame. Then, when it approaches an evil person, it will surely be killed. That is why it must be chased away.'[52]

Another example of skilful means is provided by a story centring on Eisai. One day, during a time of famine, a woman came to Eisai's temple begging for food for her family, but he was at a loss for something to give her: the temple was itself feeling the effects of the famine and there was scarcely enough food even for the monks. But rather than turn the woman away empty-handed, Eisai scraped the gilding from one of the temple's Buddha images, and offered her a handful of gold leaf, knowing that she could sell it to buy food. After the woman had left, the treasurer monk expressed his concern that such an act constituted stealing from the *Saṃgha* and challenged the master. 'Don't you know that you will go to hell for that deed?' he asked. 'I know,' replied Eisai, 'and I'll enjoy every minute of it.'[53] This story has all the more force when one considers that Eisai was a man who placed more emphasis than most on the observance of the precepts.

There is a danger that the teaching of skilful means might lead one to think that the precepts are of merely instrumental value in so far as they sustain an atmosphere conducive to awakening in the *Saṃgha*, and that in discussing the precepts one is not discussing enlightenment per se, but only the means of achieving enlightenment. But this would be misguided. Zen sees each of the precepts as having three aspects. First, there is the literal interpretation of the precept, associated with the Śrāvakayāna, 'the vehicle of the hearers', according to which Do Not Kill serves as a categorical injunction against killing and other harmful acts. Second, there is the aspect, associated with the Mahāyāna, which emphasizes the importance of compassion (and, hence, as we saw, can occasionally sanction precept-violations). Third, there is the 'Buddhayana' view, according to which the precepts are seen not as means to awakening, but as manifestations of Buddha-nature. On this account, observation of the precepts is considered to be part of what it means to be enlightened. (We will consider some of the implications of this third view presently.)

Aside from the precepts, the student of Zen learns virtue by attending to the actions of individuals more advanced in their understanding of the *Dharma*. Once again, a comparison with Aristotle is in point here. For Aristotle, one cannot know how to act by simply consulting a list of rules for right action, one must look to the *phronimos*, the man of practical wisdom, and attend to how he acts. Similarly, the student of Zen cannot rely solely on the rules codified in the form of the precepts to learn how to behave, for precisely because it can be framed as a virtue ethic, Zen practice cannot be encapsulated in a set of abstract rules. The student of Zen must therefore look to the behaviour of awakened individuals. He can look to the example of the historical Buddha (indeed for Dōgen practice was primarily an 'imitation of the Buddha'),[54] but he can also look to the stories of Zen masters

---

[52] Reihō Masunaga, *A Primer of Sōtō Zen: a translation of Dōgen's Shōbōgenzō Zuimonki* (Honolulu: East-West Center Press, 1971), pp.106-7.

[53] Tenshin Fletcher and David Scott, *Way of Zen* (Barcelona: Vega, 2001), p.51.

[54] Tsuchida Tomoaki, 'The Monastic Spirituality of Zen master Dōgen' in Takeuchi Yoshinori (ed.), *Buddhist Spirituality: Later China, Korea, Japan and the Modern World*

embodied in texts such as the *Transmission of the Lamp*. The most tangible
example of enlightenment is, however, provided by the student's teacher, who is
often looked upon as a living breathing manifestation of the *Dharma*.[55]

The fact that in learning virtue the student ought to pay attention to every one
of his master's actions, not just his 'good works', illuminates an interesting point:
that virtue is evident not only in one's expressly moral behaviour (helping others,
and so on) but in one's general demeanour. The master displays his virtue not only
when he is instructing his students or healing the sick, but when he is sweeping
leaves or washing dishes. Accordingly, a student learns virtue not only when he is
reading the *Lotus Sūtra* and nurturing his compassion for all beings, but also when
he is engaged in tasks whose ethical significance is not immediately obvious. Zen
arts such as the tea ceremony, archery and flower arranging are particularly
important in this regard. If she is to attain the fruits of the art of flower arranging,
for example, the student must develop a host of moral virtues, including inner
quiet, self-control, spiritual poverty, equanimity, humility and patience. As Gustie
Herrigel puts it in her remarkable book on the subject, 'Correct handling of flowers
refines the personality'.[56] (We will examine the connections between Zen art and
Zen ethics in more detail in the following chapters.)

I have so far been making some general observations on how Zen practice can
be interpreted in terms of virtue ethics. I would now like to focus on one practice in
detail to show how it can foster the development of insight and compassion,
namely, meditation.

The word 'Zen', recall, is a Japanese pronunciation of the Chinese 'Ch'an',
which is itself a transliteration of the Sanskrit *dhyāna* (Pali: *jhāna*), meaning,
roughly, meditation. Zen is therefore the 'meditation school' and, as one would
expect, the perfection of meditation (*zazen*) plays a key role in the development of
insight and compassion.

Let us consider the relation between *zazen* and insight. In the West, meditation
tends to be thought of as a way of escaping discursive thought – one sits in
meditation in order to take a break from thinking, to calm the constant chatter
inside one's head – and this, we are told, is the great benefit of the practice. To be
sure, this is one of the functions of meditation, but it is not the only one. In fact,
contrary to the anti-intellectual image of the religion in the West, Buddhist
traditions often view meditation as complementing one's philosophical
understanding of the teachings.[57] But can this be true of a movement as ostensibly
anti-intellectual as Zen Buddhism? To be sure, the practice of Zen cannot be
captured in a philosophical doctrine; indeed, philosophical speculation can obstruct
one's practice. It would, however, be a mistake to conclude from this that Zen
Buddhists must be ignorant of the conceptual foundations of their practice – the

(London: SCM Press, 1999), p.282. See also Keown on the Buddha as role model. *The Nature of Buddhist Ethics*, p.226.
[55] See Wright, *Philosophical Meditations*, p.17, n.41, and pp.213-14.
[56] Gustie L. Herrigel, *Zen in the Art of Flower Arangement*, translated by R. F. C. Hull (London: Souvenir Press, 1999), p.36. On the connection between Zen art and Zen ethics, see Whitehill, 'Is There a Zen Ethic?' p.27.
[57] In connection with Madhyamaka, see Williams, *Mahāyāna Buddhism*, pp.72-4.

great majority of practitioners are no doubt aware of the teachings of not-self, non-attachment, and so on. To say that reflection on these ideas should be thought of as complementing *zazen* is not to say that such reflection should be confused with the practice: philosophical reflection certainly has no place *in* the practice of *zazen*. It is only to say that one's *zazen* should ideally be set in the context of an understanding of the world within which that practice makes sense, and that one's reflections on the Buddhist teachings in less meditative moments should ideally be confirmed in *zazen*. The mindfulness of the transitory nature of thought achieved through *zazen* might complement one's philosophical understanding of the emptiness teaching, for instance;[58] or one's understanding of the not-self teaching might be deepened through the practice of unselfconscious sitting, simply following the breath. (Of course, *ideally* there should be no disjunction here at all: as Dōgen stressed, *all* one's actions should ideally be *zazen*.)

So in this way *zazen* can complement the insight into reality achieved through *prajñā*. But *prajñā* does not just involve a stark 'ontological' insight into the nature of things; as we saw above, it also involves something similar to Aristotle's conception of *phronēsis*, the practical wisdom that enables one intuitively to perceive the right thing to do in any given situation and to do it. In Zen (and especially in Sōtō traditions), the connection between *zazen* and practical wisdom is spelt out in terms of the development of the power of concentration (*joriki*), a quality which, as Kapleau writes, 'enables us even in the most sudden and unexpected situations to act instantly, without pausing to collect our wits, and in a manner wholly appropriate to the circumstances'.[59] In this respect, then, *zazen* would seem also to foster the development of the practical wisdom associated with *prajñā*.

On the connection between *zazen* and compassion, Robert Aitken has written that:

> Practicing compassion goes hand in hand with practicing realization. On your cushions in the dojo... you learn first of all to be compassionate toward yourself.[60]

But what might it mean to be compassionate toward oneself (indeed, in view of the fact that the literal meaning of compassion is 'suffering with', isn't it a misuse of words to refer to compassion for oneself?) And how is this connected to compassion for others?

In order to answer this, it is first necessary to examine the role of thought in *zazen*. *Pace* the claims of certain Rinzai masters (Ta-hui, for instance[61]) to sit in

---

[58] See Wright, *Philosophical Meditations*, p.198.
[59] Kapleau, *The Three Pillars of Zen*, pp.49-50.
[60] Aitken, *The Mind of Clover*, p.18. Cf. Chögyam Trungpa 'Renunciation and Daring' in Kaza and Kraft, *Dharma Rain*, p.263.
[61] See Izutsu, *Toward a Philosophy of Zen Buddhism*, p.165. However, bearing in mind Ta-hui's longstanding friendship with and respect for the Ts'ao-tung master, Hung-chih, it seems unlikely that he meant to condemn all practitioners of *zazen*. Perhaps he was instead chastising some practitioners for having fallen into the nihilistic understanding of emptiness described above. See Philip B. Yampolsky, 'Ch'an: A Historical Sketch' in Takeuchi

zazen is not to have drifted into unconsciousness. All kinds of thoughts can bubble up into consciousness during *zazen*: not just banal thoughts, but wholesome thoughts – startling insights, for instance – and even unwholesome thoughts such as those generated by anger, hatred and other unsettling emotions. The idea is not to chastise oneself when thoughts arise, or to try to suppress them, but just to be mindful of them, to let them come and let them go. In this way one keeps one's mind like a benevolent host keeps his home: all comers are welcomed (albeit only briefly). Thus, *zazen* is not an escape from the thorny complexities of life, but a way of confronting them, a way of turning to the world, not away from it. One could say that it is a way of becoming at one with oneself, neither clinging to the pleasant features of one's character nor fleeing from the unpleasant aspects, but of simply becoming aware of them, facing up to them. Thich Nhat Hanh offers the following advice in this regard:

> Treat your anger with the utmost respect and tenderness, for it is no other than yourself. Do not suppress it – simply be aware of it. Awareness is like the sun. When it shines on things, they are transformed.[62]

In this way, vices such as anger are transformed in the cool light of mindfulness, and the energy that was invested in them is released and turned towards the development of virtue.

The intimacy – one could say the compassion, the 'feeling with'[63] – one develops for oneself through the practice of *zazen* spills over into one's feelings for others. Having become more sensitive to the workings of one's own mind, one becomes more sympathetic to the feelings and thoughts of others. As Kapleau writes:

> Eventually zazen leads to a transformation of personality and character. Dryness, rigidity, and self-centeredness give way to flowing warmth, resiliency, and compassion, while self-indulgence and fear are transmuted into self-mastery and courage.[64]

In this way, *zazen* reinforces one's observation of the precepts. Becoming more proficient in *zazen*, one's sympathy for other beings deepens, and one comes naturally to behave in accordance with the precepts.[65] Becoming more at ease with oneself, one feels less need to lie in order to save face, for instance, and less resentment when one feels wronged. One becomes less prone to put one's fellows down or to flaunt one's own virtues. Finding contentment in *zazen*, one feels less

---

Yoshinori, (ed.), *Buddhist Spirituality: Later China, Korea, Japan and the Modern World* (London: SCM Press, 1999), p.21.

[62] Quoted in Aitken, *The Mind of Clover*, p.95. Cf. p.90.

[63] In some languages the equivalent of the English 'compassion', literally, 'suffering with', is rendered as 'feeling with'. See Milan Kundera, *The Unbearable Lightness of Being*, translated by Michael Henry Heim (London: Faber and Faber, 1984), pp.19-20.

[64] Kapleau, *The Three Pillars of Zen*, p.16.

[65] Cf. Trungpa, 'Renunciation and Daring', p.267.

inclined to take solace in alcohol, and less need to seek sexual thrills or the experiences promised by hallucinogens.[66]

The charge of amorality appraised

My response to the charge of amorality has been twofold. On the one hand, I have contended that Zen practice can be framed as a virtue ethic. On the other, I have argued that other-regarding virtues like compassion play a key role in this ethic. Now I must try to explain why, if the tradition is not at heart amoral, Zen Buddhists through the ages have been so given to deriding the practice of ethics. In doing this, I will be trying to elucidate the reasoning behind each of the three charges of amorality outlined at the beginning of this chapter. Further work will be needed to map these different responses to different traditions in Zen – to see whether, for instance, one response is more characteristic of Sung dynasty Ch'an, while another can be associated with Dōgen's Sōtō Zen.

At the start of this chapter, I identified three versions of the charge that Zen is amoral: 1) the idea that a concern to do right or be good constitutes an obstacle that must be overcome in order to attain awakening; 2) the claim that ethics is not a part of Zen practice and that it is therefore not necessary to be morally good in order to attain awakening; and 3) the idea that, whether or not morality is considered to be part of the path to awakening, it is nonetheless transcended in awakening, so that the Zen master can be thought of as being beyond good and evil.

Considering the first charge, it seems that when Zen masters portray a concern with morality as an obstacle to awakening, they are sometimes trying to draw attention to the dangers of becoming obsessed with ethical rules. The point here is not that ethics per se has no place on the Buddhist path, but that clinging to ethical rules is nonetheless clinging and hence an obstacle to awakening. Freedom from this sort of attachment could be engendered by a variety of reflections on Mahāyāna teachings. For example, one could contemplate the idea that if all things are empty, then even the precepts are ultimately empty of self-existence. Or one could reflect that from the standpoint of ultimate truth no merit is generated even by the most meritorious actions (as Bodhidharma might have said).

On the other hand, the purpose of some claims to the effect that the student of Zen should transcend ethics would seem to be to undermine, not just the urge to cling to ethical rules, but also the general tendency to conceive good and evil as two independent categories. The point here is not that good and evil do not exist, but that viewing good and evil as self-existent categories evinces an insufficient grasp of the teaching of emptiness. The following quotation from Hui-neng would seem to be directed against this particular kind of misunderstanding: 'Although you see... evil and good... you must not throw them aside, nor must you cling to

---

[66] Cf. Kapleau, *The Three Pillars of Zen*, pp.16-17.

them, nor must you be stained by them, but you must regard them as being just like the empty sky.'[67]

These are dangerous ideas, and, as ever, they should not be mistaken for propositions conveying philosophical theses. Consider, for example, the famous *kōan* attributed to Hui-neng: Not thinking of good, not thinking of evil, just at this moment, what is your original face before your mother and father were born?[68] At first sight, the implication would seem to be that thinking of good and evil are obstacles to enlightenment. But before the *kōan* is seen as a proposition conveying a thesis of 'amoralism', it should be remembered that its purpose is not to express 'Zen theory' but to inspire awakening. Thus, like other *kōan*s, it could be paraphrased as 'Show me your true nature (you who cling to ethical rules/you who cannot accept the emptiness of the categories of good and evil/you who harbour some other specific obstacle to awakening)!'

Regarding the second charge of amorality, I suggested above that one source of the view that morality is not part of the path to awakening could be the idea that practice is an ontological rather than an ethical affair which consists of the development of insight into reality (*prajñā*) rather than ethical virtue. We have already seen that this possibility cannot be ruled out. It would seem prima facie possible – with some important qualifications – that compassion might not be developed in practice but might instead arise spontaneously upon awakening. So it would seem that this particular version of the charge of amorality has some force.

Another source of the view that moral practice is not needed for awakening could be the idea that since one is already imbued with an inherently pure Buddha-nature, there is no need to cultivate compassion. The obvious response to this claim would be to say that even if we are inherently good in this sense, revealing this inherent goodness is no easy task. If it were, then there would be no need for the rigours of Zen practice. Moreover, I hope to have shown in the foregoing discussion that ethical behaviour does play an important role in revealing Buddha-nature. Practice is generally a matter of developing compassion as well as insight. That said, it could be that claims to the effect that one does not need to strive to be moral since one's Buddha-nature is inherently pure could have a therapeutic effect in some circumstances. Perhaps the student who is overawed by the considerable demands of the *Bodhisattva* Path (the liberation of *all* beings?) might benefit from being told that her nature is already boundlessly compassionate. This is just speculation. The important point is – once again – that claims to the effect that one ought not to be concerned with morality should not be read as statements of 'Zen doctrine', or anything of that sort. Instead, they should be thought of as serving therapeutic functions in certain specific situations.

[67] *The Platform Sutra of the Sixth Patriarch*, translated by Philip B. Yampolsky (New York: Columbia University Press, 1967), pp.146-7. Cf. Ikkyū: 'if one purifies one's own mind and beholds one's own nature, there remains... no duality of good and evil'. Quoted in Heinrich Dumoulin, *Zen Buddhism: A History. Vol.2: Japan* (New York: Macmillan, 1990), p.195.
[68] In the later (Sung dynasty) version of the *Platform Sūtra*, Hui-neng is said to have enlightened the monk Hui-ming by presenting him with this *kōan* atop Mount Ta-yu. (Hui-ming had chased him up the mountain to steal the robe – the symbol of transmission – from him.) See Yampolsky, *The Platform Sutra of the Sixth Patriarch*, pp.110, 134.

Turning now to the third charge, the purpose of claims to the effect that the enlightened subject is beyond good and evil could be to draw attention to the fact that the master's morality is most evident in his spontaneous actions rather than his deliberations about the right thing to do. On this reading, the Zen master has transcended *deliberating* about good and evil. Instead, he is said to perform actions, *good* actions, naturally, spontaneously, 'like feeling for one's pillow at the back of one's head at dead of night.'[69] For Zen, as for Aristotle, ethics is not a matter of consulting a list of ethical rules every time one is confronted by a moral dilemma. Instead, it is a matter of manifesting virtue, where the virtues are, so to speak, 'sedimented' or internalized dispositions to feel certain things and to act in certain ways. And because they are internalized they are expressed naturally and spontaneously in one's actions. As Stephen Clark puts it: 'The Buddhist and the Aristotelian saint alike are not pressed by self-control to do what is right... the conclusion of the practical syllogism is for them, as for animals, an action... not as it is for most of us a murmured encouragement to virtue.'[70]

Some light can be shed on the status of the Zen master's non-deliberative actions by referring to the development of the 'supramundane' perfections in the course of the *Bodhisattva* Path. Mahāyāna sources maintain that when they are informed by *prajñā* insight into emptiness the perfections (*pāramitās*) become transcendent or supramundane. Thus in exercising generosity, for instance, the *Bodhisattva* does not conceive of a gift, a giver or a recipient, but realizes that all these putative beings are empty of self-existence.[71] Nevertheless, since it has become entirely natural for him to be generous, he just gives. He has become spontaneously good. I would suggest that the same holds true of the Zen master. For the master operating at a 'supramundane' level of spiritual attainment, the perfections have, as it were, been transposed into a higher key, and they have consequently become spontaneous and natural, and therefore in this sense 'invisible'. So like the *Bodhisattva*, the master does not deliberate about the possible consequences of giving, he just gives. He does not agonize over the observation of the precepts, his behaviour is naturally in accord with them. He does not try to get his head round the emptiness teaching, he sees the world through the eye of *prajñā*. I am of course assuming here that we are referring to a fully-enlightened master. As we saw earlier, awakening is not an all or nothing affair, and it is possible that someone might have attained some degree of awakening but that their level of realization might not be so deep that the perfections have become completely internalized in this way. But against the charge that Zen is amoral (or immoral), the fully-enlightened master has not transcended morality. He has not left it behind him as a man leaves a raft on the bank once he has crossed to the

---

[69] I am paraphrasing Dōgo's (769-835) response to the question of how the *Bodhisattva* of compassion, Avalokiteśvara, manages to use his many hands and eyes. See Sekida and Grimstone, *Two Zen Classics*, p.140.

[70] Quoted in Keown, *The Nature of Buddhist Ethics*, pp.221-2.

[71] See, for instance, Conze, *The Large Sūtra on Perfect Wisdom*, p.50.

further shore.[72] The awakened man or woman has internalized morality to the extent that, as Douglas K. Mikkelson notes, the perfections have become ways of describing how he or she acts:

> from the perspective of one receiving instruction, 'do no evil' is *prescriptive*: it serves as a precept that the practitioner is to follow. But from the perspective of awakening 'do no evil' is *descriptive*: it describes the moral conduct of someone realizing/actualizing the Buddha nature.[73]

Yet the fact remains that many supposedly awakened Zen masters (and Zen mistresses, no doubt) are said to have committed actions that would appear to be thoroughly immoral. A case in point is Nan-ch'uan's murder of a cat. Are we to suppose that that act of violence was the result of Nan-ch'uan's internalizing the precepts? Are we to believe that his behaviour was, contrary to appearances, spontaneously good?

One response would be to say that this question misses the purpose of the story. As in a fairy-tale, the violence in the story of Nan-ch'uan and the cat is clearly incidental to the point being made. Perhaps the point is to convey something about the nature of objects in general; in any case, it is not meant to sanction the murder of defenceless felines. This is Robert Aitken's response, and I am largely in sympathy with it. However, for present purposes, further analysis of the cat-killing incident should prove illuminating.

If there is a 'point' to this story, then it is presumably something to do with the matter of expressing the 'suchness' of things without resorting to abstractions. In asking what the cat was, Nan-ch'uan was asking his students to express their understanding of the raw thing before them without trying to capture it in an abstract way as an exemplification of a particular concept, that of a 'cat'. As A. D. Brear writes, actions of this sort can point 'to the sheer givenness of [phenomena], free from artificial verbal distancing'.[74] One could therefore argue that Nan-ch'uan's action could be justified on account of the beneficial – i.e., awakening – effect it had on his audience. And in this sense, it could be interpreted in terms of the Mahāyāna teaching of skilful means, as outlined above in our discussion of the precepts. Perhaps, then, Nan-ch'uan's murder of the cat was justified because it was motivated by his compassionate desire to enlighten his students.

I do not find this interpretation convincing. For a precept-violation to qualify as an instance of skilful means one would expect the perpetrator of the action to have exhausted all his or her options. For instance, a case of compassionate killing would only qualify as a manifestation of skilful means if the *Bodhisattva* could see no other way to liberate beings than by killing. But in the case of Nan-ch'uan it is

---

[72] I am alluding to the famous 'raft' parable, which is often pointed to as evidence that Buddhists see morality merely as a means to attain enlightenment. See Keown's criticisms of this interpretation of the parable in *The Nature of Buddhist Ethics*, pp.92ff.

[73] Douglas K. Mikkelson, 'Who is arguing about the cat? Moral Action and Enlightenment according to Dōgen', *Philosophy East and West* 47, No.3 (July 1997), p.391.

[74] Brear, 'The nature and status of moral behavior', p.441, n.83. See also Mikkelson, 'Who is arguing about the cat?' pp.391-2.

far from clear that other options were not available. Tearing a robe in half or breaking a staff would not have had the same shock value, of course, but did Nan-ch'uan really have to kill the cat in order to make his point? In asking this are we missing the point?

In his discussion of the story of Nan-ch'uan and the cat, Dōgen affirms that, although Nan-ch'uan's action was a 'Buddha act', i.e., a manifestation of enlightenment, it would have been better if it had not been performed.[75] He maintains that if he had chosen to use a similar tactic to awaken his students, he would not have killed the cat if his students had failed to answer because killing the cat would have violated the First Precept.[76] In saying this it would seem that Dōgen is making a point about the identity of practice and realization. Just as for Dōgen *zazen* is not a means of attaining awakening, but an 'authentication' of our inherent enlightenment, so following the precepts is not a means to awakening, but a manifestation of awakening itself.[77] In holding this, Dōgen is understanding the precepts according to the 'Buddhayana' view, mentioned above. What is important to note is that this way of conceiving ethics is perfectly in accord with Keown's thesis that morality is not merely instrumental to awakening, but constitutive of it.[78] Here, as elsewhere in Zen, practising virtue does not cause enlightenment, it is an authentication of one's inherently enlightened nature.

---

[75] Mikkelson, 'Who is arguing about the cat?' p.393.

[76] Ibid. p.388. Cf. Keown, *The Nature of Buddhist Ethics*, p.155.

[77] Mikkelson, 'Who is arguing about the cat?' pp.393ff.

[78] For an illuminating discussion of Dōgen's views on ethics see Kasulis, *Zen Action, Zen Person*, pp.93-9.

Chapter Three

Environmental Ethics

In the previous chapter, I argued that Zen is neither amoral nor immoral but can be fruitfully conceived in terms of virtue ethics. I identified two key virtues at the heart of Zen, *prajñā* (insight) and *karuṇā* (compassion), and I showed how these virtues develop in practices such as meditation. In this chapter, I address the charge that Zen is inherently anthropocentric by examining the implications of Zen teachings for our moral relations with the natural environment. However, since, up to now, we have been considering Zen in terms of virtue ethics, before turning to the environmental implications of Zen it will be helpful to consider the general matter of the application of virtue ethics to environmental issues.

Environmental virtue ethics and the charge of anthropocentrism

In Chapter Two, I mentioned that virtue ethics has undergone a revival in recent years. This renewed interest was largely inspired by G. E. M. Anscombe's 1958 paper, 'Modern Moral Philosophy'.[1] In that paper, Anscombe argued that the prevailing vocabulary of 'duties' and 'moral obligations' in which discussions of ethics are conventionally framed depends on a religious context within which we are considered to be subject to the law of God. But in modern secular society, she maintained, appeals to duties, moral obligations and the like, seeming, as they do, to imply such a context, cannot be upheld. In response to this situation, Anscombe recommended that we relinquish the now hopelessly confused project of modern moral philosophy and direct our attention to the philosophy of psychology, and an analysis of the ideas of action, intention, pleasure and wanting. Should our inquiry eventually bring us to an analysis of the idea of virtue, then we will have got to the point where we can begin, as it were, to have another shot at ethics, starting, once again, with its oldest and most venerable tradition, virtue ethics.[2]

Anscombe's paper struck a chord with those philosophers who had become dissatisfied with modern ethics, preoccupied, as it is, by discussions of 'rights', 'duties' and 'obligations' and dominated by the perennial standoff between consequentialism (especially utilitarianism) and deontology. Indeed, since its

---

[1] G. E. M. Anscombe, 'Modern Moral Philosophy', *Philosophy* 33 (1958), pp.1-19.
[2] Ibid. p.15.

publication, Anscombe's general discontentment with modern ethics and her call for a return to virtue ethics has resurfaced in the work of a number of authors. Her influence is evident, for instance, in the work of Alasdair MacIntyre, who in *After Virtue* argues that modern ethics consists of a mixed bag of ideas drawn indiscriminately from a variety of incommensurable ethical traditions – talk of rights, duties and obligations mixing with appeals to empathy, compassion and moral sensitivity. Like Anscombe, MacIntyre does not recommend that we throw up our hands in a Nietzschean rejection of morality, but that we return to Aristotle and virtue ethics.[3]

One might expect the message of Anscombe et al to be welcomed by those working in environmental ethics, a field of study bedevilled by an array of intransigent problems regarding the 'rights' of natural objects and our moral 'obligations' to the natural world. Yet regardless of its popularity in other fields, the tradition of virtue ethics has been sorely overlooked by environmental ethicists.[4] There are doubtless several reasons for this. Louke van Wensveen, one of the small but growing set of writers who have treated the subject, notes that talk of virtues and vices has a rather antiquated air about it (think of references to a 'lady's virtue'), and consequently less rhetorical bite than the prevailing discourse of rights and obligations. Moreover, in a subject that often considers itself a branch of applied ethics, virtue ethicists have noticeably less practical guidance to offer on specific moral dilemmas than consequentialists or deontologists. Utilitarian calls for us to curb global warming in order to reduce the net suffering of sentient beings or deontological calls for us to respect the natural rights of higher mammals would seem to have clearer implications for how we ought to act than calls for us to cultivate certain character traits. What use are appeals to the virtues of humility or simplicity in deciding whether or not to build a bypass or whether to extend legal protection to a particular species of organism? (I will address these and other practical questions in Chapter Five.)

One reason for this lack of interest in virtue ethics could be environmental philosophy's fixation with avoiding the charge of anthropocentrism. I suspect that many radical environmental thinkers – deep ecologists, for example – would see virtue ethics and its concern with the good life as perniciously human-centred, one more manifestation of the human hubris that has spawned our modern environmental crisis. To be sure, these thinkers might acknowledge that forms of environmental concern could be conceived as virtues – they might admit that an appreciation of wild nature could be a component of the good life, for instance. But for many non-anthropocentric thinkers, to think of an appreciation of nature as a component of human well-being is to value nature not for its own sake, not for its intrinsic value, say, but only in so far as it furthers human interests, i.e., the human

[3] Alasdair MacIntyre, *After Virtue: a study in moral theory* (London: Duckworth, 1987).
[4] Robert Elliot continues this trend when he concludes his chapter on normative ethics in a recent companion to environmental philosophy with the statement that 'The prospect of a virtue-based environmental ethic seem dim'. (In Dale Jamieson, *A Companion to Environmental Philosophy* (Oxford: Blackwell, 2001), p.190.) On the neglect of virtue ethics by environmental thinkers, see Louke van Wensveen, *Dirty Virtues: The Emergence of Ecological Virtue Ethics* (New York: Humanity Books, 2000), p.19, n.7.

interest in living well. Robert Elliot is expressing this sort of scepticism regarding the application of virtue ethics to environmental issues when he writes that: 'There is a distinction to be drawn between, on the one hand, ways of treating the natural environment which we regard as admirable, desirable, constitutive of ideals of human excellence, and on the other hand, valuing the natural environment for its own sake in a completely non-instrumental way.'[5] To emphasize the attainment of ideal or virtuous character is, he claims, to be 'overly concerned with the human world'.[6]

I disagree. It seems to me perfectly reasonable to hold that valuing nature non-instrumentally – that is, valuing it for its own sake rather than for its usefulness – is constitutive of human excellence. Consider the example of a man who loves wild nature, someone like William Wordsworth or John Muir. Suppose, for the sake of argument, that that man's capacity to appreciate wild nature is a virtue, that it is constitutive of his well-being. Now to say that the nature-lover's capacity to appreciate wild nature is good for him in this sense is not to say that he values wild nature *because* it is good for him. Indeed, there is a case for saying that to value wild nature in this anthropocentric and instrumental way would not be to *appreciate* it at all. John O'Neill has illustrated this point by referring to Aristotle's treatment of friendship. For Aristotle, friendship is constitutive of human well-being, which means, very roughly, that it is good for us to have friends. However, Aristotle points out that the best sort of friendship involves caring for our friends for their own sake, not for some benefit they might bring us, and not because we think our friendship with them might contribute to our personal well-being. Similarly, there is no contradiction in conceiving of the non-instrumental appreciation of nature as a virtue, in holding, that is, that valuing nature for its own sake is good for us.[7]

So a Zen Buddhist ethic need not be thought anthropocentric simply on account of its being a virtue ethic. For it could hold that valuing nature non-instrumentally is constitutive of human well-being. We will see whether it does in fact do this in the following pages. However, it might be thought that any ethic based on Zen must be guilty of a certain degree of anthropocentrism. After all, Zen would seem to be primarily concerned with *human* awakening. Toshihiko Izutsu, for instance, writes that 'the anthropo-centric tendency of Buddhism was greatly fortified by the rise and development of the Zen sect',[8] especially after Lin-chi, a thinker who set out 'to put Man at the very centre of Zen thought'.[9] These statements would no doubt give pause to those thinkers towards the deep green pole of the environmental spectrum, for whom an adequate environmental ethic must be free of any trace of human-centredness.

---

[5] Robert Elliot, *Faking Nature: the ethics of environmental restoration* (London: Routledge, 1997), p.57.

[6] Ibid. p.57.

[7] John O'Neill, *Ecology, Policy and Politics: human well-being and the natural world* (London: Routledge, 1993), p.24.

[8] Toshihiko Izutsu, *Toward a Philosophy of Zen Buddhism* (Boulder: Prajñā Press, 1982), p.3.

[9] Ibid. p.6.

So, is Zen primarily concerned with human awakening, and is it to that degree anthropocentric? In relation to this question, it is worth considering the following passage from Malcolm David Eckel in which he refers to what he calls 'the paradox of Buddhist "anthropocentrism"':

> The tradition is genuinely concerned with the human achievement of human goals... But the achievement of self-interest is tied in an equally fundamental way to the decentering of the self.

Indeed, he continues, 'in Buddhist culture at large the cultivation of self takes the form of a decentering of the self and a concern for a wider network of life'.[10] This concern for a wider network of life clearly involves concern for other humans – otherwise it would be hard to make sense of the centrality of other-regarding virtues such as compassion in Zen practice (it is for this reason that Buddhism is not egoistic). But does this concern extend to non-human beings, and – more interestingly – if it does, to which sorts of being can it be thought of as extending to? Moreover, if environmental concern is indeed central to Zen, can the tradition be framed in terms of any pre-existing environmental ethic? These are questions this chapter will try to answer.

Sentient life

At first sight, it might seem that on account of it being a tradition of Mahāyāna Buddhism, Zen must conceive the moral community as incorporating all sentient beings. After all, we have been using the term *karuṇā* to denote, not some mundane sense of fellow-feeling, but the 'great compassion', the 'supramundane' virtue that aims at the liberation of all sentient beings. To have *karuṇā* in this sense is to seek to alleviate the suffering of all sentient beings by leading them to Buddhahood. Admittedly, on the basis of orthodox Mahāyāna cosmology, animals cannot be awakened in this lifetime (they must await a human rebirth); however, the wish to completely extinguish the suffering of others extends to all sentient beings, not just to those capable of awakening in this lifetime. That is to say that the 'moral circle' – to adopt a common image from the literature – here includes not just all humans, but all sentient beings. All sentient beings are taken to have moral standing, to be morally considerable.

It might seem that the Mahāyāna – and by implication, Zen – has something in common here with utilitarian ethics of the sort proposed by Jeremy Bentham in the eighteenth century and developed in recent years by Peter Singer. For his part, Singer, like other utilitarians, bases his ethics on a principle of equality, according to which one should give equal weight in one's moral deliberations to the like interests of all those beings affected by one's actions.[11] The moral circle is

---

[10] 'Is there a Buddhist Philosophy of Nature?' in Mary Evelyn Tucker and Duncan Ryūken Williams (eds), *Buddhism and Ecology: the interconnection of dharma and deeds* (Cambridge, Massachusetts: Harvard University Press, 1997), pp.341-2.

[11] See, for example, *Practical Ethics* (Cambridge: Cambridge University Press, 1993), p.21.

therefore held to include all and only those beings that can be said to have interests. But which beings are these? Singer points out that in order to have interests a being must be able to suffer and enjoy things. So I am acting immorally if I decide on a whim to kick a dog because the dog is a sentient being, a being capable of suffering, and it therefore has an interest in not being kicked. On the other hand, I am not acting immorally if I decide on a whim to kick a stone (unless, perhaps, I boot it at the dog), since the stone cannot suffer and so has no interest in not being kicked. Singer concludes that the criterion for inclusion in the moral circle is sentience, so that only beings that can suffer are worthy of our moral regard. Moreover, Singer argues that suffering is suffering, whatever being might be experiencing it, and so if a being suffers one is morally bound to take that suffering into account. Humans can suffer, so they are in the moral circle. But so can nonhuman animals – chimpanzees, dogs, chickens, lizards, frogs, etc. – so they are also in the moral circle. In deciding on the right course of action, then, Singer proposes that one should take into account the interests of all those beings that would be affected by it, notably the interests those beings have in not being caused to suffer. The right action will be the one that, all things being equal, leads to the greatest reduction (or the smallest increase) in the total suffering of those beings affected.[12]

Zen and Singer are certainly of a piece in rejecting the anthropocentric idea that our moral obligations extend only to humans. For Singer, there can be no moral justification for considering the suffering of a non-human animal such as a laboratory rat to be less significant than the suffering of a human.[13] Likewise, Zen inherits the general Buddhist idea that our actions towards those beings able to suffer ought to be guided by the First Precept, non-violence (*ahiṃsā*). The tradition also incorporates the distinctively Mahāyānist idea, articulated in the *Mahāparinirvāṇa Sūtra*, that all sentient beings possess the Buddha-nature and are therefore ultimately destined for Buddhahood. Although it is not obvious that someone who claims that nonhuman animals are imbued with Buddha-nature is directly attributing moral standing to those beings (and that is an issue we shall address presently), such claims certainly elevate the status of nonhuman animals, and are to that degree opposed to anthropocentrism. Furthermore, as a tradition of Eastern Mahāyāna, Zen incorporates the special regard for nonhuman animals associated with Eastern schools of Buddhism. The *Laṅkāvatāra Sūtra*, which as we saw in Chapter One was an important influence in the East, and especially on Zen, argues forcefully that ethical concern be extended to nonhuman animals.[14] Indeed, under the influence of texts such as the *Laṅkā* and the *Brahmajāla Sūtra*, many

---

[12] See Ibid. Chapter Three.

[13] Singer is, however, aware that morally-relevant differences between beings that are considered in a technical sense to be *persons* (that is, self-conscious beings, aware of themselves as distinct beings with a past and a future) and beings that are not persons emerge in conjunction with the issue of taking life (see Chapter Five of his *Practical Ethics*).

[14] See D. T. Suzuki (translator), *The Laṅkāvatāra Sūtra* (London, Routledge & Kegan Paul, 1973), (Chapter Eight).

schools of Eastern Buddhism came to promote vegetarianism, Zen monks and nuns, in particular, tending to avoid eating meat.[15]

So, both Zen and Singer maintain that all animals have moral standing on account of their capacity to suffer, but Zen augments this by maintaining that all animals are also equal in their potential for Buddhahood. Both positions are to this extent non-anthropocentric. This rejection of anthropocentrism is nicely demonstrated by the following story.[16] Two Zen priests, Shen-shan and Tung-shan, were taking a relaxing stroll through the mountains, admiring the plum blossom filling the valley below them, when suddenly a rabbit darted across the path in front of them. The two men stopped in surprise. 'How agile it was!' exclaimed Shen-shan. 'Even such a beast as a rabbit can have agility like that. How marvellous!' Tung-shan, however, though similarly impressed by the agility of the animal, reproached his friend for having used the phrase 'Even such a beast as a rabbit.' 'Think of the rabbit as a great man in disguise,' he suggested. One interpretation of this story could be that Tung-shan was drawing his colleague's attention to the teaching of rebirth, the possibility that the rabbit might have been a 'great man' in a previous life. To be sure, the idea that nonhuman beings might have been one's friend or relative in a former life often acts as a motivation for environmental concern in Buddhism.[17] However, regarding the story at hand, if the being had really been a *great* man he would not have been reborn in the form of a rabbit. For in the context of Buddhist cosmology, the rebirth of a human in the form of an animal represents a step down the spiritual ladder, as it were, because as well as leading unhappier lives, animals are seen as having less potential for spiritual development than humans (in this respect Buddhism *is* anthropocentric). Hence, rebirth of a human as an animal must be the result of the *karma* generated by evil deeds in one's human life. If a truly great man were to be reborn, he would be reborn as a human or a god rather than a rabbit. I do not think this is the point being made in the story of Tung-shan, however. It seems to me that the Zen master was rather speaking from a Mahāyāna standpoint, making the point that a rabbit possesses (or perhaps, is a manifestation of) a flawless Buddha-nature just as much as a human being.

In some very general respects, then, Zen seems in accord with the recent writings of ethicists such as Peter Singer. But before one jumps at the chance of seeing Singer's writings as a theoretical articulation of the central intuitions of Zen, it must be noted that there are some important differences between the two positions. For one thing, Singer allows the possibility that someone could do the

---

[15] See Peter Harvey, *An Introduction to Buddhist Ethics* (Cambridge: Cambridge University Press, 2000), pp.164-5.

[16] From Rev. Reirin Yamada, 'The Way to Understand Zen' in William Briggs (ed.), *Anthology of Zen* (New York: Grove Press, 1961), pp.188-9.

[17] The *Laṅkāvatāra Sūtra*, for example, cites this as a reason for being a vegetarian: '...in this long course of transmigration here, there is not one living being that... has not been your mother, or father, or brother, or sister, or son, or daughter... [this being so] how can the Bodhisattva-Mahāsattva who desires to approach all beings as if they were himself and to practise the Buddha-truths, eat the flesh of any living being...?' (p.212 (Chapter Eight), Suzuki's annotation).

right thing – that is, act in such a way as to alleviate the suffering of sentient beings – without *feeling* that that is a good thing to do. In saying this, however, Singer is very far from the Mahāyāna tradition. As we saw in Chapter Two, for the Mahāyāna the virtue of compassion is central, and compassion, of course, is a feeling. A man who did not feel for his fellow beings could not be a *Bodhisattva*.

Another, related, difference between Singer's position and that of Zen could be articulated in terms of meta-ethics. Singer's position is consequentialist in the sense that it deems an action right if it yields a good outcome – in his view, a good outcome in terms of the alleviation of suffering. But we have been interpreting Zen as a form of virtue ethic rather than a form of consequentialism. And according to the virtue ethic developed in the previous chapter, actions can be considered to be right if they are expressions of virtue, regardless of their consequences. So one could say that an action would be considered right according to Zen (and indeed Mahāyāna teachings generally) if it were motivated by a concern to liberate all beings from the round of *saṃsāra*, regardless of whether it did in fact have the best possible consequences in this respect.[18] (In fact, since his compassion should have been developed in tandem with his insight, a *Bodhisattva*'s good intentions could not misfire in this way.) Conversely, an action would be considered wrong if it were motivated by malevolence, for instance, even if, through some quirk of fate it in fact resulted in the alleviation of a great deal of suffering.[19]

The Buddha-nature of mountains, trees and rivers

We in the West are the inheritors of a philosophical tradition that has tended to deny nonhuman animals moral standing. Animals, various moral philosophers have told us, are without souls or without minds or in any case without that distinctive property which confers moral standing upon humans. In the light of such anthropocentric views, Singer's position is rightly portrayed in a positive light. He is *extending* the moral circle to include nonhuman animals, showing that they are not machines or 'brutes' or 'beasts' but have moral standing in their own right.

We have already compared and contrasted Singer's views with those of the Mahāyāna generally. But what of specifically Eastern Mahāyāna traditions such as Zen? How would they view this extension of the moral circle? Well, like other schools of the Mahāyāna they would applaud Singer's attempt to bring nonhuman animals within the fold of morality, for they would see it as being in line with their

---

[18] Admittedly, a utilitarian could reply that some form of rule-utilitarianism could accommodate the importance of motivation, arguing that actions motivated by compassion are right, not because they always maximize utility, but because the rule that actions be so motivated maximizes utility. But with this argument we are, I think, very far from anything resembling the Mahāyāna. Mahāyāna traditions do not laud the virtue of compassion simply because exercising it just so happens to decrease suffering; actions motivated by compassion have non-instrumental value.

[19] Note that these conclusions are in accord with the Buddhist idea that the moral worth of an action, that is the specific nature – good or bad – of the *karma* it generates, is a function of the choice or intention (*cetanā*) behind it.

aim to secure the liberation of all beings. Indeed, as we saw above, Eastern traditions of Mahāyāna were especially concerned to extend moral concern to nonhuman animals. But in some schools this approval would, I think, be qualified. For it seems likely that some Eastern traditions would view the idea of including all and only nonhuman animals in the moral circle in a negative light as a *limitation* of the aspirations of the Mahāyāna rather than as a praiseworthy extension of the moral circle. After all, as William LaFleur has shown, while in India the idea that all sentient beings were destined for Buddhahood was seen in a positive light as an expansion of the Great Vehicle, in China it was – ironically – perceived as a restriction. Why *deny* the promise of Buddhahood to plants and other seemingly nonsentient beings? asked the Chinese.[20] Perhaps they would have had similar qualms about Singer's position. But whether they would have or not, it can be noted that Eastern Mahāyānists did indeed tend to work with a very broad conception of the Great Vehicle, the set of beings destined for (or instantiating) Buddhahood being sometimes taken to include not only (all) animals, but also plants and even apparently non-living 'beings' such as mountains and rivers.

The extension of the Great Vehicle beyond the limits of the animal kingdom is particularly associated with the Shingon (Ch. Chen-yen) and Tendai schools of Eastern Buddhism, both of which proved important formative influences on Zen. For Chan-jan (711-782) of the latter school, Mahāyāna philosophy impelled one to consider plants and even soil as destined for Buddhahood:

> In the great assembly of the Lotus all are present – without divisions. Grass, trees, the soil on which these grow... Some are barely in motion while others make haste along the Path, but they will all in time reach the precious land of Nirvana... Who can really maintain that things inanimate lack buddhahood?[21]

In Japan, these sorts of claims chimed with traditional conceptions of the religious significance of the natural world – Shintō ideas that natural beings were inhabited by divine spirits (*kami*), for instance – and the idea of the spiritual significance of nature accordingly took root and flourished on Japanese soil.[22] It is evident, for instance, in the idea, pervasive in Japanese thought, of the inherent enlightenment (*hongaku-shisō*) of grasses and trees, rocks and mountains.[23] On this very broad conception of the Great Vehicle, all these beings were to be thought of as having Buddha-nature. Or rather, following Dōgen, these beings were to be

---

[20] William R. LaFleur, 'Saigyō and the Buddhist Value of Nature' in John Baird Callicott and Roger T. Ames (eds), *Nature in Asian Traditions of Thought* (Albany: SUNY Press, 2001), p.184.

[21] Quoted in William LaFleur, 'Enlightenment for Plants and Trees' in Stephanie Kaza and Kenneth Kraft, *Dharma Rain: Sources of Buddhist Environmentalism* (Boston: Shambhala, 2000), p.110.

[22] See LaFleur, 'Saigyō and the Buddhist Value of Nature', pp.195-6; Graham Parkes, 'Voices of Mountains, Trees, and Rivers: Kūkai, Dōgen, and a Deeper Ecology' in Tucker and Williams (eds), *Buddhism and Ecology*, p.113.

[23] See Paul L. Swanson, 'Why They Say Zen Is Not Buddhism: recent Japanese critiques of Buddha-nature' in Jamie Hubbard and Paul L. Swanson (eds), *Pruning the Bodhi Tree: The Storm over Critical Buddhism* (Honolulu: University of Hawai'i Press, 1997), p.6.

thought of as *being* Buddha-nature. As we saw in Chapter One, Dōgen, inspired no doubt by his early training in Tendai, maintained that the line in the *Mahāparinirvāṇa Sūtra*, 'All sentient beings without exception have the Buddha-nature', should be reread as, 'All is sentient being, all beings are (all being is) the Buddha-nature'. For Dōgen, mountains 'are the actualisation of the ancient buddha way',[24] and to drive this obscure point home he speaks – in terms reminiscent of the twentieth century environmental ethicist, Aldo Leopold – of considering the world from the perspective of a mountain, or of the long, slow movement of mountains through many eons of time.[25] He would, I think, have been intrigued by the speeded-up film in natural history television programmes of plants moving so quickly that they seem sentient, like animals. He might also have been impressed by the science of geology, and its discovery that the earth's surface is more fluid than it appears, that even mountains are born and die.

LaFleur has shown that in Japan natural entities such as plants, rocks and rivers were sometimes even conceived as being spiritually superior to humans. For while humans had to appropriate their enlightenment experientially – that is, realize their inherently awakened natures – trees and other natural entities were thought of as instantiating the way of the Buddha just as they were. In this sense, nature was considered to be 'in full possession of what man only still partially possesses'.[26] As such, the natural world was considered to have a religious significance, or, more precisely, a 'saving power and function'. To contemplate the natural world was to follow the way of the Buddha.[27]

This conception of the salvific power of nature is also found in Zen. For Zen poets such as Bashō, there is no separation between the way of nature and the religious path. That is why a poem ostensibly about natural phenomena could be viewed as a religious verse. Consider, for example, the following poem from Daitō (1282-1338), one of the founders of the Ōtōkan school of Rinzai:

> Rain clears from distant peaks, dew glistens frostily.
> Moonlight glazes the front of my ivied hut among the pines.
> How can I tell you how I am, right now?
> A swollen brook gushes in the valley darkened by clouds.[28]

---

[24] From the first line of his 'Mountains and Waters Sūtra', quoted in Kaza and Kraft, *Dharma Rain*, p.65.

[25] See LaFleur, 'Enlightenment for Plants and Trees', p.110.

[26] LaFleur, 'Saigyō and the Buddhist Value of Nature', p.197.

[27] Ibid. p.208.

[28] Quoted in Kaza and Kraft, *Dharma Rain*, p.77. For criticisms of the idea that the attention to natural phenomena expressed in Japanese poetry is evidence of a genuine appreciation of nature, see Arne Kalland 'Culture in Japanese Nature' in Ole Bruun and Arne Kalland, *Asian Perceptions of Nature: A Critical Approach* (Richmond: Curzon, 1996). Kalland argues that the natural phenomena referred to in *haiku* – cherry blossoms, the morning-glory, pines, the moon, etc. – 'all appear in a predictable, or conventional, way and even authors who have hardly been outside the main cities have become renowned for their sensitive praise of nature' (p.251). This is no doubt a criticism that could have been levelled at some poets, but it does not apply to men such as Bashō and Ryōkwan whose love of

To consider nature as having a salvific power is, however, not only to imbue it with a religious meaning, but also to say that the spiritual practitioner can learn from it. So to say that trees, mountains and waters exemplify Buddhahood is to say that these beings have something to teach us. And one way of expressing this is to say that these beings exemplify virtues, and that we can, in turn, learn virtue by contemplating them. To be sure, this way of putting matters is at odds with the mainstream Western traditions of virtue ethics, for which only humans can exemplify such qualities.[29] But Buddhist traditions, for their part, have not drawn such a sharp distinction. For example, in the *Jātaka* tales, the stories of the Buddha's former lives, the Buddha-to-be is often portrayed as a virtuous animal. In one tale he is said to have lived as a crane who, out of compassion, only ate fish that were already dead; in another, he is portrayed as a noble stag who sacrificed his own life in order to save one of his herd.[30] These cases are, however, rather special – after all, the individual animals depicted in these stories are not ordinary animals, but previous incarnations of the Buddha. Indeed, the positive images of nonhuman animals conveyed in these tales must, I think, be weighed against the more negative portrayals evident in other parts of the Buddhist tradition where animals are portrayed as leading lives ruled by sex, aggression and other vices.[31]

Inanimate – or perhaps I ought to say apparently inanimate – beings such as trees and mountains would not seem to be guilty of such vices, however. In fact, traditions of Eastern Mahāyāna have sometimes regarded these beings as paragons of virtue. By way of example, consider the various ways in which Zen Buddhists refer to the virtues exemplified by plants.[32] At times, the emphasis is on the 'thoughtlessness' of the plant and the spontaneity of its 'behaviour'. Thus Robert Aitken is continuing an old Buddhist tradition when he draws an analogy between the clover's spontaneous and thoughtless production of pollen and the Buddha's

---

nature is well-documented, nor does it apply to modern Zen Buddhists like Thich Nhat Hanh and John Daido Loori, whose environmental work is an expression of their practice of Zen.

[29] Although Philip Cafaro notes that the references to the virtues of animals found in the writings of modern environmental thinkers such as Aldo Leopold and Henry David Thoreau take us back to Homer, 'who could speak of the *arete* of a horse and have all Greece understand him'. ('Thoreau, Leopold, and Carson: Toward an Environmental Virtue Ethics', *Environmental Ethics* 22 (Spring 2001), p.9.) (*Areté* is the Greek term conventionally rendered as 'virtue' or 'excellence' in English.)

[30] See Harvey, *An Introduction to Buddhist Ethics*, pp.158, 162.

[31] Lambert Schmithausen, *Buddhism and Nature: the Lecture delivered on the Occasion of the EXPO 1990, An Enlarged Version with Notes* (Tokyo: The International Institute for Buddhist Studies, 1991), p.20.

[32] Or, one might say, the teachings symbolized by plants. The idea that beings such as plants exemplify the virtues of Buddhahood is in practice often inseparable from the idea that these beings symbolize teachings that can be read by someone who is suitably attentive. Thus, the hollow stem of bamboo is said to symbolize the empty core at the heart of phenomena, or a modest flower display in a room set aside for the tea ceremony is meant to symbolize the pure, unassuming attitude of mind that the ceremony requires. See Herrigel, *Zen in the Art of Flower Arrangement*, p.106.

twirling of the flower before the smiling Mahākāśyapa.[33] At other times, the focus is on the patience or steadfastness exemplified by plants. In this respect, trees, and, it seems, especially pine trees, are seen as exemplifying 'imperturbability, strength and firmness of character'.[34] For the Sōtō poet-monk Ryōkwan (1758-1831) they exemplified a divine dignity.[35] In other contexts, the emphasis is on the way plants are able to adapt themselves to their environments – in a Taoist idiom, one would say to the *Tao* – in a way in which humans often cannot. Consider, for example, the following passage from Gustie Herrigel:

> The master has seen, from the example of himself and others, how fuss, haste and impatience only bring discord into his life and his surroundings. He has listened to the plants in the wind and the storm, seen how they yield, bending and swaying, how they calmly let everything pass over their heads and so remain uninjured.[36]

Compare Katsuki Sekida's beautiful story of his encounter with an old Zen priest:

> [The priest] had been ill, and when I visited him he was sitting quietly at the window basking in the sun. A few books of haiku and a notebook were beside him. He had been composing haiku. It was a calm winter day. In the course of our conversation, he pointed to a pine grove in front of the temple and said, 'You know the Zen question, 'The Bodhisattva of Great Mercy [Avalokitesvara, or Kannon] has a thousand hands and a thousand eyes; which is the true eye?' I could not understand this for a long time. But the other day, when I looked at the pine trees bending before the cold blasts from the mountain, I suddenly realized the meaning. You see, all the boughs, branches, twigs, and leaves simultaneously bend to the wind with tremendous vigor.' He said this with a quiet but earnest gesture. I could feel his close intimacy with the pine trees. He had to convey his experience to somebody else. It was the evening glow of his life. He died a few weeks after our meeting.[37]

Some schools of the Mahāyāna spoke of a heavenly 'Pure Land' which would provide a kind of springboard to *Nirvāṇa* for those beings who were virtuous enough to be reborn there. For to be reborn in a Pure Land would be to find oneself in a spiritual paradise in which even the rustling of the leaves in the trees proclaimed the *Dharma*. Who could fail to attain awakening in such a place? For Zen, however, the Pure Land is not some far-off destination, which can only be reached by securing an auspicious rebirth, it is the very world in which we live.[38] So the truth is there in *zazen*, but it is also there in the tall beech trees outside the

---

[33] Robert Aitken, *The Mind of Clover: Essays in Zen Buddhist Ethics* (San Francisco: North Point Press, 1984), p.137.

[34] See Herrigel, *Zen in the Art of Flower Arangement*, p.84.

[35] Suzuki, *Zen and Japanese Culture*, pp.370-1.

[36] Herrigel, *Zen in the Art of Flower Arangement*, pp.22-3.

[37] Katsuki Sekida (translator), A. V. Grimstone (ed.), *Two Zen Classics: Mumonkan and Hekiganroku* (Tokyo: Weatherhill, 1977), pp.110-11. Annotations in original.

[38] See Paul Williams, *Mahāyāna Buddhism: the doctrinal foundations* (London: Routledge 1989), pp.227, 263-4.

meditation hall, reaching up into the evening sky; and it is there in the cawing of the crows as they return to roost.

Non-violence

On the face of it, it would seem that this very broad conception of the Mahāyāna as encompassing even trees, mountains and rivers would prove especially amenable to modern environmentalist concerns. And indeed, as we saw in Chapter One, Zen has proven an important source of inspiration for environmental thinkers, particularly for those towards the dark green pole of the environmental spectrum. However, it remains to be seen what implications these ideas have for environmental *ethics*.

In his book *Nonviolence to Animals, Earth, and Self in Asian Traditions*, Christopher Key Chapple suggests that the East Asian idea that plants and other natural beings are enlightened is 'uniquely ecological', implying that these beings 'are to be valued as intrinsically worthy of veneration and protection'.[39] Taking our lead from Chapple's suggestion we can ask whether the claims of Zen Buddhists that trees, mountains, rivers, and so on instantiate Buddhahood are meant to bring these beings within the purview of the First Precept, non-violence (*ahiṃsā*).[40] The first thing to note about this suggestion is that it would mark a break with traditional Buddhist understandings of non-violence. For the First Precept is traditionally considered to apply only to sentient beings, so that it serves as an injunction against intentionally killing – or more broadly, harming or injuring – humans, animals, birds, fish and insects,[41] but not plants, and certainly not mountains, rivers and other apparently insentient beings. In any case, regardless of its relation to orthodox teachings, the idea that our behaviour towards trees, mountains, and so on should be governed by non-violence would seem to over-extend the First Precept – to over-expand the moral circle, if you like – and to therefore imply an impracticable ideal. For if *all* beings are to be thought of as instantiating Buddhahood, then one would expect Zen Buddhists to see the injury of a clod of soil (whatever that means) as being on a par with the injury of an animal. Perhaps one would expect to read of Zen masters making efforts not to impinge upon anything, concerned lest they harm a morally-considerable being. One would imagine the Zen master tip-toeing around, taking care not to step on

---

[39] (Albany: SUNY Press, 1993), p.65.

[40] Even if one claims only that these beings are 'on the way' to Buddhahood, rather than actual Buddhas, one could suppose that they ought still to be viewed as sentient beings, and hence as falling within the domain of non-violence. See Steve Odin's discussion of the views of Omine Akira in his essay 'The Japanese Concept of Nature in Relation to the Environmental Ethics and Conservation Aesthetics of Aldo Leopold' in Tucker and Williams (eds), *Buddhism and Ecology*, pp.101-2.

[41] Peter Harvey, *An Introduction to Buddhism: teachings, history and practices* (Cambridge: Cambridge University Press, 1990), p.202. See also Harvey, *An Introduction to Buddhist Ethics*, p.69.

blades of grass (for they manifest Buddha-nature), carefully avoiding crushing lumps of soil beneath his feet (for they too manifest Buddha-nature).

This ideal bears some resemblance to the exacting interpretation of *ahiṃsā* propounded in Jainism, but it does not accord with the practice of Zen.[42] Zen masters, although, as we shall see, respectful of nature, do not take such extreme measures to avoid impinging on the world, so it is unlikely that in claiming that beings have Buddha-nature they mean to accord them moral standing in a way that brings them within the purview of the First Precept.[43] (In fact, Chūjin (1065-1138), a Tendai scholar, explicitly addresses this matter, maintaining that the claim that plants are endowed with Buddha-nature is made from the standpoint of ultimate truth, but that from this standpoint moral distinctions are not relevant either. It would seem to follow that the ascription of Buddha-nature to plants (and other beings) should not affect our moral obligations towards them.[44])

But if this is granted, then what should one make of the following reformulation of the First Precept presented by Thich Nhat Hanh: 'Aware of the suffering caused by the destruction of life, I vow to cultivate compassion and learn ways to protect the lives of people, animals, plants, and minerals'?[45] Is Nhat Hanh advocating that crushing clods of earth be compared to killing animals? Is he calling for the sort of extension of the First Precept I have dismissed as being out of keeping with Zen practice? I do not think he is. As we saw in Chapter Two, non-violence, like the other precepts, is not merely an injunction against performing a certain kind of action. It also has a positive aspect, so that someone whose actions were in accord with the First Precept could be said to have developed the virtue of *ahiṃsā*. All Buddhists agree that someone who had developed this virtue would radiate kindness and compassion towards sentient beings. I would hold that such a caring, gentle attitude would also be extended to plants. This is not to say that the harming of plants should be considered to be a violation of the First Precept on a

---

[42] Jainism is an Indian religion, older than Buddhism, which promotes as the highest spiritual goal the practice of *ahiṃsā* as a way of cleansing one's life-force or soul (*jīva*) of karmic accretions. It is held, moreover, that *ahiṃsā* ought to be extended to all sentient beings, which, on the Jaina conception, means not only (all) animals but also (all) plants and even elemental forces such as fire and water. Hence Jaina monks and nuns not only avoid killing insects, by covering their mouths and sweeping their path, but also avoid disturbing the elements by, say, lighting or extinguishing flames or wading into water. (See Christopher Key Chapple, 'Jainism and Buddhism' in Dale Jamieson, *A Companion to Environmental Philosophy* (Oxford: Blackwell, 2001), p.53.) To be sure, these extreme measures are partly a result of the fact that, unlike Buddhism, Jainism sees even unintentional actions as generating *karma*, so that even accidentally swallowing a fly or stepping on a daisy is thought to produce bad *karma*.
[43] Cf. Arne Kalland, 'Culture in Japanese Nature' in Ole Bruun and Arne Kalland, *Asian Perceptions of Nature: A Critical Approach* (Richmond: Curzon, 1996), p.247. Cf. also Deane Curtin, 'A State of Mind Like Water: Ecosophy T and the Buddhist Traditions', *Inquiry* 39, (1996), pp.247ff.
[44] Schmithausen, *Buddhism and Nature*, p.24.
[45] Quoted in Sallie B. King, 'Contemporary Buddhist Spirituality and Social Activism' in Takeuchi Yoshinori (ed.), *Buddhist Spirituality: Later China, Korea, Japan, and the Modern World* (London: SCM Press, 1999), p.471.

par with, say, injuring an animal. It is only to say that the gratuitous harming of plants, for instance, would be considered to be against the spirit of *ahiṃsā*. Indeed, it seems implausible to suggest that a man who had cultivated non-violence in his dealings with animals would not also be gentle in his relations with other beings.[46] This gentleness is illustrated by a story, related by D. T. Suzuki, of the Sōtō monk, Ryōkwan.[47] Suzuki tells how one day the monk noticed a bamboo shoot poking its way through the floor of his closet. Each day, Ryōkwan noted the plant's progress. However, since bamboo grows quickly, it wasn't long before the plant had grown so tall that its tip was brushing the ceiling. Ryōkwan, anxious not to impede the flourishing of the plant, tried to make a hole in the ceiling to allow the bamboo to grow through. (More precisely, Ryōkwan, ever the 'holy fool', tried to *burn* a hole in the ceiling. The roof caught fire and the entire structure burnt down!) Whether or not it would have been an 'official' violation of the First Precept to have thwarted the bamboo's growth, Ryōkwan's action was in the spirit of the First Precept, and could, I suggest, be seen as an expression of the positive virtue of non-violence.

So in reformulating the First Precept to incorporate the protection of plants and minerals, it would seem that Nhat Hanh is simply making the point that the man who has developed the virtue of non-violence would be gentle, not only in his relations with sentient beings, but with all things. And whether or not his claim can be justified in terms of the classical Buddhist teachings, he is, I think, making a point, entirely in keeping with the nature-regarding spirit of Zen, namely, that morality extends towards the natural environment as a whole, not just to humans, nor even just to those beings we deem sentient.[48]

A similar moral concern for the natural environment is expressed by John Daido Loori, at the time of writing, the abbot of Zen Mountain Monastery in New York State. Loori enjoins his students to consider the various ways in which observing the precepts affects the environment.[49] Thus he teaches that the precept of *ahiṃsā* ought to be thought of as bearing upon, not only our treatment of individual organisms, but also our relations with species, for to decimate species is 'the worst kind of killing'. 'Do not steal', on the other hand, 'means not to rape the earth', while the Third Grave Precept, 'Honour the body – do not misuse sexuality', Loori reads as an injunction against interfering in the natural order of things through genetic engineering. The Fourth Grave Precept, 'Manifest truth – do

---

[46] In this connection it can be noted that the *Vinaya* rules for monastic life prohibit monks and nuns from intentionally injuring plants, even though plants are not 'officially' protected under the First Precept. On the treatment of plants in the context of early Buddhist ethics, see Schmithausen, *Buddhism and Nature*, pp.6-8.

[47] D. T. Suzuki, *Zen and Japanese Culture* (Princeton, NJ: Princeton University Press, 1973), p.369.

[48] Holmes Rolston III also explores the possibility of basing a Zen Buddhist respect for non-sentient beings on the idea of *ahiṃsā*, although he views non-violence as a 'commandment' rather than a virtue. See his essay 'Respect for Life: Can Zen Buddhism Help in Forming an Environmental Ethic?' *Zen Buddhism Today* 7 (September 1989), p.15.

[49] John Daido Loori, 'The Precepts and the Environment' in Tucker and Williams (eds), *Buddhism and Ecology*, pp.177-84.

not lie', serves as a condemnation of the efforts of multinationals to pass themselves off as ecologically-concerned when they are in fact nothing of the sort ('greenwashing'). 'Proceed clearly – do not cloud the mind', the Fifth Grave Precept, Loori interprets as a warning not to allow our judgement to be clouded by greed, while he sees the Sixth Grave Precept, 'See the perfection – do not speak of others' errors and faults', as enjoining us to think of natural processes as inherently perfect, in need of no 'management' on our part. And so on for the other precepts. I do not think that Loori would want his teachings on this matter to be subjected to an exhaustive philosophical analysis. He would, I imagine, maintain that he is not interested in offering a defensible philosophical theory, but only in making the general point, nonetheless entirely in keeping with Zen, that our ethical concern should extend beyond the sphere of animal life to the natural environment as a whole.

Ethical holism

In bringing apparently non-sentient beings such as plants, mountains and rivers within the purview of ethics, the Zen comportment towards nature is at odds with utilitarianism, and I have rejected the idea that it can be understood on the model of Singer's position. To find an appropriate theoretical model for the Zen Buddhist attitude towards nature we will have to look elsewhere.

For one candidate, we can turn to the position of environmental ethicist J. Baird Callicott, as developed in his article 'Animal Liberation: A Triangular Affair'.[50] In that essay, Callicott coins the phrase 'humane moralism' to denote those positions, like Singer's, which accord nonhuman beings moral standing if, and only if, they are sentient. To be sure, he admits that such views represent an advance on those positions that categorically deny that any nonhuman animals have moral standing, and, in this respect, Bentham and Singer are considered to be a step up the moral ladder from inveterate anthropocentrists like Aquinas and Descartes. Yet for Callicott humane moralism is ultimately an inadequate basis for an environmental ethic. The problem here, he suggests, is that whereas humane moralism is inherently individualistic, a properly environmental ethic must be holistic. Let us try to clarify what this means. To say that humane moralist positions such as Singer's are individualistic is to say that they hold that the moral standing of beings can be determined by looking to the characteristics of those beings in themselves, irrespective of their contexts. So, on Singer's account, a rabbit has the same moral standing, whether it is languishing in the laboratory of some pharmaceutical company or hopping about in the wild. In both cases it has the same capacity to suffer, so in both cases it has the same moral standing. According to Callicott, however, such an individualistic approach cannot do justice to the moral significance of environmental concerns, and so could not form the basis for a properly environmental ethic. An environmental ethic, he maintains,

---

[50] In Louis P. Pojman (ed.), *Environmental Ethics: Readings in Theory and Application* (Belmont, California: Wadsworth, 2001), pp.52-63.

would have to take a more holistic approach in recognizing that the value of any particular being is not something that that being possesses in itself, but is instead a function of the part it plays in an environment whole, or, more precisely, a reflection of the *contribution* it makes to that whole. So according to an 'ethical holism' of this sort, a field mouse would have value, not on account of its possessing a special value-conferring property (sentience, for example), but because it plays a role in an environmental whole, as food for a kestrel, for instance, or as a fertilizer of the soil. Similarly, actions would be deemed right to the extent that they further the good of the environmental whole. As Aldo Leopold, the founding father of such holistic approaches, famously put it:

> A thing is right when it tends to preserve the integrity, stability, and beauty of the biotic community. It is wrong when it tends otherwise.[51]

The reference to beauty indicates that, unlike Singer, ethical holists such as Leopold preserve a place for feeling in their accounts of our moral relations with nature. Leopold's *Sand County Almanac* is filled with heartfelt, evocative descriptions of natural phenomena, many of which are entirely in the spirit of Zen. Moreover, just as for Leopold ethics is tied to aesthetics, so for Zen there is no clear line between a moral concern for nature and an aesthetic appreciation of it. We saw in Chapter Two that art forms such as the tea ceremony, archery and flower arranging are partly ethical practices because the virtues inherent in them are, in part, moral virtues. And many of them – perhaps all of them – bear upon one's moral relations with the natural world. Hence the aesthetic sensitivity to the world engendered by the practice of, say, flower arranging translates into a particular ethical appreciation of the world. Seeing the delicate beauty of flower arrangements, the artist comes to see the beauty inherent in all things – like a *haiku* poet, perhaps. And just as a sense of this beauty causes him to treat the flowers, twigs and pebbles with which he works with respect, so he gradually becomes gentler in his dealings with all things. His aesthetic appreciation has naturally engendered a particular ethical comportment. Furthermore, it could be that the specific kind of aesthetic sensibility fostered by Zen is especially appropriate for environmental ethics. As we saw in Chapter One, much Zen-inspired art aims at conveying the aesthetic sensibility the Japanese call *aware*, 'the sorrow-tinged appreciation of transient beauty', in Steve Odin's nice phrase.[52] This sense of impermanence is, moreover, inextricably tied to an awareness of natural cycles (think, for example, of the seasonal references (*kigo*) in *haiku*: frogs, snails or plum blossom for spring, butterflies for summer, the flowering bush clover for autumn, and so on). For Zen, the best depictions of the natural world convey the truth that phenomena are not hard-edged, substantial entities – natural kinds, for instance – but events, confluences of forces, eddies in the stream of life, if you will. This dynamic picture of the natural world strikes a chord with the writings of modern environmental thinkers such as Leopold, for whom a sense of the beauty of nature

---

[51] Aldo Leopold, *A Sand County Almanac* (New York: Oxford University Press, 1968), pp.224-5.
[52] 'The Japanese Concept of Nature' p.99.

is informed and invigorated by an understanding of the dynamism inherent in ecological relationships. For these thinkers, seeing nature as beautiful is largely a matter of appreciating the way in which natural phenomena play their part in various processes – food webs, nutrient cycles, energy flows, and the like – and of seeing how these processes fit together in a great sacramental economy of life.[53] For the Zen poet and the sensitive ecologist alike, there is a stark beauty in the decomposition of the dead mouse and in the new growth of fungi about the spot where it fell.

There are, therefore, some similarities between the aesthetic-cum-ethical concern for the biotic community advocated by ethical holists such as Leopold and the concern for the environment espoused by Zen Buddhists such as Thich Nhat Hanh and John Daido Loori. Moreover, it would seem that Zen and ethical holism show a similar awareness of the natural world as a whole. In this connection, Gary Snyder has suggested that the Chinese phrase *shan-shui* ('Mountains and waters'), so common in Buddhist accounts of the religious significance of nature, refers, not to two particular sorts of natural entity, but to 'the totality of the process of nature'.[54] So maybe in saying that mountains and waters instantiate Buddhahood Zen Buddhists are not saying that individual mountains and stretches of water ought to be accorded moral standing, but are thinking more holistically.

Would it be right, then, to say that a Zen environmental ethic would be a form of ethical holism? In support of the idea that it would, one could argue that our actions towards environmental wholes ought to be governed by the positive virtue of non-violence. For, after all, whether or not environmental wholes such as ecosystems are strictly speaking alive, they can certainly be harmed, and one might think that we ought therefore to treat them carefully, gently, non-violently. Steven C. Rockefeller is perhaps thinking along these lines when he maintains that 'the most fundamental principle of environmental protection is widely recognized today to be a variation on the theme of *ahiṃsā*, or no harming', where this concerns the prevention of environmental harms such as the elimination of endangered species.[55]

In an interesting study of the views of Kūkai (a Shingon master) and Dōgen, Graham Parkes explores the possibilities of basing a holistic environmental ethic upon Buddhist ideas. In his view, Dōgen's conception of nature can be framed as an extreme form of holism in which securing the good of the whole is deemed an overriding consideration.[56] Thus when Dōgen maintains that all beings are Buddha-nature, Parkes suggests that he is not making the implausible suggestion that all beings should be treated equally. On the contrary, 'a view of the world as... Buddha-nature would naturally lead to reverence for and respectful treatment of the totality – but would not rule out destroying certain parts of it under certain

---

[53] See Gary Snyder's essay, 'Grace' in Kaza and Kraft (eds), *Dharma Rain*, pp.450-3.
[54] 'Blue Mountains Constantly Walking' in Kaza and Kraft (eds), *Dharma Rain*, p.129.
[55] 'Buddhism, Global Ethics, and the Earth Charter' in Tucker and Williams (eds), *Buddhism and Ecology*, pp.317-8.
[56] See 'Voices of Mountains, Trees, and Rivers' in Tucker and Williams (eds), *Buddhism and Ecology*, pp.122-3.

circumstances'.[57] So respect for the 'organized totality' of Buddha-nature would in fact justify eradicating destructive beings such as the tubercle bacillus.[58] Just as one might contribute to the well-being of one's body by removing an abscess, so reverence for the Buddha-nature might lead one to remove these harmful beings.

I am not sure whether Parkes' conception of holism accords with Leopold's. Leopold has often been interpreted as presenting a version of ethical holism wherein securing the well-being of the land is held to be an overriding consideration. According to such an extreme ethical holism a thing would be right if, *and only if*, it tended to preserve the integrity, stability, and beauty of the biotic community. Defenders of Leopold have suggested alternative readings of the man's work, however.[59] In any case, whether or not Leopold is propounding such a position, it would seem that Parkes is presenting an extreme version of ethical holism of this sort as a reading of Dōgen. On this view, the prime virtue, one might suppose, is 'respect' or 'reverence' for the organized totality of the Buddha-nature, where such respect might occasionally sanction efforts to eradicate harmful beings such as tubercle bacteria.

Is such an attitude in accord with a Zen Buddhist understanding of nature? To be sure, Zen, like Buddhism generally, is holistic. The teaching of universal emptiness means that to know the nature of any element of reality one must look to its context, its environment. Nevertheless, Zen seems to embody a concern for individual phenomena at odds with extreme holism. Let us follow Parkes in considering this matter with respect to the views of Dōgen. The holistic outlook of Dōgen must, I think, be understood in terms of the Hua-yen and Tendai philosophies with which Dōgen would have been familiar and of which his own views are partly an expression. The worldview set out by those schools is certainly holistic in that it sees reality as a coherent whole formed of mutually-dependent elements, and in this sense it bears a superficial resemblance to the holism developed in the writings of Leopold. But the holism espoused in Hua-yen is subtler, and I would hold more profound, than that evident in the writings of holistic environmental thinkers. Neither Hua-yen nor Dōgen is supposing that each being forms a part of a totality which can be understood on analogy with an organic body. Matters are not so simple. Dōgen inherits the view, propounded in both Hua-yen and Tendai philosophy, that the whole is contained within each part. That is why he can claim that an awakened man can see 'the entire world in one tiny speck of dust' or 'the entire universe... in... a tall bamboo'.[60] So while for an extreme holist a being has value only to the extent that it contributes to the well-being of the whole, for Dōgen each being has a supreme worth as an embodiment of the whole. Similarly, whatever precise form it took, a Zen Buddhist environmental ethic would have to do justice to the value inherent in the details of the natural world – in the little epiphanies expressed in *haiku*, for example.

---

[57] Ibid. p.122.

[58] Ibid. pp.122-3.

[59] For example, see J. Baird Callicott, 'The Conceptual Foundations of the Land Ethic' in Pojman (ed.), *Environmental Ethics*, p.134.

[60] Dōgen, *Shōbōgenzō: The Eye and Treasury of the True Law, Vol. 1*, translated by K. Nishiyama and J. Stevens (Tokyo: Nakayama Shobō, 1976), pp.15, 89.

We will explore the metaphysics behind this idea in the next chapter. For the moment, it will suffice to note that this commitment to the worth of individual beings means that Dōgen's conception of the Buddha-nature cannot be understood along the lines of extreme holism. While an extreme holist would be willing to sacrifice individual deer in order to preserve the well-being of a particular environment, Zen thinkers would be less inclined to sanction such holistic efforts at wildlife management. Loori's criticisms of holistic approaches to wildlife management, whether they can be justified in their own terms or not, are, I think, more in keeping with Zen thought.[61]

This is not to say that Zen Buddhists would never consider such holistic approaches justified, however. Consider a situation in which one is forced to choose between culling a population of deer that has grown too large or harming the biotic community of a Scottish island which is being devastated by the presence of too many deer. The Zen Buddhist *could* be justified in choosing to cull the deer if she did so out of compassion for the deer or out of a concern not to harm the island's ecosystem. But unlike the extreme holist she would not suppose that the concern to preserve the well-being of the ecosystem must *necessarily* trump the concern not to harm the deer. The Zen approach is, as ever, more flexible than that.

Deep ecology

In the literature on environmental ethics, sympathetic mentions of Zen Buddhism are most commonly found neither in the writings of 'humane moralists' like Peter Singer nor in the work of 'ethical holists' like Aldo Leopold, but in the writings of deep ecologists. Having so far failed to find an adequate model for Zen Buddhist environmental concerns in either humane moralism or (extreme) ethical holism I would now like to consider the possibility that it is in the writings of deep ecologists such as Arne Naess and Warwick Fox that we will find an account of environmental concern more in tune with Zen.

As we saw in Chapter One, Zen has proved popular with deep ecological thinkers. Arne Naess has acknowledged Dōgen as a major inspiration,[62] while Bill Devall and George Sessions refer approvingly to Zen in articulating their conception of deep ecology.[63] Warwick Fox concludes his influential *Toward a Transpersonal Ecology* with a quotation from Dōgen, arguing that Zen is based on what he calls an 'ontologically based identification', a profound awareness of 'the fact *that* things are', which, he maintains, has important implications for

---

[61] Loori refers to the culling of deer as 'controlled genocide'. 'The Precepts and the Environment', pp.180-1. Note that Buddhism in general has trouble accounting for the ethical worth of species and environmental wholes. See Harvey, *An Introduction to Buddhist Ethics*, pp.183-4.

[62] Deane Curtin, 'A State of Mind Like Water', p.241.

[63] 'Deep Ecology' in Pojman (ed.), *Environmental Ethics*, p.158.

environmental philosophy.[64] Both Joan Halifax and Jeremy Hayward refer to Zen teachings in articulating their respective conceptions of deep ecology.[65]

So what are deep ecology and Zen supposed to have in common? First, they are thought to share a commitment to the general idea that right (that is, 'eco-friendly') action will not be generated through the 'external' pressure of moral exhortations to behave in environmentally-appropriate ways, but will arise naturally from an 'internal' transformation in how one sees the world. Thus Arne Naess admits to being 'not much interested in ethics or morals... [since] Ethics follows from how we experience the world'.[66] Zen seems to chime with this stance, for, as we saw in Chapter Two, Zen also *seems* to downplay the importance of ethics, assuming that appropriately caring behaviour must emerge naturally as a result of an enlightened way of seeing the world. (In a forthcoming study[67] I argue that to claim this is to overlook the possibility of framing both deep ecology and Zen in terms of virtue ethics. Nonetheless, it is clear that both deep ecology and Zen are generally hostile towards a particular conception of ethical life – the idea that doing right is merely a matter of conforming to ethical rules.)

Moreover, a case can be made for saying that both deep ecology and Zen advocate learning to see the world in a similar way. Although the phrase 'deep ecology' was originally conceived as an 'umbrella term' to encompass a variety of thoughtful responses to environmental issues, over the years it has become associated with a particular position on environmental matters and a specific conception of what it means to see the world aright. On this conception, the goal of deep ecology is to foster 'Self-Realization'. The first thing to note about this idea is that it is based on a singularly holistic conception of the self. According to deep ecologists such as Naess, that entity we conventionally refer to as the self does not stop at the limits of our skin. For we find that if we want to specify who or what we are we have to refer to conditions seemingly outside us. So on this account I am not a hard-edged atomic entity 'Simon James'; on the contrary, my identity depends on my being a member of a particular family, a resident of a particular town, a citizen of a particular nation, and so on. Ultimately, it could be said that I depend on the whole of nature. Deep ecologists maintain that we become aware of the extent of this more expansive self in so far as we *identify* with the interests of other beings. So I see someone slip and fall on the ice outside a High Street store and I automatically rush to help. I identify with their pain, spontaneously, naturally. In this sense, one might say that my self has expanded to include them. Finding the life of her village threatened by plans to develop a Go-Karting track on

---

[64] Warwick Fox, *Toward a Transpersonal Ecology: Developing New Foundations for Environmentalism* (Boston: Shambhala, 1990), pp.250-1, 268.

[65] See Halifax's essay 'The Third Body: Buddhism, Shamanism, and Deep Ecology' and Hayward's essay 'Ecology and the Experience of Sacredness', both in Allan Hunt Badiner (ed.), *Dharma Gaia: A Harvest of Essays in Buddhism and Ecology* (Berkeley: Parallax Press, 1990), pp.20-38 and 64-74, respectively.

[66] Quoted in Fox, *Toward a Transpersonal Ecology*, p.219. Fox provides a wealth of examples of other antinomian statements from deep ecologists in pp.217-29 of that book.

[67] David E. Cooper and Simon P. James, *Buddhism, Virtue and Environment* (Ashgate, 2004).

its outskirts, a local woman feels that she herself is threatened and she lends her voice to a campaign to protect the town with the same vigour that she would try to protect herself from harm. Deep ecologists maintain that just as we ultimately depend on the whole of nature, so there exists a particular mode of consciousness in which one identifies with nature as a whole. This is said to be the consciousness of one who has realized his or her 'great Self', and the process by which this is achieved is said to be one of 'Self-Realization'. Thus environmental activist John Seed once said that in working to protect the rainforest he does not think of himself as an individual, 'John Seed', working to protect some other entity, 'the rainforest'. He sees himself as part of the rainforest protecting itself.[68] Joanna Macy makes a similar point:

> it would not occur to me to plead with you, 'Oh, don't saw off your leg. That would be an act of violence.' It wouldn't occur to me because your leg is part of your body. Well, so are the trees in the Amazon rain basin. They are our external lungs. And we are beginning to realize that the world is our body.[69]

On the face of it, there would seem to be some striking similarities between the deep ecologists' conception of Self-Realization and the conception of Zen awakening. In the following passage, Thich Nhat Hanh would seem to be agreeing with Naess, Macy, et al when he maintains that enlightened self-interest can motivate us to care for nature:

> We classify other animals and living beings as nature, acting as if we ourselves are not part of it. Then we pose the question 'How should we deal with Nature?' We should deal with nature the way we should deal with ourselves! We should not harm ourselves; we should not harm nature... Human beings and nature are inseparable.[70]

Compare Ruben L. F. Habito, another Zen teacher:

> In rediscovering that one's true self is not separate from 'the mountains and rivers and the great earth' and all sentient beings, there is no longer anything in the universe that is outside of one's concerns... To see one's true self *as* the mountains, rivers and forests, and as the birds, dolphins and all the inhabitants of the great wide earth, constitutes a sound basis for living an ecologically sound way of life.[71]

Moreover, Philip Kapleau writes of a state in which

---

[68] Quoted in Joanna Macy, 'The Greening of the Self' in Badiner (ed.), *Dharma Gaia*, p.55.
[69] Ibid. p.62.
[70] Quoted in Harvey, *An Introduction to Buddhist Ethics*, p.151.
[71] Ruben L. F. Habito, 'Mountains and Rivers and the Great Earth: Zen and Ecology', in Tucker and Williams, *Buddhism and Ecology*, pp.170, 172; emphasis in original. Note that Habito is quoting Dōgen. Cf. James H. Austin, *Zen and the Brain* (Cambridge, Mass: MIT Press, 2000), p.652.

all of nature, mountains and rivers, are seen as oneself. In this deeper realization of oneness you will feel the preciousness of each object in the universe, rejecting nothing, since things as well as people will be seen as essential aspects of yourself.[72]

So there would seem, on the face of it, to be striking parallels between deep ecologists and Zen Buddhists on these issues. To recap: it would seem that, for both deep ecology and for Zen, people cannot be enjoined to act in environmentally-friendly ways by the imposition of moral rules, but must first learn to see the world aright. More precisely, the idea would seem to be that one must come to identify with the world, to see oneself as the world, and to cherish and protect the world as one cherishes and protects oneself. One could say that for both deep ecology and for Zen the key virtues bearing upon our relations with the natural environment are therefore the selflessness and empathy which allow one to identify with other beings and so achieve Self-Realization.

But before we down tools, satisfied that deep ecology provides an adequate model for a Zen Buddhist environmental philosophy, there are some questions that need answering. In particular, it has not yet been made clear what Self-Realization actually involves. What does it mean to identify with nature? Here, I suggest, deep ecologists often equivocate. They sometimes speak as if Self-Realization involved somehow 'taking the perspective' of nature conceived as a whole. Naess, for example, refers sympathetically to Advaita Vedānta in articulating his position, and so encourages the idea that realizing one's Self is to realize one's identity with some metaphysical Absolute – *Brahman*, perhaps.[73]

With this idea, however, we would seem to be far from Zen. For these reflections suggest that the deep ecologist's account of Self-Realization presupposes a substantial self (*ātman*), the existence of which Zen, as a form of Buddhism, cannot countenance. An argument for this conclusion could run as follows: Given that (1) Zen is a form of Buddhism, and that (2) all forms of Buddhism deny the existence of an *ātman*, and that (3) the deep ecological idea of Self-Realization presupposes the existence of such a self, one can conclude that the idea of Self-Realization is at odds with Zen.

This argument is more difficult to appraise than its simple form might suggest. Though seemingly incontrovertible, the first premise has recently been challenged by Noriaki Hakamaya and Shirō Matsumoto. In short, their reasoning is that the idea of the Buddha-nature, so important in Zen, represents a concept of an *ātman* (in fact, the Mahāyānist *Mahāparinirvāṇa Sūtra* expressly refers to it as such).[74] Therefore, by the second premise of my argument, Zen is not a form of Buddhism. I do not believe this argument is sound since I do not agree that the Buddha-nature represents an *ātman*. But I will not give my reasons for holding this view here –

---

[72] Philip Kapleau, *The Three Pillars of Zen: Teaching, Practice, and Enlightenment* (London: Rider, 1985), p.62.
[73] See Arne Naess, 'Ecosophy T: Deep Versus Shallow Ecology' in Pojman (ed.), *Environmental Ethics*, pp.151-3.
[74] See Williams, *Mahāyāna Buddhism*, pp.98ff.

venturing into this stormy debate would take us too far off course.[75] I would like to note, however, that Naess has more recently qualified his references to Advaita Vedānta, and argued that his conception of Self-Realization should *not* be thought of as presupposing the existence of an *ātman*.[76] The third premise is therefore not obviously true. Indeed, as the following passage from Jeremy Hayward indicates, perhaps the deep ecologist's idea of Self-Realization can be squared with the Buddhist teaching of not-self (*anātman*):

> Buddhists emphasize the obstacle that arises at each step on the way of this gradually widening circle of identification, namely the belief that there is a separate self at all. This obstacle is only overcome at the last stage, when the self is seen to be not separate from the space in which all that exists arises, has its being, and decays.[77]

Nevertheless, whether or not either Zen or deep ecology subscribes to a notion of an *ātman*, if Self-Realization involves one's identifying with nature conceived as a *whole*, then the deep ecologist's position reduces to an extreme form of ethical holism. For if one identifies with the whole of nature, if, say, one follows Macy in thinking (and feeling) that the whole of nature is one's body, then any individual beings that have value would have value, not in themselves, but only to the extent that they contribute to the good of that whole. In that case, culling a particular species of pest to preserve the good of 'nature' (however that is specified) could be seen as analogous to cutting one's hair or one's toenails in order to preserve the good of one's body. Now, to be sure, Zen is holistic, but we have already seen that this kind of extreme holistic perspective on environmental issues is out of keeping with the Zen Buddhist sense of the worth of individual beings.

But deep ecologists sometimes speak about Self-Realization in a way that implies that to realize one's Self is to identify with individual natural beings rather than to identify with nature as a whole. Thus Robert Aitken talks about becoming truly 'intimate' with a black bear (on the face of it, a perilous undertaking),[78] while Kapleau writes, in the passage quoted above, of feeling the preciousness of *each* object.

This commitment to the worth of individual beings is especially evident in another central tenet of deep ecology, the idea that to the extent that we identify with it nature is perceived to have intrinsic value, a value 'in itself' which ought to

---

[75] For a selection of essays by Hakamaya, Matsumoto and others, both for and against the idea that the teaching of the Buddha-nature contravenes the *anātman* teaching, see Hubbard and Swanson (eds), *Pruning the Bodhi Tree*.

[76] Curtin notes that in an unpublished paper 'the Hindu *ātman*... is explicitly rejected by Naess in favor of a Buddhist conception of no-self'. ('A State of Mind like Water', p.240.)

[77] Hayward, 'Ecology and the Experience of Sacredness', p.66. Compare the story of Shih-t'ou related in Heinrich Dumoulin, *Zen Buddhism: A History. Vol.1: India and China* (New York: Macmillan, 1988), p.73.

[78] Robert Aitken, 'Gandhi, Dogen and Deep Ecology' in George Sessions, *Deep Ecology: Living as if Nature Mattered* (Salt Lake City: Peregrine Smith Books, 1985), p.234.

be respected.[79] To be sure, deep ecologists sometimes mean by this that environmental wholes such as the biosphere have intrinsic value.[80] But at other times they seem to be saying that individual beings have this kind of value – for instance, when they express their commitment to the intrinsic value of nature in terms of the 'equal right' of all things in the biosphere to 'live and blossom'.[81]

With the idea that individual beings have intrinsic value we are, I feel, moving closer to a Zen Buddhist view of things. Nevertheless, differences between deep ecology and Zen would seem to remain. Although Naess tends to operate with a broad, non-biological conception of life, so that even 'natural wholes' such as rivers and mountains can be considered to be alive, he appears to hold that Self-Realization incorporates only one's relations with living beings.[82] But in maintaining this he seems to be introducing a distinction quite out of keeping with some important strands of Zen thought.[83] When Dōgen, for instance, maintains that we are enlightened by things, he is not only referring to living things. When he claims that all beings are Buddha-nature, he is not only referring to animals and plants, but also to walls, tiles and stones.[84]

With Dōgen's ideas we find ourselves on the edge of some very difficult conceptual terrain, and I do not intend to set out over it just yet. However, I would like to suggest, tentatively and provisionally, that it is in the deep ecologist's idea of the intrinsic value of beings that we find the closest match for a Zen Buddhist view of nature. When deep ecologists maintain that all living beings have intrinsic value, they would seem to be expressing an intuition that chimes with the positive regard for nature one finds in Zen.

It will be the purpose of the next chapter to flesh out and appraise this suggestion. For the moment, I would like to conclude this chapter by noting that however this conception of intrinsic value is spelt out, it cannot mean that all things have the sort of moral standing that Jainism attributes to sentient beings, and which leads some Jaina practitioners to take extreme practical measures to avoid impinging upon the world. If indeed Zen attributes intrinsic value to beings, then this cannot entail that any harm caused them is morally wrong, a violation of the First Precept, say. To say that a tomato has intrinsic value cannot be to say that one ought not to slice it up for a salad, although it might be to say that one ought not to gratuitously crush it underfoot or wastefully toss it in the bin. In this connection, it is interesting to note that whatever deep ecologists mean by saying that all living things have intrinsic value (and that is a question for the next chapter), they do not

---

[79] On the connection between identification and intrinsic value, see Naess, 'Ecosophy T', p.154. Naess and Sessions maintain that a commitment to the intrinsic value of 'Life on Earth' is a 'Basic Principle' of deep ecology. (Devall and Sessions, 'Deep Ecology' p.159.)
[80] See, for instance, Ibid. p.160.
[81] Ibid. p.158.
[82] See, for example, Naess, 'Ecosophy T', p.153; Devall and Sessions, 'Deep Ecology', p.160. See also Curtin, 'A State of Mind Like Water', p.245, 250. Curtin notes that in other places Naess seems to be edging towards the possibility of identifying with non-living things.
[83] As Deane Curtin argues in his very interesting article 'A State of Mind Like Water'.
[84] See Parkes, 'Voices of Mountains, Trees, and Rivers', pp.122-3.

believe that this commitment entails a 'hands-off' policy of non-interaction with the world.[85] The deep ecologist's awareness of the intrinsic value of the pine outside his door does not prevent him from felling it for timber if need be. Nor does his sense of the intrinsic value of plants stop him from eating. But it does entail that these actions are performed with a due sense of respect for the beings involved.[86] Similarly, as I argued above, a Zen Buddhist environmental ethic would not consider as exemplary a life of passive withdrawal from the world. The fact that it would not provides a reason for thinking that whatever deep ecologists mean by saying that all living beings have intrinsic value, the central intuition to which they are giving voice would be one endorsed by Zen.

---

[85] See Devall and Sessions, 'Deep Ecology', pp.158-9. Cf. Curtin, 'A State of Mind Like Water', pp.247ff.

[86] See Snyder, 'Grace'.

Chapter Four

The Intrinsic Value of Nature

The problem of the intrinsic value of nature

In Chapter Three, I compared and contrasted the Zen Buddhist view of nature with the positions of some modern environmental ethicists. Notwithstanding the general Mahāyānist concern for the welfare of all sentient beings, I rejected the suggestion that a Zen Buddhist environmental ethic would be a form of 'humane moralism' of the sort advocated by Peter Singer. I also rejected the idea that Zen represents an extreme form of 'ethical holism' of the kind arguably evident in the writings of Aldo Leopold. I argued that, in contrast to humane moralism, Zen brings apparently non-sentient beings such as plants within the purview of ethics, but that unlike extreme forms of ethical holism, it recognizes the value individual beings have in themselves, and would therefore not sanction the idea that the good of the environmental whole must always trump the good of individual beings. I found that the dual commitment to holism and the value of individual beings evident in Zen resonates with some formulations of deep ecology. In particular, the virtues of selflessness and empathy, which allow one to identify with other beings, would seem to be important in both deep ecology and Zen. I concluded the chapter by suggesting that in saying that all living beings have intrinsic value, deep ecologists seem to be espousing a view in keeping with the spirit of Zen Buddhism. In this chapter, I will try to determine whether Zen Buddhism should indeed be thought of as attributing intrinsic value to nature.

Although we came across the idea of intrinsic value in a discussion of deep ecology, references to the value beings have 'in themselves' are not the sole province of deep ecologists. Indeed, it is a perennial theme in the literature on environmental ethics that the exploitation of the environment is the result of a blindness to (or perhaps a refusal to recognize) the intrinsic value of natural beings.[1] The general story here is that Western traditions of thought have tended to

---

[1] That is, natural beings as opposed to artefacts. The phrase 'natural beings' is being used here in a non-technical sense to denote those entities with which environmental thinkers are most concerned – pandas, rare orchids, ospreys, and so on. One qualification is needed here, however. We will be addressing the question of the intrinsic value of individual beings rather than species. That said, readers might like to consider how the arguments developed in this chapter bear upon the intrinsic value of species. I am inclined to think that they apply

accord natural beings value only to the extent that they prove useful to humans, that they have tended to see nature as only instrumentally valuable. By contrast, it is said that a new, environmentally-friendly understanding of the world would value nature 'for its own sake', would conceive natural beings as having intrinsic value. In the light of such an understanding, the old oak tree, for instance, would be seen not merely as a source of timber or shade or as a decoration for the front lawn, but as valuable 'in itself', as having an intrinsic value that ought to be respected.[2]

We will investigate the meaning of these claims presently. For the moment, it need only be noted that there would seem, on the face of it, to be a problem in squaring a commitment to the intrinsic value of beings with a Buddhist conception of nature. Malcolm David Eckel is recognizing that there might be a difficulty here when he maintains that the idea of intrinsic value 'seems to suggest precisely the substantial, permanent identity that the ideas of no-self and interdependent co-origination [conditioned arising] are meant to undermine'.[3] Steven C. Rockefeller is making a similar point when he claims that 'the concept of intrinsic value suggests the existence of some fixed essence or permanent self in things, which is contrary to the Buddhist doctrines of dependent co-arising [conditioned arising], impermanence, emptiness, and no-self'.[4]

The early sections of this chapter will appraise the criticisms of Eckel and Rockefeller as they apply to Zen Buddhism. But before turning to this task, it might be helpful to clarify *why* exactly writers such as Eckel and Rockefeller

---

to species as they apply to individual beings; but I am not certain of this. Indeed, in considering the morality of the treatment of nonhuman animals, Buddhists tend to think of individual animals rather than species, partly because species cannot suffer and are to this extent not protected under the First Precept. On this interesting topic, see Peter Harvey *An Introduction to Buddhist Ethics* (Cambridge: Cambridge University Press, 2000), pp.183-4; Lambert Schmithausen, *Buddhism and Nature: the Lecture delivered on the Occasion of the EXPO 1990, An Enlarged Version with Notes* (Tokyo: The International Institute for Buddhist Studies, 1991), pp.32ff; Christopher Key Chapple, *Nonviolence to Animals, Earth, and Self in Asian Traditions* (Albany: State University of New York Press, 1993), p.46.
[2] On the idea of the intrinsic value of nature, see John O'Neill, *Ecology, Policy and Politics: Human Well-Being and the Natural World* (London: Routledge, 1993); Robert Elliot, *Faking Nature: the ethics of environmental restoration* (London: Routledge, 1997); Christopher Belshaw, *Environmental Philosophy: reason, nature and human concern* (Teddington: Acumen, 2001).
[3] 'Is there a Buddhist Philosophy of Nature?' in Mary Evelyn Tucker and Duncan Ryūken Williams (eds), *Buddhism and Ecology: the interconnection of dharma and deeds* (Cambridge, Massachusetts: Harvard University Press, 1997), p.343.
[4] 'Buddhism, Global Ethics, and the Earth Charter' in Tucker and Williams, *Buddhism and Ecology*, p.320. See also Schmithausen's claim that the Buddhist teaching of impermanence means that neither nature nor natural beings can be accorded any 'ultimate value' (*Buddhism and Nature*, p.14). These sorts of claim can be compared with the idea that the Buddhist teachings of emptiness, conditioned arising, no-self and impermanence 'negate' nature in the sense of denying natural beings any substantial existence. On this, see Eckel's discussion of the views of the Dalai Lama ('Is there a Buddhist Philosophy of Nature?' pp.328ff). See also Schmithausen's discussion of the views of Noriaki Hakamaya (*Buddhism and Nature*, pp.53-62).

believe the idea of intrinsic value jars with Buddhist thought. To do this, it will be necessary to explain something of the philosophical basis of Zen.

One of the Buddhist teachings inherited by and embodied in Zen is the teaching of emptiness (*śūnyatā*), as it was developed in the Madhyamaka or 'middle way' tradition of Buddhism. As we saw in Chapter One, this teaching states that all things lack an inherent nature, that all things are, as it were, 'empty' of self-existence. The claim here is not that nothing exists at all (always a difficult position to defend), but only that nothing exists as a substance, that is, as wholly independent of its relations to other things.[5] For Madhyamaka Buddhism, any particular thing depends for its existence on conditioning factors, upon other things, for instance. In its teaching of emptiness, Madhyamaka therefore rejects the idea, propounded by Buddhist schools such as the Vaibhāṣika Abhidharma, that all phenomenal things are constructed out of self-existent, simple elements, for it holds that on analysis even these units would reveal themselves to be empty of self-existence. Madhyamaka also rejects the idea that emptiness represents some sort of metaphysical absolute that grounds the existence of things in the world, for any absolute thus postulated would, it contends, also be empty of self-existence, and hence not an 'absolute' at all. For Madhyamaka, and also for Zen, absolutely *all* things are empty, 'emptiness' included.

Now if this is construed as a philosophical claim, then it is clearly a very bold one. However, the purpose of this chapter is not to justify or defend the Madhyamaka teaching of emptiness. I only want to note that Zen implicitly endorses the teaching.[6] My task will be to suggest one way how, given this commitment to the emptiness of all things, Zen can provide a philosophical account of the intrinsic value of individual beings. And, at first sight at least, this would seem to present quite a challenge. For even on the basis of this very cursory sketch, it would seem that the emptiness teaching could not be reconciled with the existence of any *intrinsic* properties. An argument for this could run as follows: for Madhyamaka, and hence for Zen, whatever properties one identifies as constituting the putative essence of a thing will, in the final analysis, reveal themselves to be empty of self-existence.[7] That is to say that they will reveal themselves to be functions of the thing's context, that is, as relational. According to the emptiness

---

[5] In referring to 'other things' it may seem that I am referring only to conditions seemingly 'outside' the thing. Buddhists, however, consider not only the external conditions of things but also the internal conditions, maintaining, for instance, that the tree depends for its existence, not only on sun, rain, earth, and so on, but also on its roots, trunk, leaves, etc. (see David Burton, 'Is Madhyamaka Buddhism Really the Middle Way? Emptiness and the Problem of Nihilism', *Contemporary Buddhism* 2, No.2 (2001), p.177). For the sake of simplicity, I will continue to speak in terms of the external conditions of things rather than their internal conditions in this chapter. However, I believe that the arguments I will propose apply to the internal conditions of things as well as to their external conditions.

[6] Which is not to say that Zen does not also embody other understandings of emptiness. As we saw in Chapter One, references to emptiness can mean different things in different Buddhist traditions, and Zen, for its part, was not solely the product of the Madhyamaka. For instance, later, we shall examine the question of the subject-object duality, a topic that lends itself naturally to Yogācārin conceptions of emptiness.

[7] I take the words 'thing', 'being' and 'entity' to be synonyms.

teaching, then, all properties are relational, and hence no intrinsic values can exist. And if this is the case, then no being could have a value 'in itself'. Individual organisms certainly could not, but neither could environmental wholes, for any whole thus identified (a particular species, for instance, or an ecosystem, or even the biosphere itself) would have to be considered as empty of self-existence, and hence as devoid of intrinsic properties.

Non-relational value and non-instrumental value

As they apply to Madhyamaka Buddhism, then, the reservations of Eckel and Rockefeller would seem to be justified. By virtue of its commitment to universal emptiness, Madhyamaka would not seem to be able to countenance the notion of the intrinsic value of anything. And this would seem to hold for Zen Buddhism too, incorporating, as it does, the teaching of emptiness.

But this conclusion is too hasty and need not be accepted. For one thing, it seems to rely on a dichotomy between intrinsic and relational value, which is at the very least questionable. Consider Brian Weatherson's observation that many properties seem to be both relational and intrinsic. Weatherson cites the example of the property *having longer legs than arms*, arguing that, although it seems right to say that most people have this property intrinsically – i.e., that they do not have it by virtue of their relations with other beings – the property is nonetheless relational.[8] I am not sure whether his claim is justified, but in any case there is no need for us to become entangled in the complicated metaphysical debates concerning the nature of intrinsic properties here. For it would seem that even if one grants that the emptiness teaching entails that all properties are relational, this would not preclude the possibility of developing a conception of intrinsic value consonant both with the use of that idea in environmental ethics and with Zen.

In order to see why the reservations of Eckel and Rockefeller are not justified, it is essential to note that the phrase 'intrinsic value' can be understood in several distinct ways. It seems likely that Eckel and Rockefeller are taking intrinsic value to mean non-relational value in G. E. Moore's sense, the value a thing has independently of its relations to anything else. And it would indeed seem to be difficult to justify the existence of that sort of value in the context of a commitment to emptiness, for, as we have just seen, in the context of such a commitment, all properties are conceived as being relational. Yet although this meaning would seem to be suggested by the word 'intrinsic', it is clear that many, perhaps most, environmental thinkers do not understand intrinsic value in this way. As Karen Green has argued, environmental values are generally not non-relational.[9] To demonstrate this, she points out that one cannot refer to the value of an organism in abstraction from its environment, and to illustrate the absurdity of attempting to do this she gives the example of trying to assess the value, in the abstract, of the cane

---

[8] See his account of the distinction between intrinsic and extrinsic properties in the *Stanford Encyclopaedia of Philosophy* (http://plato.stanford.edu/entries/intrinsic-extrinsic/).
[9] Karen Green, 'Two Distinctions in Environmental Goodness', *Environmental Values* 5, No.1 (February 1996), p.35.

toad. In Australia, cane toads, are (apparently) everywhere, eating everything up and causing the extinction of other species. Down under, the cane toad has a 'positive disvalue'.[10] But Green asks us to imagine a situation in which the cane toad is the sole predator on some other organism which has an even more disruptive effect on the environment – a particularly ravenous species of beetle, for instance. In such a situation, the cane toad would have a very high value.[11] The point here is that the value of the cane toad, or indeed of any organism, is relational, that is, a function of the habitat in which the organism lives.

So environmental thinkers, in calling for us to recognize environmental values, are not generally conceiving these values as non-relational. Moreover, as we shall see, this holds true even when they refer to the intrinsic value of beings. But how, then, do they understand the phrase 'intrinsic value'? It would seem that when environmentalists maintain that a particular being ought to be valued for what it is 'in itself', they are generally making the point that it should not be considered valuable only to the extent that it proves useful. In other words, rather than conceiving intrinsic value as non-relational value, most environmental thinkers seem to think of it as some kind of non-instrumental value, the value that a being has as an end in itself rather than as a means to an end. But before we rest content with this definition of intrinsic value, it must be noted that a being can have instrumental value, not only to the extent that it furthers some specifically human end, but also in so far as it promotes some end seemingly unrelated to human interests. The seal cub, for instance, could be instrumentally valuable not only because its fur and meat can be sold, but also because it might contribute to the good of the various environmental wholes of which it is a part. It might have a role in sustaining local polar bears, for instance, or in limiting the population of certain fish species. Environmental thinkers keen to promote the intrinsic value of nature are generally not lamenting the instrumental value of beings in this second sense, however. They are rather complaining that things are seen as having only instrumental value in relation to specifically *human* ends. So it would be more precise to say that environmental thinkers generally understand intrinsic value to mean the value that a being has independently of its instrumental value as a resource for humans. (That said, some environmental thinkers place further restrictions on what they mean by the intrinsic value of beings. For instance, environmental philosophers such as Holmes Rolston III argue that intrinsically valuable beings are not only non-instrumentally valuable (in the sense given above), but also objectively valuable.[12] We will consider this idea presently. For

---

[10] Ibid. p.35.

[11] One might want to object that, in this situation, the toad would be instrumentally valuable in that it is useful to the ecosystem in limiting the population of the beetle even if it is, for some reason, not in the interests of humans to curb the beetle population. Yet, as I shall argue presently, the idea of intrinsic value is generally taken by environmental thinkers to *include* the value that a being has by virtue of its contribution to the good of some environmental whole even if it *excludes* the use-value it has for humans.

[12] See, for example, his essay 'Nature for Real: Is Nature a Social Construct?' in T. D. J. Chappell, *The Philosophy of the Environment* (Edinburgh, Edinburgh University Press, 1997), pp.39-64.

the moment, it will suffice to note that whatever *else* they mean by the phrase 'intrinsic value', environmental philosophers generally mean some species of non-instrumental value, as that term has been defined above.)

The important point to note here is that there is no reason why intrinsic value, understood in this sense as non-instrumental value, need be non-relational.[13] In the example above, the cane toad in the habitat in which it is the sole predator on some particularly destructive beetle has a non-instrumental value, which would be evident to informed and concerned parties, conservationists, perhaps, or naturalists. (Admittedly, the toad could be said to have an instrumental value in that it contributes to the good of the environmental wholes of which it is part. But we can assume that it would not have instrumental value in the rather narrower sense in which we are using that term, i.e., we can imagine that it would not have value as a resource for humans.) However, as we saw, since the non-instrumental value of the toad is a function of the habitat in which the organism lives, it is clearly relational. The upshot of this is that if environmental thinkers are not understanding intrinsic value as non-relational, then there would not seem to be a problem with reconciling a commitment to the intrinsic value of individual beings with the teaching of emptiness. Or less confusingly: intrinsic value, as understood by most environmental thinkers, can be relational; and as relational its existence can be reconciled with the emptiness teaching. Eckel and Rockefeller's criticisms are therefore not justified: so far we have not been presented with a reason for dismissing an idea of the intrinsic value of individual beings based on Zen.

The charge of nihilism

We have already examined Steven Rockefeller's reservations concerning the possibility of developing a conception of intrinsic value consonant with Buddhist thought. It is worth noting that the passage quoted above continues as follows:

> In seeking a solution to this problem [i.e., the problem of developing a Buddhist conception of intrinsic value], it is important to emphasize that Buddhist philosophy and ethics do not have a quarrel with the practical meaning or bearing of the concept of intrinsic value. The relevant point is that any being with intrinsic value is worthy of respect and care.[14]

Rockefeller is surely right about this. In fact, one reason why Buddhism has been considered environmentally-friendly is because it seems to respect the non-instrumental value of natural beings. And this is particularly true of Zen Buddhism. As we have seen, the appreciation of nature has a central place in Zen, partly because of its incorporation of Taoist and (in Japan) Shintō ideas on the spiritual significance of the natural world. Whereas Indian Buddhism showed a certain (but

---

[13] See further: Shelly Kagan, 'Rethinking Intrinsic Value', *The Journal of Ethics* 2, issue 4 (1998), pp.280-3; and Tara Smith, 'Intrinsic Value: Look-Say Ethics', *The Journal of Value Inquiry* 32, issue 4 (1998), p.548.
[14] 'Buddhism, Global Ethics, and the Earth Charter', p.320. My annotation.

by no means invariable) tendency to see nature as a realm to be transcended, East Asian traditions of Buddhism such as Zen tend to use examples of natural phenomena to symbolize transcendence itself.[15] In particular, there is a tendency amongst Zen Buddhists to see ultimate truths in the details, in the 'little things' in nature. Thus, in contrast to Western depictions of the sublime – crashing waterfalls, raging storms, and the like – Zen poetry and paintings tend to focus on far less lofty phenomena: a berry dropping from a branch in a dark forest, a frog trembling on a banana leaf, a raven perched on a dry branch – things of this sort.

Environmental philosophers have, for their part, been particularly attracted to the writings of Dōgen. As we saw in Chapter Three, Arne Naess cites him as a major inspiration,[16] and a host of other environmental thinkers refer approvingly to Dōgen's thought in their work.[17] In relation to our present purpose of developing a Zen-inspired conception of intrinsic value, I would like to draw attention to Peter Harvey's claim, in his recent book on Buddhist ethics, that for Dōgen 'Each aspect of nature has an intrinsic value as part of ultimate reality, and to let go of oneself in full awareness of the sound of the rain or the cry of a monkey is to fathom this in a moment of non-dual awareness'.[18] Intuitively, Harvey's claim seems right. The picture of nature conveyed in Dōgen's writings is strikingly beautiful: as we saw in our discussion of ethical holism, it is of a world in which any particular thing is accorded a supreme significance as an embodiment of the universe as a whole, such that a man with right perception can see 'the entire world in one tiny speck of dust', or 'the entire universe... in... a tall bamboo'.[19] But what philosophical warrant have these claims? Are we to think that the world is *really* present in a speck of dust? Would a sceptic be justified in blithely dismissing these sorts of claim as 'merely' poetic? If he would, then they could hardly be used as the basis for a *philosophical* account of the intrinsic value of individual beings.

I do not think Dōgen's thoughts ought to be dismissed as 'merely' poetic, and in the following pages I will try to develop a philosophical justification for his account of the 'intrinsic value' of beings. But before doing this, I would like to formulate, and then try to refute, what I consider to be a more powerful objection to a Zen-inspired conception of intrinsic value. In order to formulate this objection, it will be necessary to consider, once again, the teaching of emptiness.

In his influential *Essays on Zen Buddhism*, D. T. Suzuki wrote that emptiness 'is not an abstraction, but an experience', and in so doing expressed a view echoed

---

[15] Eckel, 'Is there a Buddhist Philosophy of Nature?', p.339.

[16] Deane Curtin, 'A State of Mind Like Water: Ecosophy T and the Buddhist Traditions', *Inquiry* 39 (1996), p.241.

[17] For instance: Deane Curtin, both in 'A State of Mind Like Water' and in 'Dōgen, Deep Ecology, and the Ecological Self' (*Environmental Ethics* 16, No.2 (summer 1994), pp.195-213); Graham Parkes, ('Voices of Mountains, Trees, and Rivers: Kūkai, Dōgen, and a Deeper Ecology' in Tucker and Williams, *Buddhism and Ecology*, pp.111-28). As previously noted, Warwick Fox concludes his influential *Toward a Transpersonal Ecology* (Boston: Shambhala, 1990) with a quotation from Dōgen.

[18] *An Introduction to Buddhist Ethics*, p.177.

[19] Dōgen, *Shōbōgenzō: The Eye and Treasury of the True Law, Vol. 1*, translated by K. Nishiyama and J. Stevens (Tokyo: Nakayama Shobō, 1976), pp.15, 89.

throughout the Zen tradition.[20] It is said that *śūnyatā* cannot be encapsulated in words, but must be experienced directly, in enlightenment.[21] But what sort of experience could be reconciled with the teaching of emptiness? Here, of course, some will ask the perfectly reasonable question of what validity one's speculations on the nature of this experience can have if one is not enlightened. I am not enlightened, so how can I possibly imagine what it is like to experience emptiness? Moreover, even if I could claim some insight into these matters, how could I convey this experience in words? After all, the scriptures stress that insight into the empty nature of things is ineffable. Notwithstanding these objections, I will ask the cynic's indulgence in offering some speculations on what this experience might involve.

On the face of it, one might suppose that the teaching of emptiness entails the absolute non-existence of things. One might hold that to say that all things are empty is to say that they do not exist at all. This interpretation of the emptiness teaching forms the basis for a criticism that, time and again, has been levelled at Madhyamaka Buddhism, by both non-Buddhists and Buddhists from other traditions. For instance, Buddhists from one school (the Vaibhāṣika Abhidharma tradition) maintained that to deny the self-existence of certain atomic constituents of reality would be to affirm that all things are constructed but to deny the existence of any basic elements out of which things could be so constructed. And this position, they maintained, could only amount to the absurd conclusion that nothing exists at all.

The standard reply to this charge of 'nihilism' is to point out that in saying that all things are empty, Madhyamaka philosophers are not saying that they lack existence altogether, but only that they lack *self*-existence. On this reading, then, the conception of emptiness does not entail nihilism, the non-existence of all things, but rather affirms the interconnectedness of all things, the fact that all things depend for their existence on their conditions, upon other things, for instance. In this case, the teaching of emptiness, far from negating the existence of things, actually entails their (dependent) existence. For, on this account, to be real is to share in the mutual dependency of all that exists. If something were non-empty and utterly independent it could not enter into the holistic network that constitutes reality.[22] As Wittgenstein might have said, such a non-empty being would be like a wheel that can be turned though nothing else moves with it. Just as

---

[20] D. T. Suzuki, *Essays on Zen Buddhism III* (London: Luzac, 1934), p.257.

[21] If it is ultimately inappropriate to refer to emptiness as a philosophical abstraction, there are also problems with referring to it as an experience. One danger here is that the term 'experience' might be thought to encourage the idea that emptiness is experienced as an object standing over against a subject. However, for reasons I will discuss below, Zen thinkers would reject the ultimate validity of the subject-object distinction.

[22] See Nāgārjuna: 'Any factor of experience which does not participate in [conditioned arising] cannot exist. Therefore, any factor of experience not in the nature of *śūnya* cannot exist.' (Inada, Kenneth K. *Nāgārjuna: A Translation of his Mūlamadhyamakakārikā with an Introductory Essay* (Tokyo: The Hokuseido Press, 1970), Chapter 24, verse 19 (p.148).)

such a wheel would not be part of the mechanism, so such a being could not be part of reality.[23]

But this response is unconvincing. The Mādhyamika cannot avoid the charge of nihilism so easily. In order to see why the standard Madhyamaka response is inadequate, it will be helpful to interpret the teaching of emptiness in terms of the distinction between external and internal relations.

Let me explain how I will be understanding this distinction. If a thing is externally related to another thing, then that relation is not considered to be essential to the thing's nature. For instance, my coffee mug is now on my desk. But it would remain the same mug if it were on the floor or on my chest of drawers. In these respects (that is, in terms of spatial relations), the mug is said to be externally related to the desk. If, on the other hand, a thing is internally related to another thing, then the relation is considered to be essential to its nature. So the chord A minor is internally related to the chord A major, since A minor is only A minor because it *differs* by one note from A major. Or one could say that the number one is internally related to the number two, since, in order for any number to be identical to one, it must be *less than* two.[24]

In claiming that all things are empty of self-existence, Madhyamaka Buddhism must be committed to the idea that all things are only internally related. For according to the teaching of emptiness, no things enjoy that degree of independence that would allow us to speak of them as being externally related to other things. On the contrary, whatever one might identify as constituting the putative essence of a thing would, in the final analysis, reveal itself to be dependent upon its relations with other things. Yet the standard Madhyamaka response to the charge of nihilism seems to rely on the notion that things are externally related to one another. Now if indeed things were externally related to one another, then one would be justified in claiming that, even though distinct thing X is not *self*-existent, it exists to the extent that it is related to other things, and one could imagine the thing sitting at the nexus of a web of relations, or something of this sort. But this reply will not work if one considers, as one must if one is to remain true to Madhyamaka philosophy, that all things are only internally related, since the claim that all things are only internally related makes it difficult to speak of things at all.

This requires explanation. Consider two objects, X and Y, and an internal relation between them, r. Since X is internally related to Y, the relation r must be essential to its nature. So in speaking of X we are in fact implicitly referring to the relation r as well. But r, of course, cannot be specified in the absence of Y – it is, after all, a relation between X and Y. So in speaking of the essential nature of X we are in fact implicitly referring, not only to the relation r, but to Y as well. Hence X cannot be thought of as an independent entity – it is what it is only because of its

---

[23] See the reasoning leading to remark 271 in Wittgenstein's *Philosophical Investigations*, (translated by G. E. M. Anscombe (Oxford: Blackwell, 1958), p.95.

[24] Note that I am following the British Idealists' use of the term 'internal relation' rather than David Lewis's. See Lewis's *Papers in Metaphysics and Epistemology* (New York: Cambridge University Press, 1999), p.129, and especially n.16. I would like to thank Jonathan Lowe for pointing this distinction out to me.

relation to Y.[25] And this process can be continued. If all things are internally related, then Y will, in turn, be internally related to another object Z by another relation, call it r', so that in referring to Y we are implicitly referring both to r' and to Z as well. So in speaking of the essential nature of X, we are implicitly referring, not only to Y but to Z as well. And so on. If the commitment to the internal relatedness of things is thoroughgoing, this process can be continued indefinitely. And if the process can be continued in this way, then one is led to the conclusion that any particular thing is in reality not a distinct entity related in various ways to other entities, but some sort of whole, one encompassing all those entities which it at first appeared to be distinct from and related to.

   This conclusion would not be out of place in an account of the metaphysics of F. H. Bradley, the most influential of the late-nineteenth/early-twentieth century group of philosophers known as the British Idealists. Like Madhyamaka (or rather, as per my interpretation of Madhyamaka), Bradley maintained that the idea of an external relation could not be upheld. But if the idea of an external relation could not be countenanced, the proposition that all relations must be internal led to surprising results. For Bradley came to realize that to say that two or more things are internally related is to deny that those things enjoy the degree of independence that would justify references to their being related to one another. So, for Bradley, to say that two or more things are internally related to one another is to say that they are abstractions from a non-relational whole. As Peter Hylton puts it in his excellent account of Bradley's philosophy: 'By their internality, internal relations make it manifest that they are destined to be transcended in a higher unity in which the separateness of the relata, and thus the relational nature of the whole, has disappeared.'[26] So in Bradley's metaphysics, the things that apparently surround us are relegated to the status of mere appearances. The coffee mug, the desk, the pack of chewing gum, and so on: these are not things related to each other and to me in various ways. They are unreal, abstractions from a non-relational whole.[27] Notwithstanding Bradley's claim that this non-relational unity somehow 'is' its appearances, this would seem to amount to the idea that no things exist at all.[28] It was this seemingly preposterous conclusion that so offended G. E. Moore and Bertrand Russell, and which inspired the two of them to try to develop an account of the world more in tune with common sense.[29] One could imagine that Moore and Russell would have been similarly offended by the interpretation of the emptiness teaching here being discussed. For in the light of these reflections on the internal relatedness of things, one might be led to think (*might* be led to think) that to experience emptiness must be to experience no things at all. One might suppose that to experience emptiness would be to experience the disappearance or, better,

---

[25] I am here following Peter Hylton's account in *Russell, Idealism, and the Emergence of Analytic Philosophy* (Oxford: Clarendon Press, 1990), pp.54-5.

[26] Ibid. p.55.

[27] See, for instance, *Appearance and Reality* (Oxford: Clarendon Press, 1930), Chapter VIII, and also, *Essays on Truth and Reality* (Oxford: Clarendon Press, 1914), pp.238-40.

[28] F. H. Bradley, *Appearance and Reality*, pp.431-2.

[29] See Hylton's *Russell, Idealism, and the Emergence of Analytic Philosophy* for an excellent account of Moore and Russell's reaction to Bradley.

the dissolution of things. Fixing one's attention on a thing, one would find one's gaze drawn to the other things to which that thing is (internally) related, then further to the various things to which these things are (internally) related, and so on, *ad infinitum*. One would, presumably, find the thing dissolving into its conditions like a drop of water in a pool.[30] This would not mean merely that things would become indistinct, that, so to speak, their edges would blur. For even fuzzy-edged things can still be externally related to one another, and external relations cannot obtain in this state. On the contrary, it would seem (*seem*) that the dissolution of things would culminate in an experience of an undifferentiated field, a world in which, as Toshihiko Izutsu puts it, things have lost their 'essential limitations' and 'being no longer obstructed by their own ontological limits... flow into one another, reflecting each other and being reflected by each other in the limitlessly vast field of Nothingness'.[31]

On this 'nihilistic' reading, those elements of experience we in our spiritual ignorance call 'things' would be considered to be no more than projections imposed by our minds on an undifferentiated substrate. The phenomenal world would be like a show, a phantasm, a dream, as indeed it is described in some Buddhist texts.[32] To perceive emptiness would be, as it were, to see through these illusory things to the undifferentiated, non-relational field which constitutes the true nature of reality.

This nihilistic reading of the emptiness teaching can provide the basis for a more powerful objection to a Zen-inspired conception of intrinsic value. For it seems to undermine, not only the non-relational value of things, but also the non-instrumental value of things, since even this latter conception demands that we are able to identify some relatively discrete entities which could be said to be non-instrumentally valuable. But if no things exist, then no things can have even non-instrumental value.

---

[30] Once again, note that in speaking of things as 'dissolving' into their surroundings, I am referring only to the external conditions of things. See note 5. I am reminded of Masao Abe's claim that emptiness is 'expanding endlessly into all directions throughout the universe'. Masao Abe, *Zen and Western Thought*, William LaFleur (ed.) (Honolulu: University of Hawaii Press, 1989), 161. Cf. also Hegel's analysis of determinate being in his *Logic. The Logic of Hegel*, translated by William Wallace (Oxford: Clarendon Press, 1892), sections 92-3.

[31] Toshihiko Izutsu, *Toward a Philosophy of Zen Buddhism* (Boulder: Prajñā Press, 1982), p.31.

[32] E.g., *The Diamond Sutra*, section 32 (A. F. Price and Wong Mou-lam (translators), *The Diamond Sutra and The Sutra of Hui Neng* (Boulder: Shambhala, 1969), p.74). See also Burton, 'Is Madhyamaka Buddhism Really the Middle Way?' pp.179-80). I will not argue the point here, but it seems to me that this conclusion would not be warranted. For to say that all things exist in dependence on mind is not to say that mind is the only condition for their existence. Things could depend for their existence upon both mental and non-mental factors. (Similarly, to say that a thing does not exist as a mind-independent entity is not necessarily to say that it is a nothing more than a fiction.) Burton also suggests alternatives to an 'idealist' reading of the emptiness teaching.

Condensation

Yet this nihilistic interpretation of the emptiness teaching is hard to square with many of the accounts of awakening one finds in the literature of Zen. Consider, for instance, the following famous account of enlightenment from the Zen master Ch'ing-yüan (J. Seigen, d.740):

> Thirty years ago, before I began the study of Zen, I said, 'Mountains are mountains, waters are waters.' After I got an insight into the truth of Zen... I said, 'Mountains are not mountains, waters are not waters.' But now, having attained the abode of the final rest [that is, enlightenment], I say, 'Mountains are really mountains, waters are really waters.'[33]

On this account, the experience of the dissolution of things would seem to be at most a precursor to enlightenment, rather than enlightenment itself. As we saw in Chapter Two, enlightenment, though it may be preceded by a state in which things apparently dissolve into an undifferentiated background, would seem to involve the perception of distinct things. Consider also the descriptions of enlightened experience provided by Zen thinkers such as Dōgen. In these descriptions, the thing is not portrayed as dissolving into its context; on the contrary, as we saw, Dōgen maintains that the awakened observer sees the thing as somehow 'containing' the world. Indeed, in general, Zen seems to hold that to experience emptiness is not to experience the dissolution of things into a non-relational whole, but to see a world carved up into distinct things. The enlightened man or woman is said to perceive things as they 'really are', in their 'suchness' or 'thusness' (*tathatā*).

But how can the existence of distinct things be reconciled with the teaching of emptiness? To try and answer this question, let us return to the question of what, on a nihilistic reading, the experience of emptiness might be thought to involve. I have already suggested, tentatively and provisionally, that it might involve the 'dissolution' of things. But their dissolution into what? Into a non-relational field, I suggested. But what could it mean to experience such a field? For one thing, the field could not be thought of as being limited, as having boundaries, since limitation implies a relation with something it is not. This field, however, cannot be related to anything else, since on this account it represents the non-relational whole from which all things and relations are abstractions. So on this nihilistic interpretation, to experience emptiness would not be to experience a determinate being, but to experience a *limitless* undifferentiated field, a state of no-thing-ness, if you will, in which even fuzzy-edged, insubstantial things cannot exist.

But, as we saw, to experience emptiness cannot be to experience nothing (no things) at all, so this cannot be the way Zen understands the emptiness teaching. We must have taken a wrong turn somewhere. Indeed, I think it could be argued that to think of emptiness as an undifferentiated field would be to treat it as if it were unconditioned, as if it were something self-existent. But Zen holds true to its roots in Madhyamaka Buddhism in maintaining that emptiness cannot be, so to

---

[33] Quoted in Abe, *Zen and Western Thought*, p.4. My annotation.

speak, 'pinned down' as a self-existent state of pure no-thing-ness any more than it can be thought of as some sort of God-like 'pure being'; the function of the teaching is rather to draw attention to the conditioned nature of all things, emptiness included. With this in mind, one might be led to suppose that to think of emptiness as entailing the dissolution of all things into an undifferentiated field would not be to have understood emptiness at all, but to have posited the existence of some kind of *Brahman*-like Absolute in its place. And as we noted in Chapter Two, to do this would be to have become attached to emptiness, fixated by the void, and to have therefore fallen short of the thoroughgoing non-attachment that would mark a genuine appreciation of *śūnyatā*.

By contrast, Mādhyamikas and Zen Buddhists stress that emptiness is *itself* empty of self-existence, which is to say that it is conditioned by what it is not.[34] So if on our nihilistic reading emptiness reveals itself as the absence of things, it must disclose itself as conditioned by the presence of things. Hence for Zen Buddhism, as for Madhyamaka, to truly experience emptiness is not to experience a limitless undifferentiated field, a state of no-thing-ness, but to experience *things*. Things must be there in awakened experience, albeit revealed in a higher spiritual register. They must disclose themselves in the context of an experience of emptiness.

The following passage from Thich Nhat Hanh provides some insight into how things might reveal themselves in awakening:

> When we look at a chair, we see the wood, but we fail to observe the tree, the forest, the carpenter, or our own mind. When we meditate on it, we can see the entire universe in all its interwoven and interdependent relations in the chair. The presence of the wood reveals the presence of the tree. The presence of the leaf reveals the presence of the sun. The presence of the apple blossoms reveals the presence of the apple. Meditators can see the one in many, and the many in one.[35]

In this passage, Nhat Hanh would seem to be making a pronouncement, fairly standard in the Zen literature, on the mutual dependence of things, the fact that all things are empty of self-existence and depend, in various ways, upon conditioning factors. I feel, however, that his point is subtler than it might at first appear. For one thing, in trying to conceive the meditative experience here being described, it would be a mistake to think of the chair as indicating the presence of various things outside itself. The idea that it does that rests on a conception of these various things as distinct objects externally related to the chair. Yet as we saw earlier it is precisely this conception of things as externally related to one another that the emptiness teaching undermines. For this reason, Nhat Hanh maintains that the wood, tree, leaf, sun, and so on, disclose themselves *in* the chair. (As he puts it in

---

[34] See, for instance, ibid. pp.128-9. Cf. Takuan: 'If all people and things are determined to be empty, then since that determinate emptiness is itself empty, it is crucial to avoid establishing the view that simply negates.' Quoted in Minamoto Ryōen, 'Three Zen Thinkers' in Takeuchi Yoshinori (ed.), *Buddhist Spirituality: Later China, Korea, Japan and the Modern World* (London: SCM Press, 1999), p.294.

[35] *The Sun My Heart* (London: Rider, 1992), p.90.

another essay: '[Normally we imagine that] things exist outside of each other – the table outside of the flower, the sunshine outside of the cypress tree. [When we see things correctly] we see that they are inside each other – the sunshine inside the cypress tree.')[36]

This idea, strange though it is, is entirely consonant with our earlier reading of emptiness in terms of the internal relatedness of things. Earlier, we had entertained the possibility that the emptiness teaching could foster an experience of the dissolution of things. We had imagined that one's attention would be drawn from the thing to its conditions, and to the conditions of these conditions, and so on, until, at the limit, one would be left with an experience of a pure undifferentiated field. But, as the quotation from Nhat Hanh shows, the experience of emptiness could be pictured in another way. In appreciating the emptiness of the thing, Nhat Hanh's meditator does not find it dissolving into its conditions. On the contrary, he finds these conditions somehow present within the thing: the meditator sees the tree, forest, sun, and so on, *in* the chair. And this conclusion is entirely in keeping with the general idea, articulated in the Hua-yen and T'ien-t'ai schools, that each putative part of reality contains the whole. Just as in the famous metaphor of the *Avataṃsaka Sūtra* any particular jewel in Indra's Net reflects all the others, so here Nhat Hanh's chair contains all things.[37]

But, again, it is easy to misunderstand the point being made here. It would, I suggest, be an error to think of the thing as somehow containing a collection of discrete objects. In the light of a commitment to the internal relatedness of all things, such a conception cannot be upheld. To be sure, in a certain kind of meditation, one might initially see the chair as 'containing' more and more relatively distinct things – wood, tree, leaf, sun, and so on. One might imagine the thing gathering these things into itself like a whirlwind gathering debris or a plug gathering dishwater. But then, as one's meditation deepens, the commitment to emptiness must ensure that these things blur and fuse until, eventually, the thing is seen, as it were, to 'contain' the non-relational whole of emptiness.[38] One might imagine the thing gathering more and more of its conditions into itself until it finally draws its entire context into itself, that is, emptiness (or, more precisely, emptiness as conditioned by form). The thing, one might say, has 'gathered'

---

[36] 'The Sun My Heart' in Stephanie Kaza and Kenneth Kraft, *Dharma Rain: Sources of Buddhist Environmentalism* (Boston: Shambhala, 2000), p.91. My annotation.

[37] This idea also resonates with Alfred North Whitehead's discussion of the nature of events in *Science and the Modern World* (New York: Macmillan, 1925). Whitehead claims that an event 'is only itself as drawing together into its own limitation the larger whole in which it finds itself' so that 'the aspects of all things enter into its very nature' (p.96).

[38] In this connection it is worth noting Tu-shun's warning regarding the metaphor of the Jewel Net:

> Such a subtle metaphor is applied to things to help us think about them, but things are not so... These jewels only have their reflected images containing and entering each other – their substances are separate. Things are not like this, because their whole substance merges completely. (Kaza and Kraft (eds.), *Dharma Rain*, p.60.)

(Tu-shun (557-640) was the first Patriarch of the Hua-yen school.)

emptiness into itself. Alternatively, one could describe the same phenomenon by saying that emptiness has 'emptied' itself into form, into the chair. (An analogy may be helpful here: consider the way the Mona Lisa 'draws' a crowd of visitors; think of the crowd 'congregating' around the painting.)

This idea is not perhaps as odd as it might at first appear. For, after all, we do sometimes speak of individual things as intimating or 'gathering' their contexts. Think, for instance, of the way in which a particular motif embodies the entire theme of a symphony. Or consider the phenomena James Joyce once called 'epiphanies', those moments when a trivial and seemingly arbitrary event – the clink of a teaspoon against a saucer, a snatch of conversation overheard in the market – can encapsulate an entire story. In cases such as these, it does not seem absurd to say that the part in a sense 'contains' the whole. And we do sometimes speak of physical things such as chairs in this way too. For the trained observer, the relic of an ancient civilization brings with it an entire world: the shivering frontier patrol on Hadrian's Wall is there for the archaeologist in the muddy legionnaire's helmet. Consider also the phenomenon of nostalgia – the crumbling exercise book, recovered from some dusty corner of the attic, gathering a schoolyard world of warm milk and Wednesday mornings after double maths. Or consider the significance of the souvenir or the memento. And it is not only past worlds that can be gathered in this way. For there is another phenomenon, rarer but more interesting than nostalgia, when a thing, perhaps even a small, seemingly trivial thing, suddenly takes on a special significance and, as it were, condenses one's world. Phenomena of this sort play a central role in Heidegger's later writings on the nature of things. His idea is that a thing, even an ordinary, everyday thing, when attended to in an appropriately attentive way, can 'gather' the phenomenological dimensions of a rich, spiritually-satisfying world. Thus he writes that an item as seemingly innocuous as a jug can gather the brooding presence of the natural world ('the dark slumber of the earth'), the slow turning of the seasons, the community in which one lives, and even the deep longing of men and women for some relation to the divine.[39]

Perhaps Nhat Hanh is referring to a similar phenomenon. But even if he is not it has become clear that our earlier picture of emptiness as involving the 'dissolution' of things needs to be complemented by another picture wherein a thing is seen, so to speak, to 'gather' its conditions into itself. The first picture I called an experience of dissolution; this second I will call an experience of 'condensation' since I mean it to describe the phenomenon in which reality 'condenses' into particular things. It is tempting to interpret the following passage from the 'Sayings of Daikaku' in terms of this experience:

> Realisation makes every place a temple; the absolute endows all beings with the true eye. When you come to grasp it, you find it was before your eyes. If you can

---

[39] See his essay, 'The Thing', in *Poetry, Language, Thought*, translated by Albert Hofstadter (New York: Harper and Row, 1971), pp.165-86.

see clear what is before your very eyes, it is what fills the ten directions; when you see what fills the ten directions, you find it is only what is before your eyes.[40]

There is, however, a danger that all this talk of condensation might seem too grand. In seeing all reality condensed into the thing before him, one imagines the Zen master as (a caricature of) a yogi, his body sitting cross-legged in some Eastern bazaar, his mind ranging over the fiery surface of Alpha Centauri, his consciousness reaching out far beyond our galaxy. This image resonates with the way in which these ideas are presented in some Indian Mahāyāna *Sūtras*. In the *Avataṃsaka Sūtra*, for instance, one reads of *Bodhisattvas* who 'in a single atom... showed all objects in all worlds', who 'from a single pore... emitted the sounds of the teaching of all Buddhas', who 'traveled unhindered through the realm of space [and] knew all things without any impediment'.[41] But these grandiose images convey something altogether too grand to be true to the spirit of Zen, a tradition which, with typical Chinese pragmatism, has generally played down the significance of astonishing yogic feats of this sort. Moreover, they are, I think, also too grandiose, too inconceivable, for the tastes of modern readers. I do not, therefore, want to claim that Zen masters such as Dōgen, in speaking of seeing the world in a speck of dust, are claiming a cosmic omniscience of this sort.[42]

How, then, should we understand references to condensation? For my part, I do not think they should be thought of as philosophical propositions which can be assessed as true or false in their own terms. Instead, I would suggest that they be viewed as 'skilful means' designed to undercut a particular kind of philosophical delusion, namely, the idea that things are reflections or expressions of some antecedent reality. So, on this account, to say that the thing is a condensation of reality is not to propound some grand metaphysical theory, but only to reject the idea that there is anything 'behind' or 'beyond' the thing. It is to deny that the thing is an imperfect copy of a template set in a transcendent realm of Forms, for instance, or a condensation of a limitless field of Emptiness, or a worldly being imbued with a divine presence. Perhaps this is why Dōgen rejects the idea that things *have* the Buddha-nature, for to say that things possess Buddha-nature is to imply that Buddha-nature is a transcendent reality somehow inhering in the thing. And to think this is, perhaps, to be distracted from the matter at hand: the thing in its 'thusness'.

---

[40] Quoted in Tim Leggett, *Zen and the Ways* (London: Routledge & Kegan Paul, 1978), p.61.

[41] Quoted in Thomas Cleary, *Entry into the Inconceivable: an introduction to Hua-yen Buddhism* (Honolulu: University of Hawaii Press, 1983), pp.5-6.

[42] On this point, I agree with David Edward Shaner. See his essay 'The Japanese Experience of Nature' in J. Baird Callicott and Roger T. Ames (eds), *Nature in Asian Traditions of Thought* (Albany: SUNY Press, 2001), p.173.

Identification

Let us recap the argument so far. I began by arguing that the reason for thinking that Zen might find it difficult to account for the intrinsic value of individual things was that it subscribed to the idea, drawn from Madhyamaka Buddhism, that all things are empty of self-existence. But if all things are empty, then the properties of all things are relational. And if this is the case, then one might be led to wonder how any intrinsic properties could exist. I refuted this objection by noting that it interpreted intrinsic value as non-relational value, which is not the sort of value environmental thinkers are generally referring to when they speak of the intrinsic value of things. I then considered a more powerful objection to the idea of a Zen-based conception of intrinsic value. I suggested that Zen Buddhism, like the Madhyamaka tradition on which it is to a large extent based, is committed to the idea that all relations are internal, and that as a result it is, in the final analysis, committed to the idea that no things exist at all. But if no things exist, it is at the very least difficult to see how one could refer to the intrinsic value of things, even if one means by that phrase non-instrumental and not non-relational value. I hope to have shown in the foregoing discussion that this objection rests on a misconceived 'nihilistic' reading of emptiness: the idea that emptiness involves the dissolution of all things into a non-relational 'Bradleyan' Absolute. But whatever Zen means by emptiness, it cannot mean that, for such a position cannot be squared with the idea that emptiness is itself empty of self-existence and so conditioned by the presence of things. In Zen, to experience emptiness is not to experience the total absence of beings. On the contrary, the awakened experience of emptiness is said to involve the disclosure of things in their 'thusness' (*tathatā*). The charge of nihilism cannot, therefore, be upheld.

Some readers will be less than satisfied with these conclusions, however. For although I have argued that certain objections to the idea of a Zen Buddhist conception of intrinsic value cannot be sustained, I have not provided any compelling reasons for thinking that Zen does indeed subscribe to such a conception. In order to determine whether a Zen Buddhist view of nature does in fact involve anything resembling a conception of the intrinsic value of things, it will be necessary to try to imagine, once again, what it must be like to experience emptiness.

The foregoing account may have given the impression that the awakened individual *spectates* on the thing, seeing it as dissolving into or as gathering its conditions before their eyes, as it were. But that way of envisaging matters cannot be right. For I have argued that to experience emptiness must be to experience all things as internally related, and to experience *all* things as internally related would be to experience oneself as internally related to whatever one is perceiving. Moreover, in the light of Bradley's metaphysics, we have seen that to say that two or more things are internally related to each other is to say that they are ultimately not related at all, but rather abstracted from a non-relational whole. One way of expressing this point would be to say that the enlightened woman must see the object of her perception as part of herself; another would be to say that she must see herself as part of the object. Perhaps, however, it would be better to say that for the enlightened man or woman there is only the thing-presenting-itself – a single, unbroken event, from which the putative subject and the putative object are abstractions.[43] In the following passage from his essay 'The Role of Nature in Zen Buddhism', Suzuki would seem to be interpreting Ch'ing-yüan's famous realization (recounted above) as an event of this sort:

> When the mountains are seen as not standing against me, when they are dissolved into the oneness of things, they are not mountains, they cease to exist as objects of Nature. When they are seen as standing against me, as separate from me, as something unfriendly to me, they are not mountains either. The mountains are really mountains when they are assimilated into my being and I am absorbed by them.[44]

This would seem to be the kind of event *haiku* poets try to capture, a spiritual epiphany which is itself the result of an identification with the thing so intimate that one is said not to look *at* a thing, but *as* it.[45] Iris Murdoch would appear to be describing a state of absorption similar to that achieved by a *haiku* poet in the following passage:

> I am looking out of my window in an anxious and resentful state of mind, oblivious of my surroundings, brooding perhaps on some damage done to my prestige. Then suddenly I observe a hovering kestrel. In a moment everything is altered. The brooding self with its hurt vanity has disappeared. There is nothing now but kestrel. And when I return to thinking of the other matter it seems less important.[46]

What is especially interesting about this passage is the way Murdoch moves naturally between aesthetic and ethical concerns. She is using the example of the kestrel in order to make a point about beauty. But the aesthetic appreciation of the kestrel is, she says, accompanied by a selflessness or humility on her part, on the part of the observer, which would seem to have ethical implications. Murdoch finds herself party to the kestrel-presenting-itself only because she has allowed her 'brooding self' to dissipate. Elsewhere, she has the following to say about the role of humility and attentiveness in ethics and aesthetics:

> The chief enemy of excellence in morality (and also in art) is personal fantasy: the tissue of self-aggrandizing and consoling wishes and dreams which prevents one from seeing what is there outside one. Rilke said of Cézanne that he did not paint

---

[43] The following account can be usefully compared with Heidegger's of 'thinging', as developed in his essay 'The Thing'.

[44] *Zen Buddhism: Selected Writings of D. T. Suzuki*, edited by William Barrett (New York: Doubleday Anchor Books, 1956), p.240. Cf. D. T. Suzuki, *Zen and Japanese Culture* (Princeton, NJ: Princeton University Press, 1973), p.246. Note that in other places Suzuki rejects the rhetoric of identification on the grounds that it misleadingly implies the existence of a subject and an object that are somehow 'fused'. See ibid. p.359.

[45] See Lawrence Stryk (translator), *The Penguin Book of Zen Poetry* (USA: Penguin, 1977), p.23.

[46] *The Sovereignty of Good* (London: Routledge & Kegan Paul, 1970), p.84.

'I like it', he painted 'There it is.' This is not easy, and requires, in art or morals, a discipline... What I have called fantasy, the proliferation of blinding, self-centred aims and images, is itself a powerful system of energy, and most of what is called 'will' or 'willing' belongs to this system. What counteracts the system is attention to reality, inspired by, consisting of, love... Freedom is not strictly the exercise of the will, but rather the experience of accurate vision which, when this becomes appropriate, occasions action.[47]

The idea that excellence in morality and in art is the result of seeing the world aright chimes with our discussion, in Chapter Two, of insight (*prajñā*), the virtue that enables one to see the true nature of things. In that chapter, we noted that *prajñā* is not merely theoretical knowledge, but is rather a form of practical wisdom, akin in some very general respects to Aristotle's *phronēsis*, which informs how one sees the world and the way one acts in it. To see the world through the eye of *prajñā* is to be released from the attachments that normally narrow and distort one's perception, and to thereby attain a clearer view of things. Buddhists would agree with Murdoch that perceiving things clearly entails a measure of selflessness or humility on the part of the subject which has important implications for ethics. For example, when Robert Thurman claims that in the context of Mahāyāna ethics 'true compassion is not some sort of mere rule obedience... but rather action generated from the total sensitivity that compels full responsiveness to an immediate situation of suffering'[48] he is making a statement that would be endorsed by both Murdoch and Zen Buddhists. Zen and Murdoch are also alike in thinking that seeing the world clearly, in this sense, is a matter of aesthetics as well as ethics. Think of the Zen artist learning to arrange flowers or to use a paintbrush: as we saw in the previous chapters, this is in part an ethical training.

Murdoch's choice of a living being, a kestrel, to illustrate the phenomenon of selfless attentiveness is significant, for it would seem that life, and especially animate life, commands our attention in such a way that it naturally draws us out of ourselves. The life of the kestrel hovering in the dawn sky is enigmatic. Have we any conception of what it is like to be such a creature? We can, I suppose, close our eyes and try to imagine – the meadow shimmering beneath us in the morning air, each blade of grass sharply defined, the minute shifts in wind direction, the expectation of warm flesh. It is easy to anthropomorphize here, and perhaps impossible not to do so. But whatever it is like to be a kestrel, it is clear that the bird is utterly indifferent to our human concerns. The bird cared nothing for Murdoch's wounded pride, nor for the salvific effect it had on the curious human gazing at it from afar. And it is perhaps because of this very indifference that contemplating a living being can draw us out of ourselves. I remember as a boy crouching over an earthworm, watching it coil about itself on a patch of exposed soil after a rain shower. Whether or not there is anything it is like to be an earthworm – and that is a question for biologists and metaphysicians – the animal seemed to demonstrate a strange wormish purposiveness that was entirely beyond

---

[47] Ibid. p.59.
[48] R. A. F. Thurman, 'The Emptiness that is Compassion: An Essay on Buddhist Ethics', *Religious Traditions* Vol.4, no.2: p.24.

my ken. I was transfixed by it, transfixed by life. This is particularly evident in animate beings, but it is also there in plants. One can become lost in the ecstatic contemplation of a creeper, for instance, winding its slow way up a garden wall, its tendrils gripping the bricks. Or one can become enthralled by the strange gnarled figure of an old oak. There is still a life there, a purpose beyond our reckoning which draws us out of ourselves and, I would hold, ennobles us in the process.

Just as in Chapter Two we saw that the virtue of compassion is the result of the combination of selflessness and empathy, so this identification with living beings would seem to be connected to the virtue of non-violence. That is not to say that the beings identified with are necessarily brought within the fold of the First Precept. On the contrary, appreciating living beings in this way could be reconciled with harming them. (Think of the hunter lost in rapt awe of a stag he will nonetheless shoot.) To say that this experience of identification is connected to the virtue of non-violence is rather to say that someone who found herself lost, for even a moment, in the selfless appreciation of some living being would be less inclined to harm that being, or in any case more inclined to accord that being a measure of respect. (And indeed it could be argued that a respect for their quarry is the mark of the best hunters.)

These moments would seem to play an important part in Zen. Perhaps the life of an accomplished Zen Buddhist is punctuated and invigorated by these epiphanies, be they small (like my wonder at the earthworm) or great (like *kenshō*). In any case, an empathic identification with life would seem to involve the combination of several key Zen virtues: insight, selflessness, mindfulness, compassion and non-violence. Indeed, in these sorts of experience these virtues cannot be teased apart.

Intrinsic value

So far, we have been speaking in terms of virtue; however, the idea of an empathic identification with life could also be described in terms of intrinsic value. Appreciated selflessly, beings could not be seen as having merely instrumental value, as being merely useful for our purposes, for a sense of instrumentality requires an affective distance between user and used that cannot obtain in the kind of selfless appreciation of beings we are here considering. So in the eye of *prajñā*, the kestrel or earthworm or creeper must disclose itself as having a non-instrumental value, a value over and above its use-value. The kestrel could not be seen as nothing but a regulator of the local population of mice. Neither could it be seen as vermin. The creeper could not be viewed as a mere decoration. Neither could it be seen as a weed.

With the idea that becoming selflessly enthralled with a particular being involves one's valuing that being non-instrumentally, we would seem to be close to the writings of deep ecologists for whom references to transpersonal (beyond-personal) identification mix freely with talk of the intrinsic value of individual beings. So in this respect it would seem that deep ecologists were right in thinking Zen Buddhism an ally to their cause. Yet, as we saw in Chapter Three, some deep ecologists seem to restrict this sort of identification to living things. For my part, however, I do not think one need to make a sharp distinction between living and non-living beings here. Although I have, so far, been referring only to animals and plants, I do not believe only living beings can be appreciated selflessly. One might appreciate a pebble on a beach in this way, or a few flecks of cirrus cloud high in the summer sky, or an old frayed shoelace: indeed, for someone of a suitably attentive or poetic disposition anything could become the vehicle for a moment of 'unselfing', to adopt Murdoch's apt phrase.[49] And if these things were to be identified with, then they, too, would disclose themselves as having a non-instrumental value. To appreciate a thing in this way would not necessarily be to be lost in ecstatic contemplation of it. To identify with an inanimate thing one would not have to stand back from it, rapt with wonder, like Murdoch gazing up at the hovering kestrel. On the contrary, one could become 'one' with the thing through engaging with it practically, through using it. Consider the way in which one might speak of a skilled tennis player being at one with her racquet, or the instrument of a gifted musician being an extension of his body. It does not seem unreasonable to suppose that someone who had come to identify with a particular thing in this way would see that thing as having a non-instrumental value. The tennis player would treat her favourite racquet with respect, as would the pianist his piano. This conception of an identification with things achieved through practical engagement has a very Taoist flavour. We shall see in the next chapter that it was also incorporated into Zen. For the moment, it will suffice to note that although seeing things as having non-instrumental value would not necessarily preclude using them, it would preclude seeing them as nothing but resources. Things would rather be viewed as having an integrity that demands that when they are used they are used with respect. Thus the Zen master does not use his meditation cushion to soften his chair at breakfast just as the skilled carpenter does not damage his chisel by working against the grain of the wood. Both these actions would evince a blindness to the non-instrumental value of these beings. The good Zen Buddhist, by contrast, is said to be respectful in her dealings with things, as Gustie Herrigel puts it, she has developed a 'delicacy' towards her surroundings.[50] Robert Aitken is referring to a similar kind of respect for things in the following passage:

> I confess I am offended when I see zoris left every which way at the temple door, when I see someone straighten his cushion with his foot, when I see tools left in the rain. Things are altogether faithful. They follow the rules with precision. We owe them benevolence in return.[51]

Murdoch, for her part, saw things in a similar way. Consider the following recollection from her husband, John Bayley:

---

[49] *The Sovereignty of Good*, p.84.
[50] See Gustie L. Herrigel, *Zen in the Art of Flower Arangement*, translated by R. F. C. Hull (London: Souvenir Press, 1999), p.79.
[51] Aitken, *The Mind of Clover*, p.34.

The life of inanimate things was always close to her. I used to tease her about Wordsworth's flower, which the poet was confident must 'enjoy the air it breathes'. 'Never mind about flowers', Iris would say, impatiently and somewhat mysteriously. 'There are other things that matter much more'. Though good about it at the time, she also felt real sadness for abandoned bottles, and I think of it now when she stoops [i.e., after the onset of Alzheimer's] like an old tramp to pick up scraps of candy paper or cigarette ends from the pavement. She feels at one with them, and will find them a home if she can.... I think of it as her Buddhist side. She always had a strong regard for that religion... There seems no doubt that Iris's own private devotion to things finds a response in some of the tenets of Buddhism.[52]

Before continuing, it is worth pausing for a moment to consider an objection that could be made to the argument presented in this section. In Chapters Two and Three, we explored the possibilities for framing the Zen comportment towards nature in terms of virtue ethics. In this chapter we have switched to speaking about intrinsic value. Can these references to intrinsic value and virtue be reconciled? There are reasons for thinking that they cannot. For it would seem that someone who was committed to an ethic based on the idea that things have intrinsic value would hold that actions are wrong to the extent that they destroy intrinsic value, irrespective of the virtues those actions express. So someone who killed animals would be thought to have acted wrongly, even if he had acted out of a compassionate (i.e., virtuous) desire to bring what he saw as their miserable lives to a quick end.[53] (In other words, an ethic based on the idea of the intrinsic value of nature would seem to be a consequentialist ethic.) By contrast, for a virtue ethicist, it would seem that actions would be deemed wrong to the extent that they exemplified vices, and not because they destroyed intrinsic value. So someone who acted out of selfish motives would be considered to have acted wrongly, even if his actions just so happened to bring about an increase in the amount of intrinsic value in the world (think of a businessman donating money to environmental causes in an effort to appear suitably 'green'). Conversely, someone whose actions exhibited virtue – perhaps even a virtuous concern with promoting intrinsic value – would be held to have done right, even if, contrary to his desires, his actions had precisely the opposite effect and in fact resulted in a net decrease in value.

It would seem, then, that one cannot be committed both to an ethic based on the presence of intrinsic value and to a virtue ethic. But this dichotomy holds true only if one is committed to the idea that intrinsic values are *properties*. We have not been understanding intrinsic value in this way, however. According to the account set out above, to say that someone sees things as having intrinsic value is to say that he or she sees them as having a value over and above the various uses to which they can be put. One could say that these things are valued non-

---

[52] John Bayley, *Iris: A Memoir of Iris Murdoch* (London: Duckworth, 1998), pp.79-80. My annotation.

[53] For a discussion of this suggestion in its connection with Mahāyāna Buddhist ethics see Lambert Schmithausen, *Buddhism and Nature: the Lecture delivered on the Occasion of the EXPO 1990, An Enlarged Version with Notes* (Tokyo: The International Institute for Buddhist Studies, 1991), p.47.

instrumentally, which is not to say that they are imbued with some objectively existing property, non-instrumental value. The question of the ontological status of intrinsic value has therefore been left open.

There is a danger that putting matters this way might imply the subjectivist idea that value is something valuers project onto a world which, considered in itself, is evaluatively-neutral, that value is superimposed onto the world like the coloured paints added to old black and white photos. But our account of non-instrumental value implies no such thing. Indeed, the subjectivist's position relies on a distinction between the subjective and objective realms which cannot be upheld in the light of the emptiness teaching. For Zen, to see a thing as intrinsically valuable is neither to have projected a subjective value onto it, nor to have recognized some objectively existing property of it, but to have found oneself party to a single event – the thing-presenting-itself – from which subject and object can be considered abstractions.

Maybe such an event can be adequately described in terms of value, or maybe it cannot. In any case, I would like to emphasize that I have phrased my argument in terms of intrinsic value in order to counter the unsound argument that Zen cannot yield an adequate environmental ethic because it cannot endorse the idea that things have intrinsic value. But there is no need to be attached to the phrase 'intrinsic value' here. After all, those words carry a great deal of conceptual baggage. Amongst meta-ethicists, the debate rages on over how intrinsic value is to be defined, and whether or not it exists, and, if so, which entities have it. But precisely because the idea is so disputed, references to intrinsic value can, I think, sometimes distract one's attention from the concrete reality of things. So whereas the phrase was originally meant to serve the practical function of drawing attention to the overlooked non-instrumental value of things, it now serves, more often than not, as nothing more than a label for a particular philosophical can of worms. But if it serves only to distract, then even the idea of intrinsic value ought to be thrown away:

> The master Hsiang-yen asked a travelling monk where he had come from. He replied that he had come from the monastery on Mount Kuei. The master asked: 'What sort of things has the master Kuei-shan been saying lately?' The monk replied that someone had asked him what it meant that the patriarch of Zen had come from the West, in response to which the master Kuei-shan had simply held up his *fu-tzu* (a whisk symbolic of the station of Zen master or abbot). Hsiang-yen then asked what Kuei-shan's disciples had understood by this gesture. He said that it meant that mind is awakened through the concrete; reality is revealed within situations. Hsiang-yen said: 'Not bad in some sense but why are they so intent on theory?' The monk asked him how he would have explained the gesture. The master held up his *fu-tzu*.[54]

---

[54] Quoted in Dale S. Wright, *Philosophical Meditations on Zen Buddhism* (Cambridge: Cambridge University Press, 1998), p.91. Annotations Wright's own.

Chapter Five

The Charge of Quietism

The general charge

If they have been successful, the preceding chapters have refuted three objections to the idea of a Zen Buddhist environmental ethic: 1) the charge that Zen is amoral; 2) the accusation that Zen is inherently anthropocentric; and 3) the charge that Zen cannot do justice to the intrinsic value of nature. In so doing, an account of our moral relations with nature has slowly come into focus, one centred on the development of several virtues: insight into emptiness; the empathy which allows one to identify with another being; the selflessness which enables one to see the world clearly, and the compassion, non-violence and gentleness with which these virtues are inextricably linked. I have argued that someone who had developed these character traits would be inclined to treat things as having intrinsic (i.e., non-instrumental) value.

However, pragmatically-minded readers may still have doubts about the practical implications of all this. Can the Zen-inspired environmental ethic developed in Chapters Two through Four have any bearing on real-world environmental problems? The aim of this chapter is to show that Zen is not as 'quietistic' as it is often supposed to be, and that our speculations in the previous chapters do, in fact, bear upon practical issues.

Our first task will be to clarify the accusation that Zen is 'quietistic'. One version of the charge could run like this: The solutions to environmental problems are political, economic and scientific. An environmental ethic worthy of the name must be able to offer advice on these practical matters, otherwise it will simply be useless. An adequate environmental ethic must at least be able to address real-world environmental problems, even if it is not able to provide definitive solutions to them. For instance, we want environmental ethicists to advise us on whether we ought to limit carbon dioxide emissions in poorer countries at the expense of their industrialization, or whether our priority in conserving genetic diversity ought to be the preservation of species in zoological parks and botanical gardens or in the wild. But an environmental ethic based on Zen could offer no advice on these matters. Vacuous speculations on how the Zen master finds himself 'at one' with all things, or on how he 'treads lightly on earth' are of no use in resolving these real-world, practical problems.

This point can be conceded. There are all sorts of important environmental questions that Zen has little or nothing to say about. To be sure, environmentalists who also happen to be Zen Buddhists might be able to address practical problems like those mentioned above, but when they do this they will be drawing upon their technical training and experience – in conservation biology or in local politics, for example – rather than their religion. Moreover, Zen-inspired thinkers (some deep ecologists, for instance) might be able to say something about the general conceptual roots of specific environmental problems, about the way in which the problems of global warming or deforestation are ultimately an expression of a dualistic, unenlightened conception of humans versus nature, or something of that sort, and these speculations might well be philosophically interesting. But it is less clear that these thinkers will be able to derive any practical advice on the resolution of these problems from Zen, and it is practical advice that the above objection demands. So it would indeed seem that Zen would not be able to offer useful advice on real-world environmental problems such as the destruction of the ozone layer or the legal questions concerning the conservation of endangered species.

One ought not to expect Zen to provide answers to these sorts of questions, however. To maintain that it should be able to advise us on these issues would be to suppose that environmental ethics deals only with these sorts of practical, policy-oriented questions. But the discipline encompasses far more than that. Environmental ethics encompasses Wordsworth's appreciation of nature as well as the Rio Declaration, the spiritual significance of an ancient dale as much as its economic value in a cost-benefit analysis. One issue that undoubtedly falls within the purview of environmental ethics concerns the place of an appreciation of the natural world in human well-being, in the 'good life'. And it has of course been this dimension of environmental ethics that we have been primarily concerned with in this book. To be sure, questions pertaining to the character of the good life do not focus on 'hard cases', specific moral dilemmas, but instead arise from more general reflections on the best way to live. However, this does not mean that they are *im*practical considerations. Indeed, the general question of how one ought to live is an important practical issue, and one on which Zen has much to say.

But even if this is accepted, one might think that although Zen can offer advice on how one ought to live, it advises that one ought to live a life divorced from practical commitments, a life which is in some sense otherworldly or world-denying. This general charge of 'quietism' can be analysed into four interrelated accusations: 1) the charge that to say that all things have intrinsic value is ultimately to say nothing, or at least nothing that could justify action in support of environmental objectives; 2) the accusation that Zen practice advocates that one ought to renounce one's free will and live a life of unconscious obedience to the 'Way of Things', the *Tao*; 3) the idea that Zen encourages an irresponsible 'live for the moment' philosophy of life which precludes serious consideration of environmental issues; and 4) the charge that Zen advocates a withdrawal from worldly affairs into an inner world of passive meditation. The following sections will address each of these accusations in turn.

The charge of vacuousness

In the previous chapter, I argued that moments of selfless absorption in natural phenomena play an important role in Zen, and I suggested that someone who experienced things in this way would be inclined to treat them as having intrinsic (i.e., non-instrumental) value. I also claimed that a person of a suitably attentive or poetic disposition could see anything, even inanimate objects such as pebbles or shoelaces, as having this sort of value. Some readers will no doubt be sceptical of these claims. For, at first sight, it might seem that I have argued that all things have intrinsic value, and if I have indeed suggested this then it would seem that I have made a claim which is entirely vacuous. After all, surely an adequate environmental ethic would have to distinguish between those beings that have value and those that do not? To say with Christopher Ives that 'From the standpoint of *śūnyatā*, at the absolute level *all* things are relational, "empty" beings with equal intrinsic value'[1] would surely be to say nothing, or at least nothing that could have any practical ramifications. This is the objection Ian Harris is raising when he complains that to maintain, in the spirit of Hua-yen, that 'since all things are inter-related we should act in a spirit of reverence towards them all' is to say little that is of any use to ethicists. For since 'the category of "all things" includes insecticides, totalitarian regimes and nuclear weapons... [the argument] suffers from a certain vacuity from the moral perspective'. Indeed, by this reasoning, there is 'no essential difference between the proposition "all things are equally valuable" and the view that "everything is devoid of value"'.[2] In this section, we will appraise this objection. First, however, it is necessary to understand what precisely is being objected to.

To be sure, the idea of extending concern equally to all beings can serve to undermine the tendency towards sentimental attachment to 'charismatic megafauna' on the part of the public. After all, environmentalists are not solely concerned with the conservation of pandas and sea otters. In fact, Zen Buddhist writers sometimes deliberately choose to emphasize the value of the most repellent natural phenomena. Thus Bashō offers the following *haiku*:

> Fleas, lice
> The horse pissing
> Near my pillow[3]

For Zen, even the most distasteful things are worthy of a certain kind of aesthetic and ethical regard. The problem is that if Zen advocates that this concern

---

[1] Christopher Ives, *Zen Awakening and Society* (Honolulu: University of Hawaii Press, 1992), p.137. My emphasis.

[2] Ian Harris, 'Getting to Grips with Buddhist Environmentalism: A Provisional Typology', *Journal of Buddhist Ethics* 2 (1995), p.177.

[3] Quoted in D. T. Suzuki, *Zen and Japanese Culture* (Princeton, NJ: Princeton University Press, 1973), p.237. See also Francis H. Cook, 'The Jewel Net of Indra' in J. Baird Callicott and Roger T. Ames (eds), *Nature in Asian Traditions of Thought* (Albany: State University of New York Press, 2001), pp.213-29.

be extended to all beings, then it would seem to be calling for it to be extended to all manner of beings the environment would apparently be better off without. Thus Yuriko Saito would appear to be agreeing with Harris when she argues that Zen 'does not contain within it a force necessary to condemn and fight the human abuse of nature'. For 'If everything is Buddha nature... strip-mined mountains and polluted rivers must be considered as manifesting Buddha nature as much as uncultivated mountains and unpolluted rivers'.[4]

This is an important criticism – but how exactly should it be understood? Perhaps the suggestion is that in refusing to distinguish between those beings that have value and those that do not, a Zen environmental ethic would take the form of what Robert Elliot calls an 'everything ethic' – a conception of the moral community as including everything from humans to flu viruses, from river deltas to mildew.[5] And if this is the case, then it would seem that the moral circle has been expanded too far. For if Zen maintains that concern ought to be extended to all beings, without exception, then surely it is offering a conception of the moral life so attenuated as to be completely vacuous.

One problem with this objection is that it supposes that Zen is offering some kind of moral theory centred on the claim that all beings have intrinsic value. It suggests that Zen can be saddled with a particular conception of the moral circle, namely, the thesis that all beings with the property of intrinsic value (i.e., all beings) have moral standing. But this sort of concern with formulating general moral principles is of course altogether alien to Zen. In refusing to draw a line between those beings that have intrinsic value and those that do not, a Zen Buddhist environmental ethic would not be propounding the thesis that all beings have intrinsic value. In the spirit of Nāgārjuna, its aim would be deconstructive rather than constructive. More precisely, its purpose would be to undermine any vestige of dualistic thinking on the part of the practitioner (i.e., the thought that there are two categories of entity, those with intrinsic value and those without). Its aim would not be to develop a positive thesis which could itself be understood dualistically (i.e., the thesis that all things have intrinsic value, which could be contrasted with the view that, say, only some things do). So it would be wrong to suppose that a Zen master who proclaimed that all things have intrinsic value was thereby articulating the 'Zen theory of intrinsic value'. Instead, like Nāgārjuna, the master's purpose would be deconstructive, and, moreover, again like Nāgārjuna, he would have made the claim in order to achieve a specific practical end. Bearing this in mind, it would, perhaps, be better to think of the hypothetical master's statement as a 'skilful means' employed to cure his audience of a particular delusion – the idea that all things only have value in so far as they are useful for some human purpose, for example.

---

[4] Quoted in Graham Parkes, 'Voices of Mountains, Trees, and Rivers: Kūkai, Dōgen, and a Deeper Ecology' in Mary Evelyn Tucker and Duncan Ryūken Williams (eds), *Buddhism and Ecology: the interconnection of dharma and deeds* (Cambridge, Massachusetts: Harvard University Press, 1997), p.119.

[5] See Robert Elliot, 'Environmental Ethics' in Peter Singer, *A Companion to Ethics* (Oxford: Blackwell, 1991), p.288.

So for these reasons Zen should not be thought of as offering an 'everything ethic'. Moreover, if Saito's objection rests on the notion that Zen is presenting an ethic of this sort, then it is without force. However, perhaps Saito is not assuming that at all. Let us examine her objection from another angle by considering what sort of *character* it indicates. As I read Saito's words, I imagine a Zen master calmly surveying a strip-mined mountainside, seeing it not as an environmental disaster demanding attention, but as a manifestation of Buddha-nature. 'Even this is Buddha-nature,' the master says to himself. 'Let it be.' I imagine him standing back from the scene, reluctant to interfere with what, contrary to common sense, he knows to be a manifestation of spiritual perfection. So rather than lending his voice to groups protesting the devastation or lending a hand in efforts to restore the area, he sits back and contemplates the impermanence of Buddha-nature and other such topics.

This supposedly awakened master is a character we have encountered before. In Chapter Three, we saw that whatever it means to say that things have intrinsic value, it cannot mean that they are brought within the purview of the First Precept, for this would entail an exacting practical ideal quite out of keeping with Zen practice. The idea of the Zen master tip-toeing along the forest path taking care not to crush clods of soil or fallen leaves beneath his feet (for these beings, he thinks, are really Buddhas) might resonate with some aspects of Jainism, but it does not accord with Zen.

On the contrary, from a Buddhist standpoint, such a character would be thought of as being paralysed by his *attachment* to the sacredness or holiness of things. And this attachment, even though it is directed towards such an exalted object as the Buddha-nature of things, would nevertheless be seen as an attachment, and hence an obstacle to awakening. To cure him of this attachment one could point out that to say that everything is holy (in the sense of being a manifestation of Buddha-nature) is, in the final analysis, to say that nothing is holy: the idea of holiness drops out of the equation, as it were, becomes meaningless. Or, paraphrasing Bodhidharma, one could say that the highest meaning of the Buddhist teachings is that nothing is holy – there is only emptiness.[6] Or one could note, with Gary Snyder, that the idea of the sanctity or holiness of things can sometimes serve only to distract one from the reality before one's eyes:

> For those who would see directly into essential nature, the idea of the sacred is a delusion and an obstruction: it diverts us from seeing what is before our eyes: plain thusness. Roots, stems, and branches are all equally scratchy. No hierarchy, no equality.[7]

Alternatively, one could point out that the 'master' is assuming that to see things as 'condensations of emptiness' is to see them as 'manifestations of the

---

[6] Cf. K'uo-an's (J. Kakuan) commentary on the Eighth Ox-Herding Picture: 'even the idea of holiness does not obtain... A holiness before which birds offer flowers is but a farce'. Tenshin Fletcher and David Scott, *The Way of Zen* (London: Vega, 2001), p.97.

[7] 'Blue Mountains Constantly Walking' in Stephanie Kaza and Kenneth Kraft, *Dharma Rain: Sources of Buddhist Environmentalism* (Boston: Shambhala, 2000), p.130.

Absolute' and that in assuming this he is supposing, wrongly, that emptiness is an Absolute that somehow enters into things. In the West we have a tendency to see God – to imagine him descending from Heaven, imbuing the thing with His divine presence. But for Zen emptiness does not represent any kind of being, however exalted, and to see things as condensations of emptiness is not to see them as inhabited by God. As we saw in Chapter Two, if things 'condense' reality, then they also 'dissolve' into it, and so if they are in this sense everything, then they are also nothing.

Whereas the subject attached to the holiness of things would be paralysed, petrified by the spiritual perfection he sees all around him, the genuinely awakened master would *act*. To be sure, he would retain a sense of the value of things, but this awareness would not cause his joints to freeze and his tongue to fall limp in his mouth. On the contrary, in our example above, the genuinely awakened master would, I suspect, see the strip-mining for what it is, a harm. One might expect such a master to reply to Saito's objection by saying that to strip-mine a mountain is to harm the mountain (or at least to harm the myriad creatures who depend on the mountain for their existence). Maybe he would follow this up by saying that he is motivated to prevent this harm just as he would be moved to prevent someone from needlessly hacking down a sapling, and that this motivation is an expression of the virtue of non-violence. He would be motivated by non-violence to prevent the strip-mining because *ahiṃsā* does not only bear upon one's own actions; it is also a call to prevent others from violence. One attached to the holiness of things looks at the violence of the strip-mining and says 'Let it be!' But one who has eradicated all traces of the 'I am' conceit sees only violence, period, and takes measures to prevent it. He does not distinguish between his violence and the violence of another, and he therefore does not sit serenely apart from the scene of destruction, contemplating it as a panorama for his spiritual edification, safe in the knowledge that the violence being committed is not being committed by him. He sees only violence-to-be-stopped. The character suggested by Saito's objection therefore does not represent a truly enlightened master, but rather someone attached to the idea of the holiness of things and to his self. The objection that this character represents an ideal of Zen is therefore without force.

The *Tao*, determinism and freedom

As we saw in Chapter One, Zen (or more precisely, Ch'an) incorporated the Taoist idea that the best sort of life is one lived in harmony with the *Tao*. In order to achieve this unity with things it is said that a man must become so absorbed in his action that he ceases to be conscious of himself as an agent. If he is able to accomplish this then his action is said to have become 'non-action' or *wu-wei*. The idea of *wu-wei* is, perhaps, not as abstruse and inaccessible as it might appear. It is similar in some respects to the phenomenon, described by sportspeople, of being in 'the zone'. Consider the example of a tennis player finding herself totally aware of her serve, but without analysing that awareness into a subject's awareness of an object. She is mindful, not of *her* – a five foot nine inch woman with quick feet but a tendency to fluff returns – serving *the ball* (though, to be sure, she might describe the experience in these terms in retrospect), but only of *serving* – and, moreover, of, on this occasion, a perfect serve. Musicians sometimes experience a similar phenomenon. Consider a skilled musician, engrossed in his solo, finding himself 'carried away' by the music. In the midst of the solo, he is aware neither of himself as a subject nor of the piano as an object, but only of *playing*. He is, one might say, aware of beautiful playing but not of playing beautifully. In cases such as these, one is fully aware of a particular act, and, moreover, one is aware that the act is being performed well, but one is not consciously acting. For this reason, one might be disinclined to take credit for the act: the musician might say that the music 'played itself', for instance.[8] Taoists might say that in these cases the particular action must be credited to the *Tao*.[9]

This Taoist ideal of selfless action would also seem to be present in Zen. In his book, *Zen in the Art of Archery*, Eugen Herrigel recollects watching his teacher, master Kenzo Awa, shoot one arrow into the centre of a target and then split its shaft in two with another shot – in the dark. The master expressly denied having made the second shot, giving the credit to a transpersonal agency he refers to as 'It':

> I at any rate know that it is not 'I' who made the shot. 'It' shot and 'It' made the hit.[10]

In *Zen Mind, Beginner's Mind*, we find Shunryu Suzuki claiming in a similar vein that 'When we forget ourselves, we actually are the true activity of... reality itself'.[11] The implication would seem to be – *seem* to be – that by 'forgetting ourselves' in meditation we surrender our activity to some kind of super-agent, the *Tao*, perhaps. This interpretation is encouraged by the following passage from Gustie Herrigel:

> In the East, inner freedom is understood to mean adapting yourself to forms which have the significance of cosmic laws. By adapting himself to them, the pupil takes his place in a coherent world order.[12]

---

[8] The foregoing account can be compared with T. P. Kasulis's discussion of the Zen master's return to a pre-reflective immediacy (*Zen Action, Zen Person* (Honolulu: University of Hawaii Press, 1985), pp.57-60). Kasulis uses the example of a major league baseball player, who, at the moment of striking the ball is aware only of an 'unbroken hitting-of-the-baseball'.

[9] Cf. Chuang-tzu: 'When [the sage] wants to act, and to be successful, then he is moved by a force beyond him.' *The Book of Chuang Tzu*, translated by Martin Palmer, Elizabeth Breuilly, Chang Wai Ming and Jay Ramsay (London: Penguin Arkana, 1996), p.208.

[10] Eugen Herrigel, *Zen in the Art of Archery* (London: Routledge & Kegan Paul, 1976), p.83.

[11] Shunryu Suzuki, *Zen Mind, Beginner's Mind*, Trudy Dixon, ed. (New York: Weatherhill, 2000), p.79.

[12] Gustie L. Herrigel, *Zen in the Art of Flower Arrangement* (London: Souvenir Press, 1999), p.117.

Elsewhere, she refers to 'the Eastern attitude of pure, unpurposing surrender to the laws of the cosmos'.[13]

Some readers might find these statements unsettling. For they would seem to indicate that the Taoist idea of *wu-wei* represents a denial of human freedom, in the sense that achieving *wu-wei* would seem to involve surrendering one's will completely to the *Tao*. Liberal-minded thinkers might therefore worry that the 'freedom' attained by the Taoist or Zen sage is illusory, and they might imagine the sage as that classic stereotype: the Eastern mystic, having relinquished every last trace of self-consciousness, sitting in a tranquillized, beatific state, aloof from the concerns of the world. Moreover, they might worry that references to taking one's place in 'a coherent world order' indicate a metaphysical analogue of fascism, wherein it is demanded of men and women that they submit, not to the laws of the State, but to the laws of the Cosmos.

But this deterministic reading of the *Tao* cannot be upheld. In order to see why it does not hold water, it may be helpful to examine the following passage, taken from the conclusion of a paper by David Loy in which he examines the concept of *wu-wei*:

> Elsewhere I have argued that the nondualist denial of self (as in Buddhism) is equivalent to asserting that there is only the self (as in Vedānta). We would normally infer that the former implies complete determinism, the latter absolute freedom. However, if the universe is a whole (Brahman, Tao, Vijñaptimātra, and so forth) and if, as Hua Yen Buddhism develops in its image of Indra's Net, each particular is not isolated but contains and manifests the whole, then whenever 'I' act it is not 'I' but the whole universe that 'does' the action or rather *is* the action. If we accept that the universe is self-caused, then it acts freely whenever anything is done. Thus, from a nondualist perspective, complete determinism turns out to be equivalent to absolute freedom.[14]

The crux of this rather complicated argument can be rephrased in terms of the thesis developed in Chapter Four. In that chapter, I argued that if all things are internally related, then any particular thing can be thought of as a 'condensation' of reality entire, and I suggested that this might provide the metaphysical justification for the claims one occasionally finds in the literature of Zen that particular objects 'contain' the entire universe. There is no reason why this account of condensation should be restricted to things, however. For, surely, in the light of awakening, not only things, but also *actions* – a snap of the fingers, for instance, or a master's cry of '*Katsu!*' – could be considered to be condensations of reality entire. This is possible because – again, to put matters in terms of the thesis developed in Chapter Four – the internal relatedness of all things entails that any action on my part, on the part of an individual, must, so to speak, gather its conditions – and the conditions of these conditions, and the conditions of these condition, and so on – to the point where it would seem that reality as a whole is implicated in my single

[13] Ibid. p.120.
[14] David Loy,'Wei-wu-wei: Nondual action', *Philosophy East and West* 35, no.1 (January 1985), p.84.

action. This can be pictured either as my action dissolving into reality entire, or as reality entire condensing into my action (the experiences of 'dissolution' and 'condensation', respectively). To be sure, I am not to be thought of as exercising my free will in acting because in acting I am totally dependent upon forces outside myself.[15] (The Indian Mahāyānist, Śāntideva, uses a similar argument to demonstrate the folly of getting angry at someone, for if that person was not the cause of whatever annoying action they are held to have performed then what reason is there to be infuriated with them?)[16] But neither would it be correct to suppose that there is a strict determinism here because just as my freedom dissolves into reality entire, so any agency that is ascribed to reality entire must be thought of as condensing into my individual action, and in this sense, my actions are completely unconstrained and thus entirely free. As Aitken puts it, in awakening one realizes one's own 'unimpeded great action' – that is, total freedom.[17] In the light of these thoughts, both a crude commitment to the freedom of the will and an unrefined commitment to determinism would appear to be misconceived. On this understanding of *wu-wei*, one's actions are neither determined nor free (or both determined and free).

The contention that Zen advocates a passive ideal is, therefore, rather superficial. Zen does not hold that the world is entirely deterministic and that the only semblance of freedom one can therefore attain is to be gained through surrendering oneself to the *Tao*. Its view is subtler and more interesting. In any case, whether or not awakened actions can be considered to be free in the rather abstruse sense articulated above, they can be said to be free in the more conventional sense of being spontaneous, natural and unforced. In Chapter Two, we saw how the ethical virtues of the accomplished master are most evident in his spontaneous actions. But for Zen awakened action of any sort is said to be spontaneous. So the Zen master is said to respond effortlessly and naturally whether he is tending the sick or scrubbing the dishes or responding to a student in a *kōan* interview (*sanzen*). As the swordmaster, Yagyu Munenori (1571-1646) (a pupil of Takuan) put it:

> For everything there are instructions, there are ways and means which are usual. But the man who has attained (*sic*) gives them up altogether. He acts freely and spontaneously.[18]

The literature of Zen abounds with accounts of the spontaneous, albeit often baffling, actions of Zen masters. In Chapter Two, we discussed the famous story of

---

[15] Mahāyānists would not endorse Hume's conclusion that, even within the context of strict determinism, a person can be justifiably considered to be the cause of all actions that occur within his body. From a Mahāyāna standpoint, even these internal causes would be the result of causes external to the body.

[16] Śāntideva, *Bodhicaryāvatāra*, translated by Kate Crosby and Andrew Skilton (Oxford: Oxford University Press, 1996), verses 24 to 33 of Chapter Six (pp.52-3).

[17] Robert Aitken, *The Mind of Clover: Essays in Zen Buddhist Ethics* (San Francisco: North Point Press, 1984), p.110.

[18] Quoted in Fletcher and Scott, *Way of Zen*, p.157.

Nan-ch'uan and the cat. In the *Mumonkan* that story does not end with the master cutting the unfortunate animal in two, however. Reading on, one learns that later that day Nan-ch'uan came across another master, Chao-chao, and told him about the incident. Hearing the story, Chao-chao is said to have spontaneously taken off his sandal, placed it on his head, and walked away. The story ends with Nan-ch'uan remarking, enigmatically, that if Chao-chao had been present, he would have saved the cat. I will not try to unravel the meaning of this story – not least because there is probably no meaning of that sort to unravel; I will only note that here, as in so many Zen tales, the spontaneity of the master's action seems to be important. In his commentary on the story, Katsuki Sekida says of Chao-chao's action that it was 'performed as smoothly and as naturally as water running in a stream'.[19]

Why is spontaneity so valued? As we saw in Chapter Two, to say that the awakened mind is empty is to say, not that it is fixed on some object, Emptiness, but that it is held open, in a state of readiness, and so not fixed on any thing at all. Perhaps this state of readiness is best expressed in spontaneous responses. In the example above, Chao-chao had not planned his response; when he heard Nan-ch'uan's story he reacted spontaneously, and Nan-ch'uan, for his part, recognized the mark of awakening in his actions. Chao-chao's spontaneous response revealed itself to be a manifestation of an empty mind.

Drawing these separate arguments together, one can conclude that the Zen master is free – or is at least not un-free – in two senses. On the one hand, he has become aware that 'his' actions, as condensations of reality, cannot be thought of as determined. On the other, he is free in the sense that he acts spontaneously. The charge that Zen advocates surrendering one's freedom cannot, therefore, be upheld.

Responsibility, the body and the virtue of mindfulness

The second charge of quietism is well-expressed by Ruben L. F. Habito:

> the emphasis in Zen writing and teachings on 'living in the present moment' may give practitioners the misguided impression that Zen practice discourages thinking about or has nothing to do with one's individual or the earth's communal future. It may even lead to an irresponsible attitude that constantly seeks to 'seize the day' (*carpe diem*) and forgets or ignores the consequences of one's actions, passions, or omissions for one's own or others' future.[20]

The idea that Zen advocates an irresponsible, 'live for the present moment' philosophy of life has a long pedigree. Historically, it was the charge levelled at Zen Buddhists by Confucians and Neo-Confucians, who felt that Zen embodied a dangerous and immoral contempt for social issues. More recently, the charge arose

---

[19] Katsuki Sekida (translator) and A. V. Grimstone (ed.), *Two Zen Classics: Mumonkan and Hekiganroku* (Tokyo: Weatherhill, 1977), Case 14, p.60.

[20] Ruben L. F. Habito, 'Mountains and Rivers and the Great Earth: Zen and Ecology', in Tucker and Williams, *Buddhism and Ecology*, p.167.

in the debate over the merits of so-called 'Beat Zen', the interpretation of Zen chiefly associated with Allen Ginsberg, Gary Snyder, Jack Kerouac and the other writers and artists of the Beat Generation. It is on this more recent debate that we will focus.

The Beat Generation was an influential counter-cultural movement that flourished for a short period in the middle decades of the twentieth century. Some insight into its nature can be had through an analysis of the adjective 'beat'. On the one hand, the word connotes vagrancy, as in 'dead-beat': many of the Beat heroes were men (rarely women) who gave up the promise of a comfortable nine-to-five existence for a life lived amongst hoodlums, addicts and aesthetes, lived out – as the clichés have it – behind the wheel on dusty Western interstates, under the neon lights of Greyhound bus stations and in seedy downtown bars. On the other hand, the word connotes 'beatitude', spiritual ecstasy: the poverty sought by many of the Beat writers and artists was not material poverty, but spiritual poverty, the ideal to make oneself light, endlessly adaptable, to attain complete spiritual freedom. Indeed, for men like Kerouac, Ginsberg and Snyder, the word 'beat' signified nothing so much as a spiritual quest, a search for freedom and insight into the true nature of things, pursued through acid and peyote as well as through Perennial Philosophy. The Beat ideal, then, was of a simple life, unencumbered by material possessions, which emphasized the beauty and spiritual significance of each moment, combined, of course, with a refusal to abide by conventional norms. For many Beat writers, the essential elements of this vision could be found in Zen – in the iconoclastic stances of Chinese masters such as Ma-tsu, Chao-chao and Lin-chi (gleaned through the writings of Alan Watts, D. T. Suzuki, et al), and especially in the idea of the 'Zen lunatic', attached to nothing, dancing through the world, and always with a clear sense of the perfection of each everyday moment.

I have always been attracted to Beat Zen, but I think it has to be admitted that, whatever its inherent virtues as a philosophy of life, it is less than accurate as a depiction of Zen.[21] To be sure, the Zen Buddhist tradition does make much of the 'Zen lunatic', the 'holy fool' who has freed himself from all hang-ups and taken to a simple life on the road. Think of the Taoist or Zen sages of old, or of Bashō or of Ryōkwan. Or think of the ideal portrayed in the last of the famous Ox-herding pictures – the man at the final stage of awakening. He is said to 'go his own way', heedless of convention, arriving at the marketplace barefooted, bare-chested, muddied and dust-covered, carrying wine in a gourd, leading innkeepers and fishmongers in the way of the Buddha (just as Ginsberg with acid in his pockets wandered through Times Square with hustlers and dealers and addicts?).[22] To be sure, there is something of Beat Zen in these images. Yet, notwithstanding these similarities, Beat Zen seems to lack vital elements of Zen tradition. It has, for

---

[21] I should point out that it is not clear that all those writers conventionally classified as 'Beat' in fact subscribed to the conception of Zen that is referred to as Beat Zen. Some Beat writers – Gary Snyder and Philip Whalen, for instance – are, or have been, ordained Zen Buddhist priests, and are hence in a better position than I to gauge what is the 'correct' interpretation of Zen and what is not.

[22] See the discussion of this Ox-herding picture in Philip Kapleau, *The Three Pillars of Zen: Teaching, Practice, and Enlightenment* (London: Rider, 1985), pp.323-4.

instance, little to say on the discipline needed in spiritual practice. Zen traditions certainly advocate meditating in the midst of worldly activity, but this is advocated as an ideal, and, moreover, an ideal which can only be attained after a fair few hours have been spent in more formal practice, sitting in the *zendō* following one's breath, for example. Even if everyone's true nature is inherently pure, not everyone is a Hui-neng, and those who claim to have achieved awakening with little effort and no sanction are probably deluded. In this connection, it is worth remembering that the bare-chested sage depicted in the tenth Ox-herding picture has had to pass through the preceding nine stages of attainment to get there.

The idea of a freewheeling philosophy of life in which responsibility is abdicated for a '*carpe diem*' attitude would also seem to be out of keeping with the other-regarding tendencies of Zen. For, as we saw in Chapter Two, Zen practice is not just a personal matter of developing one's insight, it also embodies a keen sense of ethical responsibility in line with its Mahāyāna heritage. And from a Mahāyāna perspective, it could be argued that someone who lived a carefree, irresponsible life ever centred on the present moment would have failed to appreciate the other-regarding nature of the *Bodhisattva* Path, and would to that extent have fallen short of the selflessness and empathy integral to awakening. One could argue that a genuinely enlightened individual would instead feel an acute sense of responsibility for all beings. (And in this regard it could be noted that the Zen sage of the tenth Ox-herding picture is not a freewheeling thrill seeker but a *Bodhisattva*; and as a *Bodhisattva* he immerses himself in the evils of the world, not in a quest for new experiences, but to rescue beings from the round of *saṃsāra*.)

The idea of condensation could, once again, be used – as a skilful means, one might say – to engender such a sense of responsibility for one's actions. For in the light of that idea it would seem that each of one's actions is not a self-sufficient, isolated event, but the focus of a vast network of relations extending throughout time and space. In the words of deLancey Kapleau:

> The least act, such as eating or scratching an arm, is not at all simple. It is merely a visible moment in a network of causes and effects reaching forward into Unknowingness and back into an infinity of Silence...[23]

Waxing lyrical, one could say that to experience condensation is to realize that one's actions reverberate throughout the universe.[24] And this realization would

---

[23] Quoted in Ibid. p.280.

[24] One might suppose that the realization that each of one's actions gathers all reality would lead to a kind of paralysis, that overawed by the cosmic significance of all her deeds, the enlightened woman would find herself unable to act. However, a subject thus paralysed would, I think, be suffering from an attachment to the cosmic significance of things similar to the attachment to holiness described above. Just as the 'master' described in that section felt disinclined to act on account of his belief that all things are the Buddha-nature, so a subject paralysed by the cosmic significance of each of her actions could be said to be attached to the idea of condensation. By contrast, the genuinely enlightened subject would recognize that even her *in*action gathers all things, and that there is therefore no possibility of evading responsibility by not acting.

seem to have implications for ethics. As Philip Kapleau writes: 'the satori-realization that one is the focus of past and future time and space unavoidably carries with it a sense of fellowship and responsibility to one's family and society as a whole, alike to those who came before and those who will follow one'.[25]

Feeling the significance of one's actions in this way would seem to be intimately connected not just with other-regarding virtues such as compassion, but also with the virtue of mindfulness. For it seems reasonable to suppose that someone who felt the spiritual gravity of their actions would be motivated to be more mindful of them. In our ordinary, un-mindful 'samsaric' existence the greater proportion of our actions pass us by. On a typical evening I might find myself – or rather I *don't* find myself, that's precisely the point – slumped in my favourite chair, my arm reaching for my beer, the fingers of my other hand drumming mechanically on the TV remote. I am, perhaps, dimly aware of these actions, but I am not mindful of them. Here, as ever, I am travelling through my life with the curtains drawn. Developing mindfulness is, to a large extent, a matter of rendering these habitual actions perspicuous. It is a matter of realizing when one is slouching, of becoming aware when one is reaching for a beer, of opening one's eyes and realizing what it is one is doing right at this very moment.

It is important not to be distracted by the word 'mindful' here: becoming mindful of one's habitual actions is as much a matter of training the body as it is of training the mind. Jane Howarth has drawn attention to the fact that many of our unsustainable practices (not turning the kitchen light off, throwing the beer can in the waste bin rather than taking it to the recycling facility, and so on) are habitual.[26] Drawing upon the work of Maurice Merleau-Ponty, she argues that habitual actions are not the effects of 'consciousness directing bodily movement', but are rather manifestations of an implicit kind of bodily intelligence.[27] In these situations, one's body knows what to do, even in the absence of a determining mental attitude. Certainly, to render these practices perspicuous we must reflect on them; however, the fact remains that these habitual actions are as much bodily comportments as they are frames of mind. In this regard, it is worth noting that the literature of radical environmental ethics abounds with accounts (often caricatures) of the dominant 'modern Western' *mind*set – faith in the power of reason, a belief in the value of progress, a sense of separation from nature, and so on. Could one also speak of a characteristically Western bodily comportment? Perhaps, for instance, Western Man – or better, Technological Man – has forgotten the sensuous pleasure intrinsic to eating, and only consumes in order to live. He grabs an energy bar on the way to work to stand in for breakfast; he gobbles down his five servings of fruit and vegetables to keep healthy. He is an efficient eater. And what of the rest of his bodily life? How does Technological Man move? Does he have a characteristic posture? How does he breathe?

Let us recap the argument so far. I have suggested that contemplating the phenomenon of condensation can induce a sense of the significance of one's

---

[25] Kapleau, *The Three Pillars of Zen*, p.18.
[26] In Vernon Pratt, *Environment and Philosophy* (London: Routledge, 2000), p.71.
[27] Ibid. p.70.

actions. Moreover, I have argued that such a sense can foster the development of mindfulness, a virtue which can be directed towards one's habitual actions. But what is the connection with ethics here? One might suppose that we cannot be held *responsible* in any ethical sense for our habitual actions since they are by definition not the result of deliberation on our part. It could be argued that when I unthinkingly throw the beer can in the bin rather than setting it to one side to be recycled, I am not acting *immorally* because I have not consciously performed this action. If I had considered the action – acknowledged, for instance, that I ought to recycle the can but had not done so – then, and only then, could I be considered to be responsible for it.

It is interesting to note in this connection that Aristotle would not have agreed with this argument. For Aristotle, we are responsible for even our habitual actions because these actions result from deliberations we have made in the past concerning what sort of actions we can tolerate ourselves performing. As Terence Irwin notes:

> Aristotle's search for the origin of an action leads him beyond the actual causal sequence to the agent's attitude and character. Even if I act without deliberation and premeditation on a sudden impulse of emotion or appetite, the origin may still be in my character and decision; for the presence or strength of my desire may be the result of the character and decisions I have formed. I may have deliberately cultivated this sort of impulse, or I may have failed to do what I could reasonably be expected to do to prevent its growth. If my voluntary actions are related in this way to my decision and character, their origin is still in *me* in the relevant sense, and I am fairly held responsible for them.[28]

Like Aristotle, Zen seeks to bring our habitual actions within the purview of ethics. We are invited to become mindful of our habits, to try to identify those that are harmful, and to try to rid ourselves of them. Such reflections might, for example, encourage us to consider that every time we unthinkingly flick the light switch or leave the television on 'standby', we are, most likely, drawing upon energy generated by the combustion of fossil fuels, and are therefore making our own small contribution to global warming. Reflecting on the way in which any particular action 'gathers' a wider context can serve to focus our attention on even the smallest habitual acts (and here, once again, the idea of condensation can serve as a skilful means). Eating one's breakfast, one could contemplate the various conditions that must obtain in order to put the Frosted Flakes in the bowl: the grain nourished by the rays of the sun and by rainwater evaporated from the oceans of the world; the workers in the fields where the grain is harvested, and in the factories where it is processed into cereal, and in the shops where it is sold; the multinationals that control the production of the food and its delivery. Far from abdicating her responsibility for the solace of the present moment, the meditator feels her sense of responsibility fanning out to encompass all beings.

---

[28] Quoted in Louke van Wensveen, *Dirty Virtues: The Emergence of Ecological Virtue Ethics* (New York: Humanity Books, 2000), pp.104-5. Emphasis in original.

Maintaining such an expansive conception of things in the midst of the distractions of daily life is, however, no easy task. Short verses or *gathas* are therefore used to remind one to be mindful at every moment. Here's one from Thich Nhat Hanh, which can be used before every meal:

> In this food,
> I see clearly the presence
> of the entire universe
> supporting my existence.[29]

Here's another one, from the *Avataṃsaka Sūtra*:

> When it is time to stop and sleep,
> I vow with all beings
> to find peaceful retirement
> and a heart that is undisturbed.[30]

All this might seem very sugary sweet, and quite unpalatable to some readers. But references to the virtues of mindfulness are not the sole province of New Age sentimentalism. No lesser figure than Dōgen, for instance – himself no sentimental chap – placed great emphasis on the value of mindfulness in one's daily life. Returning from China, where he had been impressed by the spiritual significance accorded even ostensibly menial tasks in Chinese monasteries, he inculcated in his monks the virtues of maintaining mindfulness at all times, even when brushing one's teeth or using the toilet. Such mindfulness, he said, was a form of *zazen* in action.[31]

Some readers might worry that to maintain such a degree of mindfulness and to feel thus responsible for all one's actions would be to live in a state of constant guilt, continually worrying about the effects of one's actions on the environment. And this image would chime with the popular perception of environmentalists as killjoys, green Puritans. But Zen advocates no such thing. On the contrary, to be mindful at all times is to thoroughly appreciate life, to drink deeply of each moment, rather than being dulled by apathy or carried away by distraction. It is this that represents the 'live for the moment' philosophy of Zen. And, as we have seen, it is a philosophy shot through with an awareness of the consequences of one's actions and an acute sense of responsibility for all beings.

Practice and politics

The third accusation of quietism accuses Zen of promoting a withdrawal from worldly affairs into a life of passive contemplation. This charge is, once again,

---

[29] 'Meal Verses' in Kaza and Kraft, *Dharma Rain*, p.448.
[30] Quoted in Aitken, *The Mind of Clover*, p.103.
[31] Ibid. p.131.

nicely put by Ruben L. F. Habito when he writes that the 'inward turn of the Zen practitioner can militate against a commitment to an ecologically viable way of life in this way: the emphasis on "listening within" may lead to a dichotomous view of the "within" and the "without," to the extent that the practitioner disengages from the concerns of the rest of society, diminishing the individual's interest in and engagement with events in the world "outside"'.[32]

This charge calls to mind an image we have encountered before: the Eastern mystic, withdrawn from the world into a life of passive navel-gazing. There are certainly strands of Zen spirituality that seem to confirm this image – think, for instance, of Bodhidharma's legendary nine years of wall-gazing – but, on the whole, as it evolved, Zen developed a more this-worldly approach to spirituality. This development was to a large extent due to the Chinese social context within which Ch'an developed. In India, monks had traditionally been supported by the donation of alms by the laity (a transaction which, it must be noted, was not only one-way, for while the monks received food, the lay donors were thought of as receiving the more precious gift of the *Dharma*). Indeed, the *Vinaya* code for the conduct of monks expressly prohibited productive work. As we saw in Chapter One, this ban on manual labour jarred with the communitarian spirit of the Chinese, and particularly incensed the indigenous Confucians, who accused Buddhists of being freeloaders and economic parasites.[33] In answer, no doubt, to criticisms of this sort, the fourth Zen patriarch, Tao-hsin, instituted a set of reforms and so established a distinctively Chinese, communitarian form of monasticism. His conception of a monastery as a self-sufficient community caught on in China, with the result that by the early ninth century, many Zen monasteries were large enough to provide shelter, food and clothing for considerable numbers of monks and visitors. One monastery was said to have housed up to a thousand practitioners.[34]

In communities of this size, productive labour must have been a central concern, and indeed these social changes were accompanied by a new conception of the spiritual significance of work. This new attitude was exemplified in Hung-chou Zen. We saw in Chapter One that Hung-chou masters such as Ma-tsu had become convinced that undertaking some specific form of spiritual practice – more precisely, meditation – in the hope of attaining some remote goal, enlightenment, implied that practice involved striving to become something one was not. Yet if we are, each of us, already imbued with an inherently pure Buddha-nature, then viewing one's efforts in this way must be both misguided and misguiding. That is why Ma-tsu stressed that awakening is not something 'out there', external to us, but present here and now in the midst of one's everyday, worldly activities. And if this is the case, then, awakening can be manifested, not only in meditation, but in

---

[32] Habito, 'Mountains and Rivers and the Great Earth: Zen and Ecology', p.166. Note that, once again, Habito is criticizing this quietist reading of Zen.

[33] Fletcher and Scott, *Way of Zen*, p.57.

[34] Dale S. Wright, 'Four Ch'an masters' in Takeuchi Yoshinori (ed.), *Buddhist Spirituality: Later China, Korea, Japan, and The Modern World* (London: SCM Press, 1999), p.34. But see Wright, *Philosophical Meditations on Zen Buddhism* (Cambridge: Cambridge University Press, 1998), p.122, n.13.

any practice. Against the backdrop of these thoughts, even chopping wood and carrying water, ostensibly the most menial of tasks, could be viewed as spiritual practices.[35]

So in the calloused hands of Zen teachers such as Ma-tsu, the Mahāyāna teaching of the inherent purity of the Buddha-nature (combined, perhaps, with the Taoist conception of *wu-wei* manifested in one's practical engagement with the world) gave birth to a down-to-earth, distinctively Chinese conception of spirituality, one far removed from any denial of the world. The charge that Zen is solely concerned with passive navel-gazing is to this extent misguided.

Before continuing in our response to this charge, however, we should perhaps pause for a moment to consider the differences between Zen traditions on this matter. So far, we have been using the example of Hung-chou Zen to counter the accusation of quietism, and in doing this we have examined its criticisms of contemplative practices. However, it is easy to exaggerate the degree to which these traditions distanced themselves from meditative practice. The Hung-chou masters might have criticized the practice of meditation, but they did not abandon it altogether.[36] On the other hand, even those Zen traditions, such as Sōtō, that stress the importance of meditation, emphasize that *zazen* must ultimately be integrated into one's life, and that the intense awareness cultivated in the practice should be maintained in all one's activities (as we saw, Dōgen saw this as being of paramount importance).

Yet even if it is accepted that Zen subscribes to a this-worldly spirituality, one far removed from the caricature of the navel-gazing Eastern mystic, the objection could still be raised that the spirituality it advocates has little relevance for environmental ethics. Chopping wood and carrying water may be very worthy spiritual actions, if performed in the right manner, but what use are they in the face of environmental problems? Global environmental issues such as acid rain, desertification, international laws controlling the trade in animal products: all these require political action, and chopping wood and carrying water are hardly political actions. Perhaps, then, the objection that Zen advocates a rejection of social and political responsibility cannot be dismissed so easily.

Let us consider what precisely is being objected to here. If the charge is that political actions, such as lending one's voice to a political protest, cannot be spiritual practices, then it would seem to be misguided. If the Way can be manifested in *any* activities – excluding, presumably, activities that necessarily involve delusions, such as cock-fighting or badger-baiting – then it can be manifested even in political action – in environmental activism, for instance. It seems likely that many politically-engaged Zen Buddhists do indeed think of their efforts in this way. For instance, a recent anthology of essays on Buddhist environmentalism includes one section entitled 'Environmental Activism as Buddhist Practice', which consists of articles by such noted Buddhist teachers as

---

[35] Wright, 'Four Ch'an masters', p.36.

[36] Ibid. p.34. Kapleau argues that Hung-chou masters like Ma-tsu did not reject the practice of meditation, but only the idea that practice involves becoming something that one is not. That, he suggests, was the meaning of Nan-yüeh's 'polishing the tile' simile. See Kapleau, *The Three Pillars of Zen*, pp.23-5.

Philip Kapleau, the former abbot of the Rochester Zen Center, and Norman Fischer, former abbot of the Green Gulch Zen Center. To be sure, for the great majority of people it seems unlikely that sitting in an environmental protest, say, is as effective as a *spiritual* practice as the same amount of time spent in *zazen*; but it can nonetheless be a spiritual practice to a certain extent, especially when conducted by seasoned practitioners such as Kapleau and Fischer.

The charge that Zen is apolitical could be read in another way, however. It could be argued that even if some Zen Buddhists see their political action as a form of spiritual practice, Zen teachings do not themselves yield any political prescriptions. One response to this objection has already been given earlier in this chapter: Zen is concerned with self-development not with policy. Consequently, any effects it has in the political arena will be the result of changes wrought at the level of individuals. As William Ophuls puts it, a Buddhist's 'primary duty is to bring about benign changes *in himself*; indeed, for a Buddhist this is the chief way in which society can be improved, because the good society can be created only from the bottom up, not from the top down'.[37]

As one would expect, this lack of concern with policy has meant that Zen has traditionally been politically conservative.[38] Moreover, and more worryingly, this conservatism has occasionally led Zen Buddhists to accept, tacitly, and sometimes even actively support oppressive regimes in East Asia (think, for instance, of the endorsement given by some Zen figures to Japanese militarization prior to World War Two).[39] Some writers have made the further argument that Zen is in fact naturally inclined to political conservatism by its commitment to the idea that all things are the Buddha-nature and hence manifest spiritual perfection just as they are. Thus Noriaki Hakamaya argues that in Japan the concept of the Buddha-nature of all things is part of a constellation of ideas which together militate against criticism and reform of the social order. For if all things are inherently enlightened and if the world is, just as it is, in a state of spiritual harmony, then what motivation can there be to criticize the existing order? Moreover, it has been suggested that this inherent conservatism fosters, not only social inequalities, but also a lack of environmental concern, more precisely, 'an irresponsible "hands-off" disposition that contributes to pollution, reckless use of natural resources [and] littering...'.[40]

This criticism calls to mind our discussion, earlier in this chapter, of the Zen 'master' surveying the strip-mining of a mountainside, loathe to interfere in what he sees as a manifestation of spiritual perfection. I argued that someone who actually saw things in this way would not be enlightened but would instead be

---

[37] William Ophuls, 'Notes for a Buddhist Politics' in Kaza and Kraft, *Dharma Rain*, p.373. See also Philip Kapleau, 'Responsibility and Social Action' in Kaza and Kraft, *Dharma Rain*, p.242.

[38] Ives, *Zen Awakening*, pp.67-9.

[39] See Ibid. p.64.

[40] As reported by Paul L. Swanson, 'Why they say Zen is not Buddhism: recent Japanese critiques of Buddha-nature' in Jamie Hubbard and Paul L. Swanson (eds), *Pruning the Bodhi Tree: The Storm over Critical Buddhism* (Honolulu: University of Hawai'i Press, 1997), p.28.

harbouring a lingering attachment to the idea of the perfection or holiness of things, and I suggested that the genuinely enlightened individual would, by contrast, see the strip-mining for what it was – a harm – and would take steps to prevent it. That said, it must be conceded that critics such as Hakamaya are not primarily concerned with the question of how an enlightened subject would experience the world. If I understand their objections correctly, they are referring to the social implications of the idea of the universal Buddha-nature. And here, I think, they may have a point.

So, does the idea of the Buddha-nature of all things contribute to an attitude of quiet acceptance of environmental problems in Japan? Whatever its causes, the Japanese track record on environmental issues is certainly far from encouraging. Cases of significant industrial heavy metal pollution stretching back even to the Tokugawa era are well documented, and industrial pollution remains a problem in the country, dioxin emissions from waste incineration plants and the prevalence of photochemical smog in the major cities being recent causes for concern. The Japanese landscape has, moreover, been inundated with monoculture forests raised for clear cutting, and even the most inaccessible mountain streams have been dammed. Japanese companies contribute to deforestation in Southeast Asia, and continue to engage in drift-net fishing and whaling. Furthermore, studies have found that the Japanese people are singularly poorly informed and unconcerned about environmental matters when compared with, say, North Americans.[41]

Now the fact that Japan has environmental problems is not especially significant in itself. What country hasn't? The puzzle is to explain how these problems could have occurred in a land in which, as D. T. Suzuki had it, nature has been traditionally treated as a 'constant friend and companion'.[42] It could be argued that the country's environmental troubles are the result of the Japanese having rushed to embrace Western technology, and having forgotten, in the process, their intellectual heritage and the love of nature it embodied.[43] This thesis would, however, seem to be undermined by evidence of anthropogenic environmental devastation on the islands prior to the Meiji Restoration.[44] By contrast, some commentators have suggested that indigenous conceptions of the natural world might actually have contributed to Japan's environmental problems. For writers such as Arne Kalland, the traditional Japanese 'love of nature' – if it may be so described – is in fact directed towards a highly stylized aesthetic abstraction: a world of picturesque landscapes viewed from afar, of gardens carefully arranged to give the semblance of naturalness, of aesthetic symbols (the cherry blossom, the

---

[41] See Arne Kalland and Pamela J. Asquith, 'Japanese Perceptions of Nature: Ideals and Illusions' in Pamela J. Asquith and Arne Kalland (eds), *Japanese Images of Nature: Cultural Perspectives* (Richmond: Curzon, 1997), pp.6-7. See also J. Baird Callicott, *Earth's Insights: A Survey of Ecological Ethics from the Mediterranean Basin to the Australian Outback* (Berekley: University of California Press, 1994), pp.102-3.
[42] Suzuki, *Zen and Japanese Culture*, p.334.
[43] This is the diagnosis proffered by Allan G. Grapard. See his essay 'Nature and Culture in Japan' in Michael Tobias (ed.), *Deep Ecology* (San Diego, CA: Avant Books, 1985), pp.240-55.
[44] See Kalland and Asquith, 'Japanese Perceptions of Nature', pp.5-6.

moon, pine trees glimpsed through the rain) to be captured in verse for the edification of human beings.[45] Moreover, the argument continues, there is no place in this singularly anthropocentric view of nature for the preservation of wild things for what they are in themselves, irrespective of their relations to human beings. Indeed, Kalland argues that the Japanese have an 'abhorrence towards nature in the raw'.[46] In the light of these thoughts, it would seem that the Japanese sensitivity to nature is far removed from the concerns of Western environmentalists. Augustin Berque argues that it was for that reason that 'the Japanese could at the same time love and respect nature and beauty, on the one hand, and on the other let their environment become, during the sixties, one of the most polluted and disfigured in the world'.[47] Perhaps, as critics such as Hakamaya suggest, environmental concerns could be neglected in this way because of a quietist attitude fostered, to some extent, by the conception of the Buddha-nature of all things. Further work will be needed to determine whether this is in fact the case.

However, whether this turns out to be the case or not, I do not see why Zen need be inherently conservative and quietist. One could argue that, although self-development is its primary focus, ideas inspired by Zen Buddhist teachings could be used as the basis for a critique of modern society. Kapleau is endorsing this idea when he asks, rhetorically, whether there is hypocrisy in 'a Buddhism that lectures individuals on their delusions, but has nothing to say about the deluding political and economic conditions that reinforce these'.[48] Indeed, from a Buddhist perspective one could make all sorts of criticisms of existing social orders. One could argue that material inequalities in the world, and in particular those between the richest and poorest nations, are so marked that people either lack the minimal material conditions needed to pursue the *Dharma* or find themselves so distracted by the buzz and whirl of consumer society that they are unwilling to make the effort to develop themselves as people. One could argue, further, that capitalism takes selfishness to be a fact of human nature rather than a problem to be solved; that it encourages excessive consumption, rather than regarding greed as a vice; that it tranquillizes its citizens through the media and through an education system that upholds the value of instrumental rationality to the detriment of training in character.[49] And if there is no reason why Zen need be politically quietist, then there is also no reason why it must remain silent on practical environmental issues. One could draw upon Buddhist teachings in arguing that drift-net fishing and whaling are acts of violence, and hence opposed to the virtue of *ahiṃsā*, as, less obviously, are excessive logging and shortsighted damming policies, and, perhaps, the planting of monoculture forests. Or one could argue that the profligate consumption of resources and the wasteful attitudes it brings in tow are the

---

[45] See, for instance, Arne Kalland, 'Culture in Japanese Nature' in Ole Bruun and Arne Kalland, *Asian Perceptions of Nature: A Critical Approach* (Richmond: Curzon, 1996), pp.243-57.

[46] Ibid. p.254.

[47] Quoted in Callicott, *Earths Insights*, p.105.

[48] Kapleau, 'Responsibility and Social Action', p.244.

[49] See Ophuls, 'Notes for a Buddhist Politics' for interesting discussions of these and other suggestions.

expressions of the vice of greed; or that trade in endangered species, or some forms of animal experimentation, or battery farming, create suffering – *vast* amounts of suffering – and should therefore be condemned from a Buddhist standpoint. Or one could argue, more positively, that concern for the environment can be analysed into a variety of virtues – compassion, say, or non-violence or mindfulness – which it ought to be the job of the education system to foster.

These are only bare sketches of some directions that such a line of enquiry might take. In this book, I have not been primarily concerned with these sorts of practical prescriptions. My aim has instead been to show the role of environmental concern in human well-being. Yet I think that the general attempt to derive practical prescriptions from Buddhist ideas is potentially fruitful, and a project worth continuing, so long as it does not degenerate into the presentation of unrealistic political or environmental utopias. I will not continue this line of enquiry here, however. For this is a book specifically about Zen Buddhism, and although the practical prescriptions canvassed above have been inspired by Buddhist teachings and are apparently in keeping with Zen, they are not specifically *Zen* Buddhist. But does this mean that a Zen Buddhist need have no truck with them?

Conclusion

The negative aim of this book was to refute a set of objections to the idea that Zen might have anything to contribute to environmental ethics. To this end, Chapters Two through Five, aimed to refute four theses: 1) Zen is amoral, and therefore cannot be used as the basis for an ethic of any sort; 2) Zen is anthropocentric, and so cannot yield an environmental ethic; 3) Zen cannot accommodate any conception of the intrinsic value of things; and 4) Zen is irredeemably quietist and otherworldly, and so can have no bearing on practical environmental matters. By writing about the philosophical ramifications of Zen, I have also tried to refute the general idea that Zen is mystical nonsense not amenable to serious academic investigation.

It is possible that the very act of articulating these objections has planted worries in the heads of readers that were not already there. So maybe now readers find themselves troubled by the thought that Zen might be inherently quietistic (for example) when they formerly entertained no doubts in this area. In response to this possibility, I can only say that this is necessarily a risk that must be taken by any author who wishes to deal fairly with criticisms of Zen. In each chapter, I tried to show why anyone might think the theses articulated above compelling, before attempting to refute them. So to show that Zen is not quietistic, I first tried to explain why anyone might think it quietistic in the first place. If, however, this book has achieved its (negative) aim, readers who had been inclined to doubt the intellectual credibility of Zen for the reasons canvassed above will now be persuaded otherwise. I hope that anyone thus persuaded will now feel free to turn to the practice of Zen. But even if they do not, and whether or not they share my belief that Zen has much to offer environmental ethics, I hope to have shown that there is an illuminating discussion to be had here, that the debate concerning Zen and environmental ethics is a live one. To say this is to reject two possibilities. It is to reject the assumption made in many of the more popular accounts of Zen that the tradition is unquestionably environmentalist, and that no argument is needed to support this conclusion. It is also to reject the assumption that anyone who draws the conclusion that Zen does in fact have something to offer environmental ethics must be uncritically accepting the fashionable or romantic view that Zen is inherently 'green'. These are both extreme views and I reject them.

I chose to adopt a negative aim in this book in order to avoid giving the impression that my purpose was to congeal Zen Buddhism into a philosophical theory, for that would be a project wholly opposed to the anti-intellectualist spirit of the tradition. So, for example, I was careful to point out in Chapter Four that my aim was not to argue that Zen does in fact subscribe to the thesis that things have intrinsic value, but to counter the unsound argument that because of its commitment to the teaching of emptiness, Zen would not be able to accommodate any conception of intrinsic value. Nevertheless, for all my care to avoid theorization, it is clear that through the course of this book a specific philosophical theory, a particular environmental ethic, has taken shape. Before turning to the question of whether this means that I have, contrary to my wishes, congealed Zen into a philosophical theory, let us consider what this theory actually amounts to.

I have argued that certain character traits – primarily, insight, compassion, non-violence, selflessness and mindfulness – are environmental virtues. In calling these traits *environmental* virtues I have meant that they each have implications for our relations to the non-human environment. In calling them environmental *virtues* I have meant that they are constituents of well-being, so that to live the most fulfilling kind of life is to live a life that exemplifies insight, compassion, non-violence, and so on. I have followed Buddhist tradition in maintaining that the most fulfilling kind of life is the enlightened life, one marked by a sense of joy, freedom, appreciation of beauty, warm feelings for others, as well as the satisfaction of knowing the true nature of things.

I have argued that the virtue of insight (*prajñā*) expresses itself in a certain comportment towards the world. To have developed this virtue would be to have attained the kind of intimacy with things one might associate with an artist. To see a thing with the 'eye of *prajñā*' would not be to see it as an object standing over against oneself, but to have 'become' the thing, as Zen Buddhists say. I have suggested that to have the virtue of insight would be to treat things as having an intrinsic value, that the insightful man or woman would not regard whatever being he or she was faced with merely as a resource, but would instead see it as having a non-instrumental value. Hence insight is an *environmental* virtue.

I have argued that this kind of insight into the nature of things is not confined to the sphere of the intellect, but arises and persists in dependence upon other more practical virtues. That is to say that as one internalizes the teachings of emptiness, etc., and so develops the virtue of insight, one also learns to feel and act in ways appropriate to that vision of the world. Hence insight comes as part of a 'package deal', bound up with virtues such as compassion, non-violence, selflessness and mindfulness. Moreover, like insight, these virtues are environmental virtues in the sense that they imply certain kinds of positive regard for the non-human environment. Thus to be compassionate is to feel compassion for all sentient beings, human and non-human, and to act so as to alleviate their suffering. To be non-violent is to treat all beings with respect and not as merely instrumentally valuable. To be selfless is not to be self-abnegating, but to be non-attached to oneself, and to therefore be free of the desire to greedily consume as many natural resources as possible. To be mindful is to have made one's actions one's own, not to be carried through life by the inertia of habit, and to be aware of the consequences of one's actions, environmental or otherwise.

So does this environmental ethic represent an attempt to congeal Zen Buddhism into a philosophical theory? Is this my account of 'Zen thought', all nicely tied up and expressed in under a thousand words? It is not. For one thing, it is not clear that such a thing as 'Zen thought' exists. Perhaps Zen is unified, not by a set of doctrines, but by a set of practices, so that what makes a Zen Buddhist a Zen Buddhist is not their subscribing to a particular set of ideas but their engaging in a particular family of practices, *zazen*, say. In any case, even if such a thing as 'Zen thought' were to exist, it would certainly not be a monolithic entity. The Zen of Bodhidharma is, as we have seen, quite different from the Zen of Hui-neng, which is, in turn, quite different from the Zen of Dōgen. In this book – or rather in Chapters Two through Five – I have drawn indiscriminately from various Zen traditions as I saw fit in order to make this or that particular point. So in Chapter Two I advised critics who think Zen amoral to look again at the writings of Hui-neng. Or in Chapter Four I tried to show that the work of Dōgen could be drawn upon to counter the idea that Zen cannot accommodate any conception of the intrinsic value of things. In sketching the philosophical position that has emerged in the course of this book, I have drawn together my claims from each chapter. But in doing this I have gathered together a variety of different forms of Zen into a sort of Zen Buddhist casserole: Dōgen mixed with Hui-neng, with a dash of Ma-tsu, garnished with a pinch of D. T. Suzuki, and so on. For this reason, it ought not to be assumed that the philosophical position outlined above represents any particular form of Zen Buddhism. Perhaps no such form ever existed. In view of this, I would like the philosophical position developed above to be thought of as an environmental ethic *inspired* by Zen Buddhism, rather than a 'Zen Buddhist environmental ethic'. It may have been inspired by Zen, but it does not represent Zen, and it therefore stands or falls on its own merits. And so if the negative result of this book was to refute a series of objections to the idea that Zen might have anything to contribute to environmental ethics, the positive result was to develop an environmental ethic inspired by Zen.

Shunryu Suzuki's *Zen Mind, Beginner's Mind*; Robert Aitken's *The Mind of Clover* – these are 'Zen books' in the sense that they are written by accomplished Zen teachers and convey something of the spirit of Zen. I, on the other hand, have written a book *about* Zen. And like most books about Zen, this one has made Zen out to be more complicated than it in fact is. It might have given the misleading impression that to achieve any insight into Zen one must come to understand some very abstruse matters regarding the conceptual connections between virtue and well-being and the internal relatedness of things, and so on. But Zen is simpler than this book has made it out to be. Zen teachers assure us that one does not have to get one's head around the abstruse philosophy of emptiness and so on in order to attain *satori*. It is said that by simply practising Zen – by concentrating on the breath, say, or on *Mu* – these matters will resolve themselves of their own accord, so that through practice one will come directly to experience the world in the way Buddhist texts describe it. It is said that one will then recognize that all philosophical descriptions of the world fail to hit the mark. On this note, it is perhaps time to take our leave of philosophy for the moment. One can become too attached to philosophy, as to anything else.

Bibliography

Abe, Masao. *Zen and Western Thought*, edited by William LaFleur (Honolulu: University of Hawaii Press, 1989).

Aitken, Robert. *The Mind of Clover: Essays in Zen Buddhist Ethics* (San Francisco: North Point Press, 1984).

Aitken, Robert. 'Gandhi, Dogen and Deep Ecology', in George Sessions, *Deep Ecology: Living as if Nature Mattered* (Salt Lake City: Peregrine Smith Books, 1985), pp.232-5.

Anscombe, G. E. M. 'Modern Moral Philosophy', *Philosophy* 33 (1958): 1-19.

Aristotle. *Nicomachean Ethics*, translated by David Ross, revised by J. L. Ackrill and J. O. Urmson (Oxford: Oxford University Press, 1998).

Austin, James H. *Zen and the Brain* (Cambridge, Mass: MIT Press, 2000).

Baron, M. W., Petit, P. and Slote, M. *Three Methods in Ethics: A Debate* (Oxford: Blackwell, 1997).

Bayley, John. *Iris: A Memoir of Iris Murdoch* (London: Duckworth, 1998).

Belshaw, Christopher. *Environmental Philosophy: reason, nature and human concern* (Teddington: Acumen, 2001).

Blofeld, John (translator). *The Zen Teaching of Huang Po on the Transmission of Mind* (London: The Buddhist Society, 1968).

Bradley, F. H. *Essays on Truth and Reality* (Oxford: Clarendon Press, 1914).

Bradley, F. H. *Appearance and Reality* (Oxford: Clarendon Press, 1930).

Brear, A. D. 'The nature and status of moral behavior in Zen Buddhist tradition', *Philosophy East and West* 24, no.4 (1974): 429-41.

Burton, David. 'Is Madhyamaka Buddhism Really the Middle Way? Emptiness and the Problem of Nihilism', *Contemporary Buddhism* 2, No.2 (2001): 177-90.

Buswell, Robert E. 'The Koryo Period', in Takeuchi Yoshinori (ed.), *Buddhist Spirituality: Later China, Korea, Japan and the Modern World* (London: SCM Press, 1999), pp.79-108.

Cafaro, Philip. 'Thoreau, Leopold, and Carson: Toward an Environmental Virtue Ethics', *Environmental Ethics* 22 (Spring 2001): 3-17.

Callicott, J. Baird. *Earth's Insights: A Survey of Ecological Ethics from the Mediterranean Basin to the Australian Outback* (Berkeley: University of California Press, 1994).

Callicott, J. Baird. 'The Conceptual Foundations of the Land Ethic' in Louis P. Pojman (ed.), *Environmental Ethics: Readings in Theory and Application* (Belmont, California: Wadsworth, 2001), pp.126-36.

Callicott, J. Baird. 'Animal Liberation: A Triangular Affair', in Louis P. Pojman, (ed.), *Environmental Ethics: Readings in Theory and Application* (Belmont, California: Wadsworth, 2001), pp.52-63.

Chang, G. C. C. *The Practice of Zen* (London: Rider & Company, 1960).

Chapple, Christopher Key. *Nonviolence to Animals, Earth, and Self in Asian Traditions* (Albany: SUNY Press, 1993).

Chapple, Christopher Key. 'Jainism and Buddhism', in Dale Jamieson, *A Companion to Environmental Philosophy* (Oxford: Blackwell, 2001), pp.52-66.

Chuang-tzu. *See under* Palmer, Martin.

Ching, Julia. 'The Encounter of Ch'an with Confucianism', in Takeuchi Yoshinori (ed.), *Buddhist Spirituality: Later China, Korea, Japan, and the Modern World* (London: SCM Press, 1999), pp.44-53.

Cleary, Thomas. *Entry into the Inconceivable: An Introduction to Hua-yen Buddhism* (Honolulu: University of Hawaii Press, 1983).

Cleary, Thomas. *Rational Zen: the Mind of Dōgen Zenji* (Boston: Shambhala, 1992).

Conze, Edward (translator). *The Large Sutra on Perfect Wisdom* (Delhi: Motilal Banarsidass, 1990).

Cook, Francis H. 'The Jewel Net of Indra', in J. Baird Callicott and Roger T. Ames (eds), *Nature in Asian Traditions of Thought* (Albany: State University of New York Press, 2001), pp.213-29.

Cooper, David E. *World Philosophies: an historical introduction, 2nd edition* (Oxford: Blackwell, 2003).

Cooper, David E. and James, Simon P. *Buddhism, Virtue and Environment* (Ashgate, forthcoming).

Curtin, Deane. 'Dōgen, Deep Ecology, and the Ecological Self', *Environmental Ethics* 16, No.2 (summer 1994): 195-213.

Curtin, Deane. 'A State of Mind Like Water: Ecosophy T and the Buddhist Traditions', *Inquiry* 39, (1996): 239-53.

Devall, B. and Sessions, G. 'Deep Ecology', in Louis P. Pojman (ed.), *Environmental Ethics: Readings in Theory and Application* (Belmont, California: Wadsworth, 2001), pp.157-61.

Dōgen. *See under* Nishiyama, K. and Stevens, J. *and* Masunaga, Reihō.

Dumoulin, Heinrich. *Zen Buddhism: A History. Vol.1: India and China* (New York: Macmillan, 1988).

Dumoulin, Heinrich. *Zen Buddhism: A History. Vol.2: Japan* (New York: Macmillan, 1990).

Eckel, Malcolm David, 'Is there a Buddhist Philosophy of Nature?', in Mary Evelyn Tucker and Duncan Ryūken Williams (eds), *Buddhism and Ecology: the interconnection of dharma and deeds* (Cambridge, Massachusetts: Harvard University Press, 1997), pp.327-49.

Elliot, Robert. 'Environmental Ethics', in Peter Singer, *A Companion to Ethics* (Oxford: Blackwell, 1993), pp.284-93.

Elliot, Robert. *Faking Nature: the ethics of environmental restoration* (London: Routledge, 1997).

Elliot, Robert. 'Normative ethics', in Dale Jamieson (ed.), *A Companion to Environmental Philosophy* (Oxford: Blackwell, 2001), pp.177-91.

Fletcher, T. and Scott, D. *Way of Zen* (Barcelona: Vega, 2001).

Fox, Warwick. *Toward a Transpersonal Ecology* (Boston: Shambhala, 1990).

Grapard, Allan G. 'Nature and Culture in Japan', in Michael Tobias (ed.), *Deep Ecology* (San Diego: Avant Books, 1985), pp.240-55.

Green, Karen. 'Two Distinctions in Environmental Goodness', *Environmental Values* 5, No.1 (February 1996): 31-46.

Habito, Ruben L. F. 'Mountains and Rivers and the Great Earth: Zen and Ecology', in Mary Evelyn Tucker and Duncan Ryūken Williams, *Buddhism and Ecology: the interconnection of dharma and deeds* (Cambridge, Massachusetts: Harvard University Press, 1997), pp.165-75.

Hakuin. *See under* Yampolsky, Philip B.

Halifax, Joan. 'The Third Body: Buddhism, Shamanism, and Deep Ecology', in Allan Hunt Badiner (ed.), *Dharma Gaia: A Harvest of Essays in Buddhism and Ecology* (Berkeley: Parallax Press, 1990), pp.20-38.

Hargrove, Eugene C. 'Foreword', to J. Baird Callicott and Roger T. Ames (eds), *Nature in Asian Traditions of Thought* (Albany: State University of New York Press, 2001), pp.xiii-xxi.

Harris, Ian. 'Getting to Grips with Buddhist Environmentalism: A Provisional Typology', *Journal of Buddhist Ethics* 2, (1995): 173-90.

Harvey, Peter. *An Introduction to Buddhism: teachings, history and practices* (Cambridge: Cambridge University Press, 1990).

Harvey, Peter. *An Introduction to Buddhist Ethics* (Cambridge: Cambridge University Press, 2000).

Hayward, Jeremy. 'Ecology and the Experience of Sacredness', in Allan Hunt Badiner (ed.), *Dharma Gaia: A Harvest of Essays in Buddhism and Ecology* (Berkeley: Parallax Press, 1990), pp.64-74.

Hegel, G. W. F. *The Logic of Hegel*, translated by William Wallace (Oxford: Clarendon Press, 1892).

Heidegger, Martin. 'The Thing', in *Poetry, Language, Thought*, translated by Albert Hofstadter (New York: Harper and Row, 1971), pp.165-86.

Heidegger, Martin. *Being and Time*, translated by John Macquarrie and Edward Robinson (Oxford: Blackwell, 1996).

Herrigel, Eugen. *Zen in the Art of Archery*, translated by R. F. C. Hull (London: Routledge & Kegan Paul, 1976).

Herrigel, Gustie L. *Zen in the Art of Flower Arrangement: an introduction to the spirit of the Japanese art of flower arrangement*, translated by R. F. C. Hull (London: Souvenir Press, 1999).

Horner, I. B. (translator). *Majjhima Nikāya; Middle Length Sayings*, 3 vols. (London: PTS, 1954-9).

Hubbard, J. and Swanson, P. L. (eds), *Pruning the Bodhi Tree: The Storm over Critical Buddhism* (Honolulu: University of Hawai'i Press, 1997).

Huang-po. *See under* Blofeld, John.

Hui-neng. *See under* Yampolsky, Philip B.

Hylton, Peter. *Russell, Idealism, and the Emergence of Analytic Philosophy* (Oxford: Clarendon Press, 1990).

Inada, Kenneth K. *Nāgārjuna: A Translation of his Mūlamadhyamakakārikā with an Introductory Essay* (Tokyo: The Hokuseido Press, 1970).

Ives, Christopher. *Zen Awakening and Society* (Honolulu: University of Hawaii Press, 1992).

Izutsu, Toshihiko. *Toward a Philosophy of Zen Buddhism* (Boulder: Prajñā Press, 1982).

Kagan, Shelly. 'Rethinking Intrinsic Value', *The Journal of Ethics* 2, issue 4 (1998): 277-97.

Kalland, Arne. 'Culture in Japanese Nature', in Ole Bruun and Arne Kalland, *Asian Perceptions of Nature: A Critical Approach* (Richmond: Curzon, 1996), pp.243-57.

Kalland, Arne and Asquith, Pamela J. 'Japanese Perceptions of Nature: Ideals and Illusions', in Pamela J. Asquith and Arne Kalland (eds), *Japanese Images of Nature: Cultural Perspectives* (Richmond: Curzon, 1997), pp.1-35.

Kalupahana, David J. *A History of Buddhist Philosophy: continuities and discontinuities* (Delhi: Motilal Banarsidass, 1994).

Kapleau, Philip. *The Three Pillars of Zen: Teaching, Practice, and Enlightenment* (London: Rider, 1985).

Kapleau, Philip. 'Responsibility and Social Action', in Stephanie Kaza and Kenneth Kraft, *Dharma Rain: Sources of Buddhist Environmentalism* (Boston: Shambhala, 2000), pp.241-5.

Kasulis, Thomas P. *Zen Action, Zen Person* (Honolulu: University of Hawaii Press, 1985).

Kasulis, Thomas P. 'Ch'an Spirituality', in Takeuchi Yoshinori (ed.), *Buddhist Spirituality: Later China, Korea, Japan, and the Modern World* (London: SCM Press, 1999), pp.24-32.

Kaza, S. and Kraft, K. (eds). *Dharma Rain: Sources of Buddhist Environmentalism* (Boston: Shambhala, 2000).

Keenan, John P. 'Yogācāra in China', in Takeuchi Yoshinori (ed.), *Buddhist Spirituality: Indian, Southeast Asian, Tibetan, Early Chinese* (London: SCM Press, 1994), pp.365-72.

Keown, Damien. *The Nature of Buddhist Ethics* (Basingstoke: Palgrave, 2001).

King, Sallie B. 'Contemporary Buddhist Spirituality and Social Activism', in Takeuchi Yoshinori (ed.), *Buddhist Spirituality: Later China, Korea, Japan, and the Modern World* (London: SCM Press, 1999), pp.455-81.

Kundera, Milan. *The Unbearable Lightness of Being*, translated by Michael Henry Heim (London: Faber and Faber, 1984),

LaFleur, William R. 'Enlightenment for Plants and Trees', in Stephanie Kaza and Kenneth Kraft (eds), *Dharma Rain: Sources of Buddhist Environmentalism* (Boston: Shambhala, 2000), pp.109-16.

LaFleur, William R. 'Saigyō and the Buddhist Value of Nature', in J. Baird Callicott and Roger T. Ames (eds), *Nature in Asian Traditions of Thought* (Albany: SUNY Press, 2001), pp.183-209.

Lai, Whalen W. 'The Three Jewels in China' in Takeuchi Yoshinori (ed.), *Buddhist Spirituality: Indian, Southeast Asian, Tibetan, Early Chinese* (London: SCM Press, 1994), pp.275-342.

Lao-tzu. *See under* Lau, D. C.

Lau, D. C. (translator). *Tao Te Ching* (Middlesex: Penguin, 1982).

Leggett, Tim. *Zen and the Ways* (London: Routledge & Kegan Paul, 1978).

Leopold, Aldo. *A Sand County Almanac* (New York: Oxford University Press, 1968).

Lewis, David. *Papers in Metaphysics and Epistemology* (New York: Cambridge University Press, 1999).

Loori, John Daido. 'The Precepts and the Environment', in Mary Evelyn Tucker and Duncan Ryūken Williams (eds), *Buddhism and Ecology: the interconnection of dharma and deeds* (Cambridge, Massachusetts: Harvard University Press, 1997), pp.177-84.

Loy, David. 'Wei-wu-wei: Nondual action', *Philosophy East and West* 35, no.1 (January 1985): 73-86.

MacIntyre, Alasdair. *After Virtue: a study in moral theory* (London: Duckworth, 1987).

Macy, Joanna. 'The Greening of the Self', in Allan Hunt Badiner (ed.), *Dharma Gaia: A Harvest of Essays in Buddhism and Ecology* (Berkeley, California: Parallax Press, 1990), pp.53-63.

Masunaga, Reihō. *A Primer of Sōtō Zen: a translation of Dōgen's Shōbōgenzō zuimonki* (Honolulu: East-West Center Press, 1971).

Mikkelson, Douglas, K. 'Who is arguing about the cat? Moral Action and Enlightenment according to Dōgen', *Philosophy East and West* 47, no.3 (July 1997): 383-97.

Mohr, Michel. 'Hakuin', in Takeuchi Yoshinori (ed.), *Buddhist Spirituality: Later China, Korea, Japan, and the Modern World* (London: SCM Press, 1999), pp.307-28.

Murdoch, Iris. *The Sovereignty of Good* (London: Routledge & Kegan Paul, 1970).

Naess, Arne. 'Ecosophy T: Deep Versus Shallow Ecology', in Louis P. Pojman (ed.), *Environmental Ethics: Readings in Theory and Application* (Belmont, California: Wadsworth, 2001), pp.150-7.

Nāgārjuna. *See under* Inada, Kenneth K.

Nhat Hanh, Thich. *The Sun My Heart* (London: Rider, 1992).

Nhat Hanh, Thich. 'The Sun My Heart', in Stephanie Kaza and Kenneth Kraft (eds), *Dharma Rain: Sources of Buddhist Environmentalism* (Boston: Shambhala, 2000), pp.83-91.

Nhat Hanh, Thich 'Meal Verses', in Stephanie Kaza and Kenneth Kraft (eds), *Dharma Rain: Sources of Buddhist Environmentalism* (Boston: Shambhala, 2000), pp.448-9.

Nishiyama, K. and Stevens, J. (translators). *Shōbōgenzō: The Eye and Treasury of the True Law* (4 volumes) (Tokyo: Nakayama Shobō, 1976).

Odin, Steve. 'The Japanese Concept of Nature in Relation to the Environmental Ethics and Conservation Aesthetics of Aldo Leopold', in Mary Evelyn Tucker and Duncan Ryūken Williams (eds), *Buddhism and Ecology: the interconnection of dharma and deeds* (Cambridge, Massachusetts: Harvard University Press, 1997), pp.89-109.

O'Neill, John. *Ecology, Policy and Politics: Human Well-Being and the Natural World* (London: Routledge, 1993).

Ophuls, William 'Notes for a Buddhist Politics', in Stephanie Kaza and Kenneth Kraft (eds), *Dharma Rain: Sources of Buddhist Environmentalism* (Boston: Shambhala, 2000), pp.369-78.

Palmer, M., Breuilly, E., Wai Ming, C. and Ramsay, J. (translators). *The Book of Chuang Tzu* (London: Penguin Arkana, 1996).

Parkes, Graham. 'Voices of Mountains, Trees, and Rivers: Kūkai, Dōgen, and a Deeper Ecology', in Mary Evelyn Tucker and Duncan Ryūken Williams (eds), *Buddhism and Ecology: the interconnection of dharma and deeds* (Cambridge, Massachusetts: Harvard University Press, 1997), pp.111-28.

Passmore, John. *Man's Responsibility for Nature: Ecological Problems and Western Traditions, 2nd ed.* (London: Duckworth, 1980).

Pratt, Vernon. *Environment and Philosophy* (London: Routledge, 2000).

Price, A. F. and Mou-lam, W. (translators). *The Diamond Sutra and The Sutra of Hui Neng* (Boulder: Shambhala, 1969).

Rockefeller, Steven. 'Buddhism, Global Ethics, and the Earth Charter', in Mary Evelyn Tucker and Duncan Ryūken Williams (eds), *Buddhism and Ecology: the interconnection of dharma and deeds* (Cambridge, Massachusetts: Harvard University Press, 1997), pp.313-24.

Rolston, Holmes, III. 'Respect for Life: Can Zen Buddhism Help in Forming an Environmental Ethic?', *Zen Buddhism Today* 7 (September 1989): 11-30.

Rolston, Holmes, III. 'Nature for Real: Is Nature a Social Construct?', in T. D. J. Chappell (ed.), *The Philosophy of the Environment* (Edinburgh, Edinburgh University Press, 1997), pp.38-64.

Ryōen, Minamoto. 'Three Zen Thinkers', in Takeuchi Yoshinori (ed.), *Buddhist Spirituality: Later China, Korea, Japan and the Modern World* (London: SCM Press, 1999), pp.291-306.

Śāntideva. *Bodhicaryāvatāra*, translated by Kate Crosby and Andrew Skilton (Oxford: Oxford University Press, 1996).

Schmithausen, Lambert. *Buddhism and Nature: the Lecture delivered on the Occasion of the EXPO 1990, An Enlarged Version with Notes* (Tokyo: The International Institute for Buddhist Studies, 1991).

Sekida, K. (translator) and Grimstone, A. V. (ed.). *Two Zen Classics: Mumonkan and Hekiganroku* (Tokyo: Weatherhill, 1977).

Senzaki, N. and Reps, P. (translators). *Zen Flesh, Zen Bones* (Middlesex: Penguin, 1957).

Shaner, David Edward. 'The Japanese Experience of Nature', in J. Baird Callicott and Roger T. Ames (eds), *Nature in Asian Traditions of Thought* (Albany: SUNY Press, 2001), pp.163-82.

Singer, Peter. *Practical Ethics, 2nd ed.* (Cambridge: Cambridge University Press, 1993).

Smith, Tara. 'Intrinsic Value: Look-Say Ethics', *The Journal of Value Inquiry* 32, issue 4 (1998): 539-53.

Snyder, Gary. 'Blue Mountains Constantly Walking', in Stephanie Kaza and Kenneth Kraft (eds), *Dharma Rain: Sources of Buddhist Environmentalism* (Boston: Shambhala, 2000), pp.125-41.

Snyder, Gary. 'Grace', in Stephanie Kaza and Kenneth Kraft (eds), *Dharma Rain: Sources of Buddhist Environmentalism* (Boston: Shambhala, 2000), pp.450-3.

Sponberg, Alan. 'Green Buddhism and the Hierarchy of Compassion', in Mary Evelyn Tucker and Duncan Ryūken Williams, (eds), *Buddhism and Ecology: the interconnection of dharma and deeds* (Cambridge, Massachusetts: Harvard University Press, 1997), pp.351-76.

Statman, Daniel. (ed.). *Virtue Ethics: A Critical Reader* (Edinburgh: Edinburgh University Press, 1997).

Stryk, Lawrence. (translator). *The Penguin Book of Zen Poetry* (USA: Penguin, 1977).

Suzuki, D. T. *Essays on Zen Buddhism III* (London: Luzac, 1934).

Suzuki, D. T. *Zen Buddhism: Selected Writings of D. T. Suzuki*, edited by William Barrett (New York: Doubleday Anchor Books, 1956).

Suzuki, D. T. *Zen and Japanese Culture* (Princeton, NJ: Princeton University Press, 1973).

Suzuki, D. T. (translator). *The Laṅkāvatāra Sūtra* (London, Routledge & Kegan Paul, 1973).

Suzuki, Shunryu. *Zen Mind, Beginner's Mind*, edited by Trudy Dixon (New York: Weatherhill, 2000).

Swanson, Paul L. 'Why they say Zen is not Buddhism: recent Japanese critiques of Buddha-nature', in Jamie Hubbard and Paul L. Swanson (eds), *Pruning the Bodhi Tree: The Storm over Critical Buddhism* (Honolulu: University of Hawai'i Press, 1997), pp.3-29.

Thurman, R. A. F. 'The Emptiness that is Compassion: An Essay on Buddhist Ethics', *Religious Traditions* 4, no.2 (1981): 11-34.

Tomoaki, Tsuchida. 'The Monastic Spirituality of Zen Master Dōgen', in Takeuchi Yoshinori (ed.), *Buddhist Spirituality: Later China, Korea, Japan and the Modern World* (London: SCM Press, 1999), pp.274-90.

Trungpa, Chögyam, 'Renunciation and Daring', in Stephanie Kaza and Kenneth Kraft (eds), *Dharma Rain: Sources of Buddhist Environmentalism* (Boston: Shambhala, 2000), pp.261-71.

Tucker, Mary E. and Ryūken Williams, D. (eds). *Buddhism and Ecology: the interconnection of dharma and deeds* (Cambridge, Massachusetts: Harvard University Press, 1997.

Tu-shun. 'The Jewel Net of Indra', in Stephanie Kaza and Kenneth Kraft (eds), *Dharma Rain: Sources of Buddhist Environmentalism* (Boston: Shambhala, 2000), pp.58-61.

van Wensveen, Louke. *Dirty Virtues: The Emergence of Ecological Virtue Ethics* (New York: Humanity Books, 2000).

Weatherson, Brian. 'Intrinsic vs. extrinsic properties', *Stanford Encyclopaedia of Philosophy* (http://plato.stanford.edu/entries/intrinsic-extrinsic/).

White, Lynn. 'The historical roots of our ecologic crisis', in Louis P. Pojman (ed.), *Environmental Ethics: readings in theory and application* (Belmont, CA: Wadsworth, 2001), pp.13-18.

Whitehead, Alfred North. *Science and the Modern World* (New York: Macmillan, 1925).

Whitehill, James. 'Is There a Zen Ethic?', *The Eastern Buddhist* 20 (Spring 1987): 9-33.

Whitehill, James. 'Buddhism and the Virtues', in Damien Keown (ed.), *Contemporary Buddhist Ethics* (Richmond: Curzon, 2000), pp.17-36.

Williams, Bernard. *Ethics and the Limits of Philosophy* (London: Fontana/Collins, 1985).

Williams, Paul. *Mahāyāna Buddhism: the doctrinal foundations* (London: Routledge 1989).

Wittgenstein, Ludwig. *Philosophical Investigations*, translated by G. E. M. Anscombe (Oxford: Blackwell, 1958).

Wright, Dale S. *Philosophical Meditations on Zen Buddhism* (Cambridge: Cambridge University Press, 1998).

Wright, Dale S. 'Four Ch'an Masters', in Takeuchi Yoshinori (ed.), *Buddhist Spirituality: Later China, Korea, Japan, and the Modern World* (London: SCM Press, 1999), pp.33-43.

Yamada, Rev. Reirin. 'The Way to Understand Zen', in William Briggs (ed.), *Anthology of Zen* (New York: Grove Press, 1961), pp.187-9.

Yampolsky, Philip B. (translator). *The Platform Sutra of the Sixth Patriarch* (New York: Columbia University Press, 1967).

Yampolsky, Philip B. (translator). *The Zen Master Hakuin: Selected Writings* (New York: Columbia University Press, 1971).

Yampolsky, Philip B. 'Ch'an: a historical sketch', in Takeuchi Yoshinori (ed.), *Buddhist Spirituality: Later China, Korea, Japan, and the Modern World* (London: SCM Press, 1999), pp.3-23.

Yampolsky, Philip B. 'Zen: a historical sketch', in Takeuchi Yoshinori (ed.), *Buddhist Spirituality: Later China, Korea, Japan, and the Modern World* (London: SCM Press, 1999), pp.256-73.

Yoshinori, Takeuchi. (ed.). *Buddhist Spirituality: Indian, Southeast Asian, Tibetan, Early Chinese* (London: SCM Press, 1994).

Index